THE POWER OF HERBAL REMEDIES

A HOLISTIC HEALING GUIDEBOOK TO ACHIEVE WELLNESS, BEAUTY AND STRESS RELIEF WITH NATURAL AND SIMPLE APPROACHES

JESS EMILE

CONTENTS

INTRODUCTION

Did you know that in ancient times, herbal remedies were not just alternative options but mainstream medicine? These natural healers have been trusted across continents and cultures, bearing witness to their efficacy and integral role in human health. Today, as many of us find ourselves increasingly disillusioned with the often impersonal nature of modern healthcare, there's a remarkable shift back to these roots—quite literally.

This rekindled interest isn't just a trend. Recent studies suggest that more than 38% of adults are now turning to natural remedies and herbal treatments, seeking solutions that align with a holistic approach to health. This surge is not merely about dissatisfaction with conventional medicine but about empowering oneself with healing solutions that are gentle, effective, and harmonious with our bodies.

I am one of those who found solace and solutions in the green world of plants. My journey into herbalism began at a young age, influenced by a family legacy steeped in traditional healing practices. Over the years, my passion for understanding and utilizing herbal remedies has only deepened. It has become my mission to share this knowledge with those who are seeking out the natural ways to enhance health, beauty, and manage stress.

This natural remedy guidebook is crafted to demystify the world of herbal medicine. This book is designed to equip you with the knowledge to use readily available herbs to treat common ailments, enhance your beauty regimen, and elevate your mental well-being. From soothing teas to healing baths, each remedy has been selected for its effectiveness and ease of preparation.

What sets this book apart is its commitment to simplicity and safety. As we explore various herbs, I've included crucial information on potential interactions with drugs, ensuring that you remain safe as you explore these natural treatments. This guide doesn't just list remedies; it educates on the safe, informed use of herbs to enrich your life.

Structured to be your go-to resource, the book is divided into intuitive sections covering everything from daily wellness and women's health issues to stress relief and beauty solutions. Whether you're a novice to herbal remedies or looking to expand your existing knowledge, the layout is designed to help you easily navigate through the information, with an index for quick reference.

I understand the skepticism and concerns that come with trying something new, especially when it involves your health. That's why each page of this book is grounded in research and enriched with personal insights that aim to reassure and inspire you.

So, I invite you, with an open heart and mind, to explore the empowering world of herbal remedies. The plants are waiting to share their healing powers; are you ready to receive them? Let this book be your guide to a more natural, informed, and vibrant way of living.

As my grandmother often said, "Nature's bounty holds the secrets to our wellness." Let us tap into this ancient wisdom together and rediscover the joy of natural healing. Welcome to a journey that promises not just health, but a profound connection with the natural world around us.

FOUNDATIONS OF HERBAL REMEDIES

Herbal remedies, with their rich tapestry of history and tradition, are more than just supplements—they are a bridge to a world where nature and healing converge. As you step into this verdant landscape, consider the humble dandelion: often dismissed as a mere weed, yet its roots and leaves have been used for centuries to detoxify the liver and soothe digestive discomfort. This transformation from the mundane to the medicinal is not just about the herbs themselves but about understanding the language of herbalism. This first chapter is designed to equip you with the foundational knowledge to confidently navigate the complex yet fascinating world of herbal remedies. Here, you will learn to decode the terminology that is the bedrock of herbal practices, ensuring that you can both comprehend and utilize these tools to enhance your health and wellbeing effectively.

1.1 DECODING HERBAL TERMINOLOGY: A BEGINNER'S GUIDE

In the realm of herbal remedies, terminology isn't just jargon; it's the key to unlocking the full potential of these natural healers. Understanding these terms ensures you can follow recipes and make remedies correctly, maximizing their benefits while minimizing risks.

Tinctures, for instance, are alcohol-based extracts of herbs. The alcohol acts as a solvent that pulls out the active compounds of the herbs, preserving these potent properties in a concentrated liquid form. Tinctures are valued for their long shelf life and ease of assimilation into the body. They are typically administered in small doses, measured in drops, which can be added to water or tea.

Salves are another fundamental herbal preparation. They are thick, ointment-like substances made by combining herbs with waxy substances like beeswax, which are then applied topically. Salves are particularly effective for skin-related issues, from dry skin and eczema to minor cuts and bruises, as they create a protective barrier over the skin, allowing the herbal extracts to be absorbed directly at the site of discomfort.

Moving on, adaptogens are a class of herbs that are turning heads in the wellness community for their unique ability to help the body resist and adapt to stress, whether physical, environmental, or emotional. Herbs like ashwagandha and rhodiola fall into this category and are often used to improve stamina, reduce fatigue, and support the adrenal system.

Essential oils are highly concentrated plant extracts obtained through steam distillation, cold pressing, or resin tapping. Known for their aromatic and therapeutic properties, essential oils are used in a variety of ways, from inhalation to topical application. However, due to their concentration, they should be used with caution, often diluted in a carrier oil to prevent skin irritation.

Misunderstandings can arise with terms like these. For example, tinctures and essential oils might both be extracts, but they are used quite differently due to their concentration and the solvents involved. Similarly, the term 'adaptogen' is sometimes mistakenly applied to any herb that boosts energy, but true adaptogens must meet specific criteria, including reducing stress-induced impairments and fatigue.

The precision of language in herbalism is not about pedantry. Each term encapsulates a wealth of information about the preparation, use, and benefits of a remedy. For example, knowing the difference between a decoction and an infusion (both methods of extracting herbal properties through water) can impact the potency and effectiveness of your remedy. A decoction is used for harder substances like roots or bark, requiring a longer, more vigorous extraction, whereas an infusion is best for delicate parts like leaves or flowers, preserving their volatile compounds.

Understanding and using the correct terminology in herbalism not only enhances communication among those in the field but also ensures that you are applying these practices safely and effectively. As we continue to explore the vast world of herbal remedies, this foundational knowledge will serve as your guide, helping you to make informed decisions about the herbs you choose and the methods you employ to integrate them into your life for health and healing.

How to Make a Herbal Remedy Tincture: Simple Step-by-Step Guide

WHAT YOU NEED:

1. **Herbs**: Fresh or dried. Popular choices include echinacea, chamomile, or valerian.
2. **Alcohol**: Vodka or brandy, at least 80 proof (40% alcohol content).
3. **Glass Jar**: A mason jar or any clean, airtight glass container.
4. **Cheesecloth or Strainer**: For filtering the tincture.
5. **Dropper Bottles**: For storing the finished tincture.

STEPS TO MAKE A TINCTURE:

1. Prepare the Herbs:

- **Fresh Herbs**: Chop finely to expose more surface area.
- **Dried Herbs**: Crush or break into smaller pieces.

2. Fill the Jar with Herbs:

- Fill the jar about halfway with the herbs. This allows room for the alcohol.

3. Add Alcohol:

- Pour the alcohol over the herbs, completely covering them.
- Leave about an inch of space at the top of the jar.
- The alcohol should fully submerge the herbs.

4. Seal and Shake:

- Seal the jar tightly with a lid.
- Shake the jar well to mix the herbs and alcohol.

5. Store and Wait:

- Place the jar in a cool, dark place.
- Shake the jar every day or every few days to keep the mixture well-blended.
- Let the tincture sit for at least 4-6 weeks. The longer it sits, the stronger it will be.

6. Strain the Tincture:

- After the waiting period, place cheesecloth or a strainer over a clean bowl.

- Pour the mixture through the cheesecloth to filter out the herbs.
- Squeeze the cheesecloth to extract as much liquid as possible.

7. Transfer to Dropper Bottles:

- Use a funnel to pour the strained liquid into dropper bottles for easy use.
- Label the bottles with the name of the herb and the date.

TIPS:

- **Ratios**: A common ratio is 1 part fresh herbs to 2 parts alcohol or 1 part dried herbs to 5 parts alcohol.
- **Alcohol Alternatives**: For non-alcoholic tinctures, use apple cider vinegar or glycerin, though they may not extract as many beneficial compounds.

HOW TO USE:

- Tinctures are usually taken by placing a few drops under the tongue or diluted in water or tea. Follow dosage instructions specific to the herb used.

This process ensures that you capture the potent compounds of the herbs in a form that is easy to use and has a long shelf life.

How to Make a Herbal Remedy Salve: Simple Step-by-Step Guide

WHAT YOU NEED:

1. **Herbs**: Dried herbs such as calendula, comfrey, or lavender.
2. **Carrier Oil**: Olive oil, coconut oil, or any other vegetable oil.
3. **Beeswax**: Helps solidify the salve.
4. **Double Boiler**: Or a heatproof bowl and saucepan.

5. **Cheesecloth or Strainer**: For filtering the infused oil.
6. **Glass Jar or Tin**: For storing the finished salve.

STEPS TO MAKE A SALVE:

1. Infuse the Oil with Herbs:

- **Ratio**: Use 1 cup of dried herbs for every 2 cups of oil.
- **Double Boiler Method**: Place the herbs and oil in a double boiler. Heat gently on low for 2-3 hours, ensuring the oil does not boil.
- **Alternative Method**: Place herbs and oil in a jar, seal, and leave in a sunny spot for 2-3 weeks, shaking occasionally.

2. Strain the Infused Oil:

- After the infusion period, strain the oil through cheesecloth or a fine strainer into a clean bowl to remove the herb solids.
- Squeeze the cheesecloth to get as much oil out as possible.

3. Measure the Beeswax:

- Use approximately 1 ounce (about 2 tablespoons) of beeswax for every cup of infused oil.

4. Melt the Beeswax:

- Place the strained oil and beeswax in a double boiler or heatproof bowl over a saucepan of simmering water.
- Heat gently until the beeswax is fully melted, stirring occasionally.

5. Mix Well:

- Once the beeswax is melted, stir the mixture well to ensure the oil and beeswax are fully combined.

6. Pour into Containers:

- Carefully pour the hot mixture into glass jars or tins.
- Let the salve cool and solidify completely before sealing with lids.

7. Label the Containers:

- Label the jars with the name of the salve and the date.

TIPS:

- **Essential Oils**: Add a few drops of essential oil (like lavender or tea tree oil) to the mixture after removing it from heat for added benefits and fragrance.
- **Testing Consistency**: Before pouring into containers, you can test the consistency by placing a small amount on a spoon and putting it in the freezer for a minute. Adjust by adding more beeswax to harden or more oil to soften.

HOW TO USE:

- Apply the salve to the skin as needed for moisturizing, healing minor cuts, soothing insect bites, or relieving dry skin.

This process ensures you create a potent, natural salve that can be used for various skin ailments and is free from synthetic ingredients.

How to Make a Herbal Remedy Adaptogen: Simple Step-by-Step Guide

WHAT YOU NEED:

1. **Adaptogenic Herbs**: Popular choices include ashwagandha, rhodiola, holy basil, or ginseng.
2. **Water**: For decoctions (if using roots or bark) or teas (if using leaves and flowers).
3. **Alcohol (Optional)**: For tinctures.
4. **Glass Jar**: For tinctures.
5. **Cheesecloth or Strainer**: For filtering.
6. **Dropper Bottles**: For tinctures.

TYPES OF ADAPTOGEN PREPARATIONS:

1. **Tea/Infusion (for Leaves and Flowers)**
2. **Decoction (for Roots and Bark)**
3. **Tincture (Alcohol Extract)**

STEPS FOR EACH PREPARATION:

1. Making an Adaptogen Tea/Infusion:

1. Boil Water:

- Boil about 2 cups of water.

2. Add Herbs:

- Place 1-2 teaspoons of dried adaptogenic herbs (like holy basil) or a handful of fresh herbs into a teapot or infuser.

3. Pour Water:

- Pour the boiling water over the herbs.

4. Steep:

- Cover and let the herbs steep for 10-15 minutes.

5. Strain and Serve:

- Strain the herbs using a fine strainer or cheesecloth.
- Pour the tea into a cup and enjoy.

2. Making an Adaptogen Decoction:

1. Prepare the Herbs:

- Use 1-2 tablespoons of dried roots or bark (like ashwagandha or ginseng) or a handful of fresh.

2. Simmer:

- Place the herbs in a saucepan with about 4 cups of water.
- Bring to a boil, then reduce to a simmer.

3. Cook:

- Simmer for 20-30 minutes, partially covered.

4. Strain and Serve:

- Strain the decoction using a fine strainer or cheesecloth.
- Pour into a cup and enjoy.

3. Making an Adaptogen Tincture:

1. Prepare the Herbs:

- Use dried adaptogenic herbs (like rhodiola or ashwagandha).

- Chop or crush the herbs to increase the surface area.

2. Fill the Jar:

- Fill a glass jar halfway with the dried herbs.

3. Add Alcohol:

- Pour vodka or brandy (at least 80 proof) over the herbs, filling the jar.
- Ensure the herbs are fully submerged.

4. Seal and Shake:

- Seal the jar tightly.
- Shake well to mix the herbs and alcohol.

5. Store and Shake:

- Store the jar in a cool, dark place.
- Shake the jar every day or two.
- Let the mixture sit for at least 4-6 weeks.

6. Strain:

- After 4-6 weeks, strain the tincture through cheesecloth or a fine strainer into a clean bowl.
- Squeeze the cheesecloth to extract as much liquid as possible.

7. Transfer to Dropper Bottles:

- Use a funnel to pour the tincture into dropper bottles.
- Label with the herb name and date.

Tips:

- **Dosage**: For tea, drink 1-2 cups daily. For tinctures, take 1-2 droppersful (1-2 ml) 1-3 times a day, as needed.
- **Combining Adaptogens**: You can combine different adaptogenic herbs in your preparations for a synergistic effect.
- **Storage**: Store teas and decoctions in the refrigerator for up to a week. Tinctures have a long shelf life and can be stored in a cool, dark place for up to a year.

These preparations allow you to harness the benefits of adaptogenic herbs to help your body adapt to stress and maintain balance.

How to Make a Herbal Remedy Essential Oil: Simple Step-by-Step Guide

What You Need:

1. **Fresh Herbs or Plants**: Common choices include lavender, peppermint, eucalyptus, or rosemary.
2. **Carrier Oil**: Olive oil, jojoba oil, or sweet almond oil.
3. **Glass Jar**: A clean, airtight glass container.
4. **Distillation Equipment**: For steam distillation (optional, for advanced method).
5. **Cheesecloth or Strainer**: For filtering.
6. **Dark Glass Bottles**: For storing the finished essential oil.

Methods to Extract Essential Oils:

1. **Infusion (Simpler Method)**
2. **Steam Distillation (Advanced Method)**

STEPS FOR EACH METHOD:

1. Infusion Method (Simpler):

1. Harvest Fresh Herbs:

- Choose fresh, aromatic herbs.
- Rinse and pat them dry to remove any dirt or insects.

2. Prepare the Jar:

- Fill the glass jar halfway with fresh herbs, lightly packed.

3. Add Carrier Oil:

- Pour a carrier oil over the herbs, fully submerging them.
- Leave about an inch of space at the top of the jar.

4. Seal and Store:

- Seal the jar tightly.
- Place the jar in a sunny spot for 2-3 weeks.
- Shake the jar gently every day.

5. Strain the Oil:

- After the infusion period, strain the oil through cheesecloth or a fine strainer into a clean bowl.
- Squeeze the cheesecloth to extract as much oil as possible.

6. Store the Essential Oil:

- Pour the strained oil into dark glass bottles.
- Label the bottles with the herb name and date.

2. Steam Distillation Method (Advanced):

1. Harvest Fresh Herbs:

- Choose fresh, aromatic herbs.
- Rinse and pat them dry to remove any dirt or insects.

2. Set Up the Distillation Apparatus:

- Place the herbs in the distillation flask.
- Add water to the flask, ensuring it doesn't touch the herbs.
- Attach the condenser and collection tube.

3. Heat the Flask:

- Heat the water to create steam.
- The steam will pass through the herbs, carrying the essential oils with it.

4. Condense the Steam:

- The steam will travel through the condenser and cool down, turning back into liquid.
- The liquid will collect in the collection tube, separating into water and essential oil layers.

5. Separate the Essential Oil:

- Carefully extract the essential oil from the top layer using a pipette or dropper.

6. Store the Essential Oil:

- Transfer the essential oil to dark glass bottles.
- Label the bottles with the herb name and date.

TIPS:

- **Infusion Oil Quality**: Infused oils are less concentrated than distilled essential oils but still hold the aromatic and therapeutic properties of the herbs.
- **Storage**: Store essential oils in a cool, dark place to maintain their potency and shelf life.
- **Carrier Oil Choice**: Use high-quality, cold-pressed carrier oils for the best results.

HOW TO USE:

- **Aromatherapy**: Add a few drops to a diffuser.
- **Topical Application**: Dilute with a carrier oil before applying to the skin.
- **Massage**: Mix with a carrier oil for therapeutic massages.

These methods provide you with natural, homemade essential oils that capture the essence and benefits of the herbs. The infusion method is simpler and accessible, while steam distillation is more advanced and yields pure essential oils.

1.2 THE HISTORY AND EVOLUTION OF HERBAL MEDICINE

Herbal medicine, with its roots deeply entrenched in ancient soils, has been a cornerstone of health and wellness for millennia. It is a testament to the enduring wisdom of our ancestors who utilized the flora around them for healing and nurturing. The journey of herbal medicine through various cultures and epochs not only highlights its significance but also its dynamic evolution into the practices we recognize today.

The origins of herbal medicine can be traced back to ancient civilizations. In ancient Egypt, for instance, papyrus texts as early as 1500

BCE meticulously cataloged herbs like garlic and juniper for their medicinal properties. Similarly, in ancient China, the foundational text, "The Shennong Bencao Jing," penned around the 3rd century, detailed hundreds of medicinal plants and their uses, laying the groundwork for Traditional Chinese Medicine. Meanwhile, in ancient India, Ayurveda developed as a holistic approach to health, which included the use of herbs based on their energies and the effects they had on the individual body types known as doshas.

These ancient practices significantly influenced Western herbal medicine, particularly through the works of scholars during the Renaissance, such as Paracelsus, who introduced the doctrine of signatures. This theory suggested that herbs resembling various parts of the body could be used to treat ailments of those body parts, a concept that mirrored earlier holistic approaches seen in other cultures. Furthermore, the "Materia Medica," written by Dioscorides in the first century AD, served as one of the most influential herbal texts throughout the Middle Ages, describing the properties and uses of over 600 plants.

As we transitioned into the modern era, the impact of these historical texts and practices on contemporary herbal medicine became increasingly evident. While the advent of synthetic drugs led to a decline in the use of herbal remedies in the West for a time, there has been a resurgence of interest in natural health practices. This revival is partly due to the growing body of scientific research that supports the efficacy of herbal treatments and a collective desire to return to more sustainable, holistic approaches to healthcare.

Today, herbal medicine is integrated into modern practices in various ways. Many herbal compounds are the basis for pharmaceutical medications, while holistic therapists incorporate herbal treatments into complementary health approaches. This integration underscores the adaptability and enduring relevance of herbal medicine in our continuing quest for health and well-being.

Significant figures in herbalism, such as Hildegard von Bingen and Nicholas Culpeper, have also played pivotal roles in shaping modern perceptions of herbal medicine. Hildegard, a 12th-century healer, emphasized the connection between the environment and human health, while Culpeper's 17th-century works democratized medical knowledge by describing the uses of British herbs in the vernacular, making it accessible to the common people.

The evolution of herbal medicine is a rich tapestry woven from diverse threads of human experience, culture, and innovation. From ancient healers to modern-day herbalists, the knowledge passed down through generations has grown and adapted, yet the essence remains the same—to live in harmony with nature and utilize its gifts for health and healing. As we continue to explore and study the vast botanical world, it is clear that the journey of herbal medicine is far from complete, promising new discoveries and innovations that will continue to enrich our lives.

1.3 SAFETY FIRST: UNDERSTANDING HERB-DRUG INTERACTIONS

Navigating the use of herbal remedies requires not only an appreciation of their benefits but also an understanding of their interactions with pharmaceuticals. This is particularly crucial for anyone currently under medication, as the natural compounds in herbs can influence the effectiveness and processing of drugs within your body. For example, St. John's Wort, a herb celebrated for its ability to alleviate mild to moderate depression, can also accelerate the breakdown of medications in the liver, including antidepressants. This interaction can lead to reduced blood levels of the medication, diminishing its efficacy and potentially leading to a resurgence of depressive symptoms.

The mechanism behind such interactions often involves the way certain herbal compounds influence the activity of enzymes responsible for metabolizing drugs in the liver, primarily the cytochrome

P450 enzyme family. When St. John's Wort is taken, it induces these enzymes to metabolize drugs more rapidly than usual, a process not limited to antidepressants but also affecting drugs like blood thinners, birth control pills, and certain cancer therapies, among others. Another poignant example is grapefruit juice, which, while not an herb, similarly affects drug metabolism by inhibiting the same liver enzymes, leading to increased levels of certain drugs in the bloodstream, which can be potentially hazardous.

Given these complexities, it is paramount to approach herbal remedies with informed caution. The first step in ensuring safe use is to always consult with a healthcare provider before starting any new herbal regimen, especially if you are currently taking other medications. This dialogue is crucial as it allows for an assessment of potential interactions based on your specific health profile and the medications you are taking.

Additionally, understanding the importance of correct dosing and administration of herbs cannot be overstated. Just as with conventional medicines, the efficacy of herbal treatments largely depends on their being used appropriately. This includes not only how much and how often an herb is taken but also the form in which it is consumed. For instance, teas generally offer a milder dose of herbs compared to extracts or tinctures, which are much more concentrated and require more careful dosing. Furthermore, factors such as the time of day you take the herb and whether it is taken with or without food can influence its effects and interactions with other medications.

Ensuring you follow guidelines for safe usage also involves maintaining open lines of communication with your healthcare provider throughout your herbal therapy journey. This includes regular monitoring of any health changes and adjusting your herbal regimen in consultation with your provider to avoid adverse interactions. Always ensure that any herbal supplements you take are from reputable sources and clearly labeled, providing transparency about the ingredients and their concentrations. This vigilance helps safeguard against the risks associated with adulterated or misidentified products, which can lead to unexpected and unwanted drug interactions.

In sum, while the world of herbal remedies offers a promising adjunct to conventional medical treatments, it demands a cautious and informed approach. By understanding the potential interactions between herbs and pharmaceuticals, consulting healthcare professionals, and adhering to recommended guidelines for usage, you can safely integrate the benefits of herbal medicine into your healthcare regimen, ensuring that the natural solutions you turn to for health and wellness enhance rather than compromise your medical care.

1.4 HOW TO SOURCE AND SELECT QUALITY HERBS

Selecting high-quality herbs is akin to choosing fresh produce. Just as you'd scrutinize fruits and vegetables for freshness and quality, the same level of attention is needed when picking herbs for medicinal use. The criteria for selection are crucial because the potency and effectiveness of your herbal remedies are directly influenced by the herb's condition. Fresh herbs should look vibrant and lively, not wilted or discolored, which can indicate age or poor handling. The color should be rich and consistent, characteristic of the herb's natural hue. Aroma is another vital factor; fresh, quality herbs will have a strong, distinct smell that should be immediately recognizable and pleasant, not musty or faint, which can suggest they've been stored improperly or for too long.

When evaluating suppliers and retailers, consider their sourcing and handling practices. A reputable supplier should be transparent about where their herbs come from and how they are grown. Ideally, herbs should be organic, ensuring they haven't been treated with pesticides or other harmful chemicals that could compromise their medicinal qualities and your health. Ethical sourcing is also important; it involves sustainable harvesting practices that protect the environment and ensure that natural resources are not depleted. When possible, support local herb farmers or gatherers who use responsible practices, as this not only promotes sustainability but also contributes to the local economy.

Understanding labels on herbal products is crucial for making informed choices. Labels should provide comprehensive information about the herb, including its scientific name, which can prevent confusion with herbs of similar common names, and its origin, which can affect its medicinal qualities due to differences in soil and growing conditions. The label should also indicate the part of the plant used, as different parts can have different uses and efficacy. Purity is another important factor; the label should confirm that the herb is free from fillers or additives, which can dilute the herb's effectiveness and introduce unwanted substances into your body.

The decision between foraging for herbs or buying them involves several considerations. Foraging allows you to connect with nature and ensures that you get the freshest herbs possible. It can be a rewarding experience that enhances your understanding of herbal properties and their natural environments. However, foraging requires a good knowledge of plant identification to avoid picking the wrong herb, which can be dangerous. It also requires access to unpolluted natural areas, which may not be available to everyone. On the other hand, buying herbs is more convenient and often provides access to a wider variety of herbs than what might be available locally. However, when buying, you rely on the supplier for quality and purity, which underscores the importance of choosing reputable retailers.

Whether you decide to forage or buy your herbs, the key is to ensure that they are of the highest quality to maximize the health benefits they can provide. This involves being diligent and informed about sourcing, handling, and storing herbs, whether you gather them yourself or purchase them from a supplier. Quality should never be compromised when it comes to your health, and understanding how to select the best herbs is an essential skill for anyone interested in herbal medicine.

1.5 SETTING UP YOUR HERBAL REMEDY TOOLKIT

When venturing into the world of herbal remedies, having the right tools and workspace not only makes the process of creating these natural solutions easier but also more enjoyable. Think of this as setting up your own mini apothecary at home—a place where health and wellness are crafted with your own hands. Essential tools for your toolkit include mortars and pestles, which are invaluable for grinding herbs and spices to release their full potency. Measuring spoons are crucial for ensuring the correct dosages, while various storage containers such as glass jars with tight-fitting lids are perfect for storing dried herbs and keeping your tinctures, salves, and oils safe from light and air, which can degrade their quality.

Another key component is a good quality knife and cutting board, dedicated solely to your herbal crafting. This will ensure that your materials are prepared consistently, which is crucial for the efficacy of your remedies. Additionally, having a fine mesh strainer or cheesecloth is essential for filtering tinctures and teas, ensuring clarity and purity in your final product. For those who plan to venture into making their own creams and lotions, a double boiler is a must-have for gently heating and mixing ingredients.

Creating a dedicated space for your herbal activities does more than just centralize your efforts; it helps in maintaining the integrity of your products. This space should be well-ventilated, away from direct sunlight, and at a consistent temperature to ensure the herbs do not degrade prematurely. It should also be away from household contaminants and not be a multi-use space where food is prepared or chemicals are stored. Ideally, this would be a small nook or corner of your kitchen or pantry that can be devoted entirely to your herbal practices. Here, you can install some shelving to organize your herbs and tools neatly, ensuring everything is easily accessible.

Cleanliness and organization are not just about aesthetics; they are critical to the success of your herbal preparations. Herbs are highly absorbent, and their medicinal qualities can be compromised by dust, dirt, or exposure to strong household odors. Ensure that your workspace and all tools are cleaned thoroughly before and after each use. Regular cleaning prevents cross-contamination between different herbs and keeps your space conducive to creating pure, effective remedies. Organizing your herbs and tools not only saves time but also minimizes the risk of errors in your preparations. Labeling each jar and container clearly with the herb name, date of storage, and any other pertinent details such as weight or concentration will help maintain an effective workflow and ensure the longevity and efficacy of your stored materials.

To further your practice in herbal medicine, it is beneficial to have a list of resources where you can access high-quality tools and educational materials. For tools and supplies, online retailers such as Mountain Rose Herbs and Starwest Botanicals offer a wide range of high-quality, ethically sourced herbs and herbal preparation tools. Additionally, joining local herbalist groups or online forums can provide support and further learning opportunities. These communities can be invaluable for sharing tips, recipes, and experiences that can enhance your herbal knowledge and skills.

As you set up your own herbal remedy toolkit, remember that each tool and each herb you choose is a step toward greater self-reliance in managing your health. This space, whether it's a small table in the corner of your room or a designated counter in your kitchen, is where you'll harness the natural potency of the earth's bounty, blending science and tradition to nurture your health and that of your loved ones. With each herb you store and each remedy you create, you're building a bridge to a more natural, empowered form of wellness that resonates through every aspect of your life.

EVERYDAY HERBAL SOLUTIONS

Imagine a day where instead of reaching for a bottle of painkillers to address a nagging headache, you turn to a soothing tea made from leaves you've blended yourself, or a lavender-scented salve you've crafted with care. This isn't just an exercise in imagination, but a practical and empowering reality that herbal remedies offer. Headaches, whether they're tension-related or migraines, can disrupt your daily life, and finding a natural way to manage them not only alleviates pain but also enhances your overall well-being. In this chapter, we explore how herbs like peppermint, lavender, and feverfew can be transformative in dealing with headaches, detailing their use, preparation, and the preventative strategies that can reduce their occurrence.

2.1 ESSENTIAL HERBAL SUPPLEMENTS AND THEIR BENEFITS

In a world increasingly inclined toward holistic health, herbal supplements stand out for their ability to enhance general well-being naturally. Key among these are ginger, turmeric, and garlic—each with its own portfolio of health benefits, backed by both historical use and modern scientific research. Ginger, for instance, has been revered across various cultures for its ability to soothe digestive disturbances and combat nausea. It contains gingerol, a substance with powerful anti-inflammatory and antioxidant properties. Studies have shown that ginger can significantly reduce symptoms of osteoarthritis, especially in the knee, and may even surpass conventional pain medication in some cases without the side effects associated with pharmaceuticals.

Turmeric, characterized by its vibrant yellow color, is another powerhouse supplement. Curcumin, the active compound in turmeric, is celebrated for its potent anti-inflammatory effects and capacity as an antioxidant. Research suggests that curcumin can match the effectiveness of some anti-inflammatory drugs, potentially offering relief for conditions from arthritis to inflammatory bowel disease. Furthermore, it's being studied for its potential in preventing (and possibly treating) cancer, with early results showing it can affect cancer growth, development, and spread at the molecular level. Additionally, the role of curcumin in boosting brain function and lowering the risk of brain diseases links closely to its ability to increase levels of brain-derived neurotrophic factor (BDNF), a type of growth hormone that functions in your brain.

Garlic, used since antiquity for its medicinal properties, remains a staple in natural health for its immune-boosting effects. It is rich in compounds such as allicin, which have been proven to reduce the risk of common illnesses like the cold or flu. Regular garlic supplementation is shown to lower cholesterol levels, and may also have beneficial effects on blood pressure, making it a valuable ally in heart health. The broad-spectrum antimicrobial properties of garlic—effective against bacteria, viruses, fungi, and parasites—add to its profile as a versatile, preventive supplement.

Incorporating these supplements into daily routines can be both simple and transformative. Starting the day with a turmeric latte, for example, can provide a morning boost of anti-inflammatory goodness, while adding freshly grated ginger to a smoothie or tea can invigorate your digestive system and ward off nausea. Garlic, easily integrated into meals, can be taken in the form of chopped cloves in cooking or as a daily supplement to fortify the body's defenses. The key is consistency; the regular inclusion of these supplements maximizes their therapeutic benefits.

Customizing herbal regimens to fit individual health needs and conditions is crucial for maximizing the therapeutic potential of herbal supplements. While the general benefits of ginger, turmeric, and garlic are applicable to many, specific health conditions can benefit from targeted herbal protocols. For instance, someone dealing with inflammatory conditions might increase their intake of turmeric, while those frequently battling infections could focus more on garlic. It's important to adjust dosages and combinations of these herbs based on personal health status and goals, ideally under the guidance of a healthcare provider knowledgeable in both herbal medicine and conventional treatments. This tailored approach ensures that each individual can harness the most effective and personalized benefits from their herbal supplements, leading to better overall health outcomes.

Navigating the world of herbal supplements requires a balance of knowledge, consistency, and personalization. By understanding the specific benefits and potential applications of ginger, turmeric, and garlic, and integrating them thoughtfully into daily life, you can significantly enhance your health and well-being. Remember, the most effective health strategies are those tailored to your unique needs and circumstances—a principle that holds true whether you're exploring the rich world of herbal supplements or any other aspect of natural health.

Herbal Remedy Recipe for Digestion with Marshmallow Root and Ginger

WHAT YOU NEED:

1. **Marshmallow Root** (dried): 1 tablespoon
2. **Fresh Ginger Root**: 1-inch piece
3. **Water**: 2 cups
4. **Honey** (optional): For taste

STEPS TO PREPARE:

1. Prepare the Ingredients:

- **Marshmallow Root**: Measure out 1 tablespoon of dried marshmallow root.
- **Ginger Root**: Peel and slice the fresh ginger root into thin pieces.

2. Boil the Water:

- Pour 2 cups of water into a saucepan.
- Bring the water to a boil.

3. Add Ginger:

- Once the water is boiling, add the sliced ginger.
- Reduce the heat and let it simmer for about 10 minutes.

4. Add Marshmallow Root:

- After simmering the ginger, add the dried marshmallow root to the saucepan.
- Let it simmer for another 5 minutes. Marshmallow root

should not be boiled for long periods to preserve its beneficial properties.

5. Remove from Heat:

- Turn off the heat and let the mixture steep for an additional 5-10 minutes.

6. Strain the Tea:

- Pour the mixture through a fine strainer or cheesecloth into a teapot or directly into cups to remove the ginger and marshmallow root pieces.

7. Add Honey (Optional):

- If desired, add honey to taste for sweetness and additional soothing properties.

8. Serve:

- Pour the strained tea into a cup and enjoy.

TIPS:

- **Dosage**: Drink 1-2 cups daily, especially after meals, to help with digestion.
- **Storage**: If you make a larger batch, store the tea in the refrigerator for up to 3 days. Reheat as needed.

BENEFITS:

- **Marshmallow Root**: Known for its soothing properties, marshmallow root helps coat the digestive tract, reducing irritation and inflammation.

- **Ginger**: A well-known digestive aid, ginger helps stimulate digestion, reduce nausea, and alleviate bloating.

This simple herbal tea combines the soothing properties of marshmallow root with the digestive benefits of ginger, making it a natural remedy to support healthy digestion.

Herbal Remedy Recipe for a Turmeric Latte (Golden Milk) to Aid in Anti-Inflammatory Properties and Arthritis

WHAT YOU NEED:

1. **Turmeric Powder**: 1 teaspoon
2. **Fresh Ginger Root**: 1/2-inch piece (or 1/2 teaspoon ginger powder)
3. **Cinnamon Powder**: 1/2 teaspoon
4. **Black Pepper**: A pinch (helps with the absorption of turmeric)
5. **Milk**: 2 cups (dairy or plant-based, such as almond, coconut, or oat milk)
6. **Honey or Maple Syrup**: 1 teaspoon (optional, for sweetness)
7. **Coconut Oil or Ghee**: 1 teaspoon (optional, for added creaminess and health benefits)
8. **Vanilla Extract**: 1/4 teaspoon (optional, for flavor)

STEPS TO PREPARE:

1. Prepare the Ingredients:

- **Fresh Ginger**: Peel and finely grate or mince the ginger root.
- Measure out the turmeric powder, cinnamon powder, and black pepper.

2. Heat the Milk:

- Pour 2 cups of milk into a small saucepan.

- Heat the milk over medium heat until it is warm, but not boiling.

3. Add Spices:

- Add the turmeric powder, grated or powdered ginger, cinnamon powder, and black pepper to the warm milk.
- Stir well to combine all the ingredients.

4. Simmer the Mixture:

- Reduce the heat to low and let the mixture simmer for about 5-10 minutes, stirring occasionally. This helps the flavors meld and allows the turmeric to fully dissolve.

5. Add Sweetener and Fat (Optional):

- If using, add 1 teaspoon of honey or maple syrup for sweetness.
- Add 1 teaspoon of coconut oil or ghee for added creaminess and health benefits.
- Stir well to incorporate.

6. Add Vanilla Extract (Optional):

- If using, add 1/4 teaspoon of vanilla extract for additional flavor.
- Stir to combine.

7. Strain (if needed):

- If using fresh ginger, you may want to strain the mixture through a fine-mesh strainer to remove the ginger pieces before serving.

8. Serve:

- Pour the turmeric latte into a mug and enjoy warm.

TIPS:

- **Dosage**: Drink one cup daily, especially in the evening for its calming and anti-inflammatory effects.
- **Storage**: If making a larger batch, store the turmeric latte in the refrigerator for up to 3 days. Reheat before drinking.

BENEFITS:

- **Turmeric**: Contains curcumin, which has powerful anti-inflammatory and antioxidant properties, beneficial for reducing inflammation and pain associated with arthritis.
- **Ginger**: Adds additional anti-inflammatory and digestive benefits.
- **Cinnamon**: Helps regulate blood sugar levels and adds a warm flavor.
- **Black Pepper**: Enhances the absorption of curcumin from turmeric.
- **Coconut Oil/Ghee**: Healthy fats that aid in the absorption of turmeric and provide additional anti-inflammatory benefits.

This delicious and soothing turmeric latte, also known as golden milk, combines powerful anti-inflammatory ingredients to help manage arthritis symptoms and promote overall health.

2.2 HERBS FOR HEADACHE RELIEF AND PREVENTION

Headaches can often be a signal from your body that something is amiss, be it stress, dehydration, or hormonal changes. Thankfully, nature offers a palette of herbal remedies that not only relieve pain but also help address the underlying causes. Peppermint, for instance, is more than just a refreshing flavor for candies; it has significant analgesic properties that can soothe headaches. The menthol in peppermint oil helps relax the muscles and ease pain, making it an excellent remedy for tension headaches. Lavender, renowned for its calming aroma, is another ally against headaches, particularly those triggered by stress or lack of sleep. Its sedative properties help reduce muscle tension and promote relaxation, providing relief from headache pain. Feverfew, less known but equally potent, has been used for centuries to treat migraines. Its ability to reduce inflammation and prevent the contraction of blood vessels in the brain makes it a valuable herb for preventing migraines before they start.

Preparation Methods

Turning these herbs into remedies can be both a therapeutic process and a way to personalize your healthcare. For peppermint, a simple tea can be effective. Just steep fresh or dried peppermint leaves in boiling water for about 10 minutes, then strain and sip. The warmth and the menthol can soothe your headache as you drink. Lavender, on the other hand, works well in a tincture or as an essential oil. A lavender oil massage can be particularly soothing when applied to the temples and the back of the neck. As for feverfew, it can be taken as a capsule or tablet, but for those who prefer a more direct approach, chewing on a few leaves daily can help prevent migraines, though it's important to note that it has a bitter taste and isn't suitable for everyone.

Preventative Herbal Strategies

Incorporating these herbs into your daily routine can also serve as a preventive measure against headaches. Consider starting your day with a cup of peppermint tea or ending it with a lavender-scented bath. Such practices not only reduce the immediate discomfort but can also diminish the frequency of headaches over time. Additionally, lifestyle adjustments such as maintaining proper hydration, ensuring adequate sleep, and managing stress through mindfulness or yoga can amplify the benefits of these herbal remedies, creating a holistic approach to headache prevention. Incorporating a daily routine of peppermint tea and using lavender oil during periods of high stress can significantly reduce the frequency and intensity of headaches. Similarly, for those who struggle with migraines, the regular use of feverfew supplements can decrease the occurrence of migraine episodes.

Herbal remedies offer a gentle yet effective way to manage headaches, providing relief while also nurturing your body's natural healing abilities. By understanding and utilizing the therapeutic properties of herbs like peppermint, lavender, and feverfew, you can not only alleviate pain but also enhance your overall health and well-being. As you integrate these herbal solutions into your life, you may find that they offer more than just physical relief—they can also bring a sense of calm and balance, enriching your daily experience.

Peppermint Tea for Headache Relief

INGREDIENTS:

1. 1 tablespoon fresh peppermint leaves (or 1 teaspoon dried peppermint leaves)
2. 1 cup boiling water
3. 1 teaspoon honey (optional)
4. Lemon slice (optional)

INSTRUCTIONS:

1. Prepare the Peppermint:

- If using fresh peppermint leaves, rinse them thoroughly under cold water.
- If using dried peppermint leaves, measure out 1 teaspoon.

2. Boil Water:

- Bring 1 cup of water to a rolling boil.

3. Steep the Tea:

- Place the peppermint leaves in a teapot or a mug.
- Pour the boiling water over the leaves.
- Cover and let the tea steep for about 5-10 minutes. The longer you steep, the stronger the flavor.

4. Strain the Leaves:

- If you used loose leaves, strain the tea into another mug to remove the leaves.
- If you used a tea infuser, simply remove it from the mug.

5. Add Honey and Lemon (Optional):

- Stir in a teaspoon of honey if you prefer a sweeter taste.
- Add a slice of lemon for additional flavor and a boost of vitamin C.

6. Serve and Enjoy:

- Sip the tea slowly and relax. The peppermint can help to relax muscles and improve blood flow, which may alleviate headache symptoms.

TIPS:

- **Fresh vs. Dried:** Fresh peppermint leaves tend to have a more vibrant flavor, but dried leaves work well too and are convenient to store.

- **Peppermint Oil:** For an extra boost, you can add a drop of food-grade peppermint oil to the tea, but use this sparingly as it's very potent.
- **Aromatherapy:** Inhaling the steam from the peppermint tea while it steeps can also provide relief.

Herbal Remedy Recipe for a Lavender Tincture

WHAT YOU NEED:

1. **Dried Lavender Flowers**: 1 cup (fresh lavender flowers can also be used, double the amount if using fresh)
2. **Alcohol**: Vodka or brandy, at least 80 proof (40% alcohol content)
3. **Glass Jar**: A clean, airtight glass container
4. **Cheesecloth or Strainer**: For filtering
5. **Dark Glass Dropper Bottles**: For storing the finished tincture
6. **Label and Pen**: For labeling the tincture

STEPS TO PREPARE:

1. Prepare the Lavender:

- If using fresh lavender flowers, rinse them thoroughly and pat them dry. If using dried lavender, ensure they are free from any moisture and contaminants.

2. Fill the Jar:

- Place the lavender flowers in the glass jar, filling it about halfway for dried lavender, or up to three-quarters full for fresh lavender.

3. Add Alcohol:

- Pour the alcohol over the lavender flowers, making sure they are completely submerged.
- Leave about an inch of space at the top of the jar.

4. Seal and Shake:

- Seal the jar tightly with a lid.
- Shake the jar well to mix the lavender and alcohol.

5. Store and Shake:

- Place the jar in a cool, dark place.
- Shake the jar every day or every few days to keep the mixture well-blended.
- Let the tincture sit for at least 4-6 weeks. The longer it sits, the stronger it will be.

6. Strain the Tincture:

- After the waiting period, place cheesecloth or a fine strainer over a clean bowl.
- Pour the mixture through the cheesecloth to filter out the lavender flowers.
- Squeeze the cheesecloth to extract as much liquid as possible.

7. Transfer to Dropper Bottles:

- Use a funnel to pour the strained liquid into dark glass dropper bottles.
- Label the bottles with the name of the tincture and the date.

TIPS:

- **Ratio**: A common ratio is 1 part fresh lavender flowers to 2 parts alcohol or 1 part dried lavender flowers to 5 parts alcohol.
- **Alcohol Alternatives**: For non-alcoholic tinctures, you can use apple cider vinegar or glycerin, though they may not extract as many beneficial compounds.

BENEFITS OF LAVENDER TINCTURE:

- **Calming and Relaxing**: Lavender is well-known for its calming and relaxing properties, which can help reduce stress, anxiety, and promote better sleep.
- **Digestive Aid**: Lavender can help alleviate digestive issues such as bloating, gas, and indigestion.
- **Pain Relief**: It has mild analgesic properties that can help with headaches, muscle pain, and menstrual cramps.
- **Anti-inflammatory and Antimicrobial**: Lavender has anti-inflammatory and antimicrobial properties, making it useful for minor wounds, insect bites, and skin irritations.

HOW TO USE:

- **Dosage**: Take 1-2 droppersful (1-2 ml) of lavender tincture diluted in a small amount of water or juice up to three times a day, as needed.
- **Sleep Aid**: For better sleep, take a dose 30 minutes before bedtime.
- **Stress Relief**: Use during the day to help manage stress and anxiety.

This lavender tincture is a versatile herbal remedy that captures the therapeutic benefits of lavender, offering a natural way to promote relaxation, aid digestion, and relieve minor pains and skin irritations.

2.3 NATURAL HERBAL REMEDIES FOR DIGESTIVE HEALTH

Digestive issues can often be as frustrating as they are common, with symptoms like bloating, indigestion, and acid reflux affecting a significant part of the population daily. Fortunately, nature offers a variety of herbs that can help soothe and support the digestive system, making it easier to enjoy meals and lead a comfortable life. Ginger, chamomile, and dandelion stand out as three botanicals with remarkable digestive benefits. Ginger, with its sharp, invigorating aroma and taste, is well-known for its ability to alleviate nausea and stimulate digestive juices, aiding the digestion process efficiently. Chamomile, a herb celebrated for its gentle, soothing qualities, can calm an upset stomach and reduce inflammation in the digestive tract, making it perfect for those evenings when you need a peaceful end to your day. Dandelion, often overlooked and removed as a common weed, is actually a powerhouse of digestion support, stimulating appetite and promoting healthy liver function.

For those looking to incorporate these herbs into their diet, various recipes can enhance digestive health while providing enjoyable culinary experiences. Herbal teas are a straightforward and effective way to consume these herbs. For instance, a simple ginger tea can be made by steeping fresh ginger slices in boiling water for several minutes, which helps to extract the beneficial compounds. Adding a little honey or lemon can enhance the flavor and add additional digestive benefits. Chamomile tea, made from dried chamomile flowers, is another excellent choice for evenings, as it can help soothe the stomach and prepare the body for a restful sleep. For those who might enjoy a slightly bitter flavor, dandelion root tea can be a potent digestive aid. Roasting dandelion root before steeping it in hot water can help mellow its bitter taste and bring out a rich, coffee-like flavor.

Introducing herbal bitters into your diet is another effective strategy for improving digestive health. Bitters, which have been used for centuries across various cultures, work by stimulating the digestive system to produce digestive enzymes, bile, and stomach acid. This process enhances digestion and absorption of nutrients while reducing symptoms of indigestion and bloating. Making your own herbal bitters at home can be a rewarding process that allows you to tailor the ingredients to your specific digestive needs. A simple recipe might include alcohol such as vodka or brandy, infused with a blend of bitter herbs such as dandelion, ginger, and a touch of orange peel for flavor. The mixture should be allowed to infuse for about a month before straining and storing in a clean bottle. A few drops of this homemade bitter can be taken before meals to prime the digestive system.

To seamlessly incorporate these digestive herbs into your daily meals, start by adding grated fresh ginger to your dishes, such as stir-fries or smoothies. Chamomile can be used to make a soothing after-dinner tea, which not only aids digestion but also helps you unwind at the end of the day. Dandelion leaves are excellent in salads and are best when picked young; they add a pleasantly bitter crunch that complements sweeter salad ingredients. For a more integrated approach, consider planning meals that naturally incorporate these herbs. For example, a dinner featuring a ginger stir-fry, a fresh dandelion green salad, and a cup of chamomile tea for dessert can provide a full spectrum of digestive benefits while delighting your palate.

The beauty of using herbs for digestive health lies not only in their effectiveness but also in their ability to integrate naturally into daily life, offering a gentle, nourishing way to support your body's digestive processes. By choosing to incorporate these natural remedies, you're not just easing discomfort but also enriching your overall approach to health with traditions that have supported wellness for generations.

Herbal Remedy Recipe for Ginger and Dandelion Root Tea

WHAT YOU NEED:

1. **Fresh Ginger Root**: 1-inch piece
2. **Dandelion Root (dried)**: 1 tablespoon (or 1 small fresh dandelion root)
3. **Water**: 2 cups
4. **Honey or Lemon** (optional): For taste

STEPS TO PREPARE:

1. Prepare the Ingredients:

- **Ginger Root**: Peel and slice the fresh ginger root into thin pieces.
- **Dandelion Root**: If using fresh dandelion root, rinse thoroughly and chop into small pieces. If using dried dandelion root, measure out 1 tablespoon.

2. Boil the Water:

- Pour 2 cups of water into a saucepan.
- Bring the water to a boil.

3. Add Ginger and Dandelion Root:

- Once the water is boiling, add the sliced ginger and dandelion root to the saucepan.

4. Simmer:

- Reduce the heat and let the mixture simmer for about 10-15 minutes.

- Cover the saucepan with a lid to keep the steam in and enhance the infusion process.

5. Remove from Heat:

- Turn off the heat and let the mixture steep for an additional 5 minutes.

6. Strain the Tea:

- Pour the mixture through a fine strainer or cheesecloth into a teapot or directly into cups to remove the ginger and dandelion root pieces.

7. Add Honey or Lemon (Optional):

- If desired, add honey for sweetness and lemon for additional flavor and health benefits.

8. Serve:

- Pour the strained tea into a cup and enjoy.

TIPS:

- **Dosage**: Drink 1-2 cups daily, especially after meals, to help with digestion and detoxification.
- **Storage**: If you make a larger batch, store the tea in the refrigerator for up to 3 days. Reheat as needed.

BENEFITS:

1. Ginger:

- **Digestive Aid**: Ginger helps stimulate digestion, reduce nausea, and alleviate bloating.
- **Anti-inflammatory**: It has potent anti-inflammatory properties that can help reduce inflammation and pain.
- **Immune Boosting**: Ginger supports the immune system and helps fight infections.

2. Dandelion Root:

- **Liver Health**: Dandelion root is known for its liver-detoxifying properties, promoting healthy liver function.
- **Digestive Health**: It acts as a mild laxative, helping to improve digestion and relieve constipation.
- **Diuretic**: Dandelion root helps increase urine production, aiding in detoxification and reducing water retention.
- **Anti-inflammatory**: It has anti-inflammatory properties that can help reduce inflammation in the body.

This ginger and dandelion root tea combines the powerful benefits of both herbs to support digestion, detoxification, and overall health. It's a natural and effective way to promote well-being and address common health concerns.

Herbal Bitters Remedy for Digestive Health

INGREDIENTS:

1. 1 cup dried dandelion root
2. 1 cup dried ginger root
3. 1 cup dried orange peel
4. 1 quart (4 cups) high-proof alcohol (such as vodka or brandy)

5. 1 quart-sized glass jar with a tight-fitting lid
6. Cheesecloth or fine strainer
7. Amber glass dropper bottles for storage

INSTRUCTIONS:

1. Prepare the Ingredients:

- Measure out 1 cup each of dried dandelion root, dried ginger root, and dried orange peel.

2. Combine in a Jar:

- Place the dandelion root, ginger root, and orange peel into the quart-sized glass jar.

3. Add Alcohol:

- Pour the high-proof alcohol over the herbs, ensuring they are fully submerged.

4. Seal and Store:

- Seal the jar tightly with the lid.
- Store the jar in a cool, dark place for 4-6 weeks. Shake the jar gently every few days to help the infusion process.

5. Strain the Mixture:

- After 4-6 weeks, strain the mixture through cheesecloth or a fine strainer to remove the herbs.
- Transfer the strained liquid into amber glass dropper bottles for storage.

DOSAGE:

- Take 1-2 dropperfuls (approximately 1/4 to 1/2 teaspoon) of the herbal bitters before or after meals to aid digestion.
- Bitters can be taken straight, diluted in water, or added to a small amount of juice.

TIPS:

- **Storage:** Keep the bitters in a cool, dark place. Properly stored, they can last for up to a year.
- **Customization:** You can adjust the recipe by adding other digestive herbs such as fennel seeds, gentian root, or chamomile flowers.

2.4 HERBAL TEAS FOR ENERGY AND VITALITY

In the rhythm of daily life, maintaining consistent energy levels can sometimes feel like an uphill battle. It's tempting to reach for a quick fix like a cup of coffee, but there's a more sustainable way to invigorate your body and mind: herbal teas. Not only do these natural brews offer a boost without the harsh effects of caffeine, but they also provide a range of other health benefits that support your overall vitality. Let's explore some remarkable herbs like ginseng, guarana, and green tea, each known for their energizing properties.

Ginseng, revered in traditional Chinese medicine for centuries, stands out for its ability to increase energy and reduce fatigue. It works by enhancing the efficiency of your body's energy production in cells, helping you feel more alert and less stressed. Guarana, a powerhouse of natural caffeine, offers a longer-lasting stimulation than coffee. Its seeds contain about twice the concentration of caffeine found in coffee beans, making it a potent ingredient for energy-boosting teas. However, it's the controlled release in guarana that helps prevent the jitters and crashes often associated with coffee.

Green tea, rich in antioxidants and a moderate amount of caffeine, provides a gentler rise in energy. The presence of L-theanine in green tea helps in smoothing out caffeine's stimulatory effects, offering a balanced boost that enhances alertness without causing nervousness.

Creating your own energy-boosting tea blends allows you to enjoy the synergistic benefits of these herbs. When blending teas, it's important to consider both flavor and function. A basic blend could combine green tea for its mild caffeine, ginseng for stamina, and a touch of dried citrus peel for a refreshing flavor. To make this blend, start with two parts green tea, one part ginseng root, and a half-part of dried citrus peel. Mix these ingredients in a bowl or jar, then steep about one teaspoon of the blend per cup of hot water for five to seven minutes. This tea is ideal for mornings or early afternoons when you need a natural boost to tackle your day.

Timing your consumption of these teas can be as important as the ingredients themselves. Morning is typically the best time to enjoy an energy-boosting tea, setting a positive tone for the rest of your day. Drinking these teas early ensures that the natural stimulants do their work when you most need them, without interfering with your night-time routine. However, if you find your energy waning in the early afternoon, a cup of green tea can be a perfect pick-me-up that won't disrupt your sleep. It's crucial to avoid consuming energizing herbs late in the evening as they can delay sleep and disrupt your natural sleep cycle.

The sustainable energy provided by herbal teas contrasts sharply with the short bursts offered by traditional caffeinated beverages like coffee or energy drinks. While these beverages can provide an immediate jolt, they often lead to an energy crash that can leave you feeling more exhausted than before. Herbal teas, on the other hand, support your body's natural energy systems, offering a smoother, more sustained lift that doesn't compromise your health. Over time, regular consumption of these teas can contribute to improved endurance, reduced fatigue, and a greater sense of well-being, making them a valuable addition to your daily routine.

Incorporating these energy-boosting herbal teas into your daily regimen is more than just a way to ward off sleepiness—it's a step towards embracing a lifestyle that values long-term health and vitality. As you sip these invigorating brews, consider not only the immediate benefits but also the broader impact they have on your wellness journey. With each cup, you're nurturing your body with nature's best resources, fostering resilience against the ebbs and flows of daily energy demands.

Herbal Energy Tea Recipe with Green Tea, Ginseng, and Dried Citrus Peel

INGREDIENTS:

1. 1 tablespoon green tea leaves (or 1 green tea bag)
2. 1 teaspoon dried ginseng root (sliced or powdered)
3. 1 teaspoon dried citrus peel (orange or lemon)
4. 2 cups boiling water
5. Honey or lemon (optional, for taste)

INSTRUCTIONS:

1. Prepare the Ingredients:

- Measure out 1 tablespoon of green tea leaves or use a green tea bag.
- Measure out 1 teaspoon of dried ginseng root.
- Measure out 1 teaspoon of dried citrus peel.

2. Combine in a Teapot:

- Place the green tea leaves, ginseng root, and citrus peel into a teapot or a large mug.

3. Add Boiling Water:

- Pour 2 cups of boiling water over the mixture.

4. Steep the Tea:

- Cover and let the tea steep for 5-10 minutes. The longer it steeps, the stronger the flavor and the more potent the infusion.

5. Strain and Serve:

- If using loose ingredients, strain the tea into another mug to remove the solids.
- If using a tea infuser or bag, simply remove it from the mug.

6. Add Honey or Lemon (Optional):

- Stir in honey or add a slice of lemon if desired for additional flavor and sweetness.

Dosage:

- Drink 1-2 cups of this herbal energy tea in the morning or early afternoon for an energy boost. Avoid drinking too late in the day to prevent interference with sleep.

Tips:

- **Storage:** Store any unused dried ingredients in a cool, dark place in an airtight container.
- **Customization:** Adjust the amounts of ginseng and citrus peel to suit your taste preferences. You can also add other energizing herbs like peppermint or rosemary for a different flavor profile.

2.5 CALMING HERBS FOR STRESS AND ANXIETY RELIEF

In the bustling rhythm of modern life, stress and anxiety can often shadow our days, making it difficult to find moments of peace and relaxation. Fortunately, nature offers a gentle reprieve with herbs like ashwagandha, valerian root, and passionflower, known for their calming effects. These herbs serve as natural anxiolytics, providing a soothing influence on the nervous system and helping to restore a sense of calm in times of emotional turmoil.

Ashwagandha, a revered herb in Ayurvedic medicine, stands out for its adaptogenic properties, helping the body manage stress more effectively. It works by moderating the stress response, reducing cortisol levels, and enhancing overall resilience to emotional and physical stressors. For those who find themselves constantly 'on edge', ashwagandha can be a cornerstone for restoring balance. Valerian root, with its sedative qualities, is particularly effective in easing anxiety and promoting relaxation. It acts on the brain's GABA receptors, mimicking the action of GABA, a neurotransmitter that helps regulate nerve cells and calm anxiety. Teas and tinctures made from valerian root are excellent for evening use, as they prepare the body and mind for a restful night. Passionflower, another powerful ally, contains flavonoids that soothe the nervous system, making it an ideal choice for those who experience frequent anxiety attacks. Its ability to reduce brain activity helps achieve a quieter state of mind, allowing for moments of tranquility amidst daily chaos.

The preparation of these herbs can be tailored to individual needs and preferences. For a simple, soothing tea, mix equal parts of dried ashwagandha, valerian root, and passionflower. Steep in hot water for about 10 minutes before straining. This herbal tea can be consumed in the evening to unwind after a stressful day or during moments of heightened anxiety to restore a sense of calm. For those who prefer a quicker, more concentrated form, tinctures are ideal. You can create a tincture by macerating the dried herbs in alcohol for several weeks, then straining the mixture. This method extracts the active compounds more efficiently, providing a potent remedy that can be taken in small doses throughout the day. Inhalations offer immediate relief and can be especially beneficial during anxiety attacks. Adding a few drops of passionflower extract to hot water and inhaling the steam can help alleviate anxiety symptoms quickly and effectively.

Integrating these calming herbs into daily routines can enhance their effectiveness and provide continuous support for stress management. Incorporating a cup of herbal tea into your evening ritual or taking a few drops of tincture in moments of stress can help maintain a calm baseline throughout the day. For a deeper relaxation experience, consider adding these herbs to your bath. A warm bath infused with a sachet of calming herbs can provide a double benefit of soothing both the mind and the body. Preparing a bath sachet is simple: just fill a small cloth bag with dried herbs, tie it securely, and let it steep in the bathwater as you soak.

Linking the use of calming herbs with mindfulness practices can further enhance their benefits. Mindfulness meditation, focused on the breath, can be particularly effective when combined with the soothing properties of these herbs. Before beginning a meditation session, sipping on a cup of passionflower tea can help ease your mind into a more receptive state for mindfulness practice. This combination not only helps in reducing current stress and anxiety levels but also builds long-term resilience against future stress.

By choosing to incorporate ashwagandha, valerian root, and passion-flower into your life, you embrace a natural path to managing stress and anxiety. These herbs offer a gentle yet powerful way to enhance your mental health, providing a foundation of calm that can help you navigate life's challenges with grace and tranquility. As you integrate these herbal remedies and practices into your routine, you cultivate a deeper connection to the natural world, one that nourishes both your body and your spirit.

Herbal Remedy Recipe for Ashwagandha, Valerian Root, and Passionflower Tea

WHAT YOU NEED:

1. **Ashwagandha Root (dried)**: 1 teaspoon
2. **Valerian Root (dried)**: 1 teaspoon
3. **Passionflower (dried)**: 1 teaspoon
4. **Water**: 2 cups
5. **Honey or Lemon** (optional): For taste

STEPS TO PREPARE:

1. Boil the Water:

- Pour 2 cups of water into a saucepan.
- Bring the water to a boil.

2. Add Valerian Root:

- Once the water is boiling, add the dried valerian root to the saucepan.
- Reduce the heat and let it simmer for about 10 minutes. Valerian root needs a longer simmering time to extract its beneficial compounds.

3. Add Ashwagandha Root:

- After simmering the valerian root, add the dried ashwagandha root to the saucepan.
- Continue to simmer for another 5-10 minutes.

4. Add Passionflower:

- After simmering the valerian and ashwagandha roots, add the dried passionflower to the mixture.
- Let it simmer for an additional 5 minutes. Passionflower does not require as long to infuse.

5. Remove from Heat:

- Turn off the heat and let the mixture steep for an additional 5 minutes to ensure all the herbs are fully infused.

6. Strain the Tea:

- Pour the mixture through a fine strainer or cheesecloth into a teapot or directly into cups to remove the herb pieces.

7. Add Honey or Lemon (Optional):

- If desired, add honey for sweetness or a slice of lemon for additional flavor and health benefits.

8. Serve:

- Pour the strained tea into a cup and enjoy.

Tips:

- **Dosage**: Drink 1 cup in the evening before bedtime to promote relaxation and restful sleep.
- **Storage**: If you make a larger batch, store the tea in the refrigerator for up to 3 days. Reheat as needed.

BENEFITS:

1. Ashwagandha:

- **Stress Reduction**: Ashwagandha is an adaptogen that helps the body manage stress and anxiety.
- **Improves Sleep**: It has sedative properties that promote restful sleep.
- **Boosts Immunity**: Supports overall health and strengthens the immune system.

2. Valerian Root:

- **Natural Sedative**: Valerian root is well-known for its ability to promote relaxation and improve sleep quality.
- **Reduces Anxiety**: It has calming effects that help reduce anxiety and nervous tension.
- **Muscle Relaxant**: Helps relieve muscle tension and spasms.

3. Passionflower:

- **Anxiety Relief**: Passionflower is effective in reducing anxiety and calming the mind.
- **Improves Sleep**: It helps improve the quality of sleep by promoting relaxation.
- **Mood Enhancement**: Passionflower has mild antidepressant properties that can improve mood.

This herbal tea combines the calming and stress-relieving properties of ashwagandha, valerian root, and passionflower, making it an excellent remedy for promoting relaxation, reducing anxiety, and improving sleep quality.

Herbal Remedy Recipe for Ashwagandha, Valerian Root, and
Passionflower Tincture

WHAT YOU NEED:

1. **Ashwagandha Root (dried)**: 1 part
2. **Valerian Root (dried)**: 1 part
3. **Passionflower (dried)**: 1 part
4. **Alcohol**: Vodka or brandy, at least 80 proof (40% alcohol content)
5. **Glass Jar**: A clean, airtight glass container
6. **Cheesecloth or Strainer**: For filtering
7. **Dark Glass Dropper Bottles**: For storing the finished tincture
8. **Label and Pen**: For labeling the tincture

STEPS TO PREPARE:

1. Prepare the Herbs:

- Measure equal parts of dried ashwagandha root, valerian root, and passionflower. For example, use 1 cup of each herb if you want to make a larger batch.

2. Fill the Jar:

- Place the dried herbs into the glass jar, filling it about halfway.

3. Add Alcohol:

- Pour the alcohol over the herbs, making sure they are completely submerged. Leave about an inch of space at the top of the jar.

4. Seal and Shake:

- Seal the jar tightly with a lid.
- Shake the jar well to mix the herbs and alcohol.

5. Store and Shake:

- Place the jar in a cool, dark place.
- Shake the jar every day or every few days to keep the mixture well-blended.
- Let the tincture sit for at least 4-6 weeks. The longer it sits, the stronger it will be.

6. Strain the Tincture:

- After the waiting period, place cheesecloth or a fine strainer over a clean bowl.
- Pour the mixture through the cheesecloth to filter out the herb solids.
- Squeeze the cheesecloth to extract as much liquid as possible.

7. Transfer to Dropper Bottles:

- Use a funnel to pour the strained liquid into dark glass dropper bottles.
- Label the bottles with the name of the tincture and the date.

DOSAGE INSTRUCTIONS:

- **Standard Dose**: Take 1-2 droppersful (1-2 ml) of the tincture up to three times a day.
- **For Sleep**: Take 1-2 droppersful (1-2 ml) about 30 minutes before bedtime to promote relaxation and improve sleep quality.

- **Anxiety and Stress Relief**: Take 1-2 droppersful (1-2 ml) during the day as needed to help manage stress and reduce anxiety.

2.6 HERBAL SOLUTIONS FOR SLEEP DISORDERS

In the quiet moments of the night, when the world slows down and the demands of the day fade into the background, sleep should naturally follow. Yet, for many, this isn't the case. Sleep disorders are a common struggle, with countless individuals lying awake, yearning for a rest that seems just out of reach. However, the natural world offers solace in the form of sleep-promoting herbs such as lavender, hops, and chamomile. These herbs, known for their gentle sedative properties, interact with the nervous system in ways that encourage relaxation and support the natural sleep cycle.

Lavender, often celebrated for its soothing aroma, is more than just a pleasant scent. It contains compounds like linalool and linalyl acetate, which have been shown to interact with neurotransmitters in the brain to reduce agitation and promote relaxation. This makes lavender an excellent aid for those who find it hard to unwind after a busy day. Hops, another powerful ally, have been used traditionally in herbal medicine to treat insomnia and restlessness. The bitter acids in hops, such as humulone and lupulone, have sedative effects on the central nervous system, helping to shorten the time it takes to fall asleep. Chamomile, with its mild sedative effects, is perhaps one of the most well-known sleep aids. Its calming effects are attributed to the flavonoid apigenin, which binds to benzodiazepine receptors in the brain, subtly promoting drowsiness and improving the quality of sleep.

Creating a bedtime ritual incorporating these herbs can significantly enhance their effectiveness. One delightful way to do this is by crafting a sleep-promoting herbal pillow. Mixing dried lavender, hops, and chamomile in a small cloth bag and placing it near your pillow releases subtle aromas that enhance the sleep environment, making it more conducive to restful sleep. Alternatively, crafting a sleep spray by diluting essential oils from these herbs in water and misting it around your sleeping area can create a calm, fragrant atmosphere that eases the transition into sleep.

Herbal sleep supplements, such as teas or capsules containing these herbs, are another effective method for combating sleep disorders. When using herbal supplements, it's crucial to consider the dosage and potential interactions with other medications. Generally, it's recommended to start with the lowest effective dose and adjust as needed based on your response. For instance, a cup of chamomile tea about 30 minutes before bedtime can be a good starting point. For those taking other medications, particularly sedatives or antidepressants, consulting with a healthcare provider before starting any herbal supplement is essential. This ensures safety, especially since herbs like hops can potentiate the effects of sedative drugs, leading to excessive drowsiness.

Tailoring herbal sleep solutions to fit your specific needs can transform how you approach your sleep problems. If you have difficulty falling asleep, a regimen that includes drinking chamomile tea and using a lavender sleep spray might be most beneficial. For those who find themselves waking up frequently during the night, incorporating more hops into their nighttime routine could be more effective. It's also beneficial to consider the broader aspects of your sleep hygiene when integrating herbal remedies. This includes maintaining a regular sleep schedule, ensuring your sleeping environment is dark and cool, and avoiding stimulants like caffeine and electronics in the evening. By considering these factors alongside your use of sleep-promoting herbs, you create a comprehensive plan that addresses your sleep issues from multiple angles, enhancing your chances of achieving restful, uninterrupted sleep.

In this way, herbs do more than merely treat symptoms; they enhance your overall quality of life by improving one of its most fundamental aspects—your sleep. As you incorporate these herbal solutions into your nightly routine, you not only find relief from sleep disorders but also embrace a lifestyle that honors and nurtures your body's natural rhythms and needs.

Herbal Remedy Recipes for Better Sleep

Lavender, Hops, and Chamomile Tea

INGREDIENTS:

1. 1 teaspoon dried lavender flowers
2. 1 teaspoon dried hops flowers
3. 1 teaspoon dried chamomile flowers
4. 2 cups boiling water
5. Honey (optional, for taste)

INSTRUCTIONS:

1. Prepare the Ingredients:

- Measure out 1 teaspoon each of dried lavender flowers, hops flowers, and chamomile flowers.

2. Combine in a Teapot:

- Place the lavender, hops, and chamomile into a teapot or a large mug.

3. Add Boiling Water:

- Pour 2 cups of boiling water over the herbal mixture.

4. Steep the Tea:

- Cover and let the tea steep for 10-15 minutes. The longer it steeps, the stronger the infusion.

5. Strain and Serve:

- If using loose ingredients, strain the tea into another mug to remove the solids.
- If using a tea infuser, simply remove it from the mug.

6. Add Honey (Optional):

- Stir in honey if desired for additional sweetness.

DOSAGE:

- Drink 1 cup of this herbal tea about 30 minutes to an hour before bedtime to promote relaxation and improve sleep quality.

Herbal Sleep Tincture

INGREDIENTS:

1. 1/2 cup dried lavender flowers
2. 1/2 cup dried hops flowers
3. 1/2 cup dried chamomile flowers
4. 2 cups high-proof alcohol (such as vodka)
5. Quart-sized glass jar with a tight-fitting lid
6. Cheesecloth or fine strainer
7. Amber glass dropper bottles for storage

INSTRUCTIONS:

1. Prepare the Ingredients:

- Measure out 1/2 cup each of dried lavender flowers, hops flowers, and chamomile flowers.

2. Combine in a Jar:

- Place the lavender, hops, and chamomile into the quart-sized glass jar.

3. Add Alcohol:

- Pour the high-proof alcohol over the herbs, ensuring they are fully submerged.

4. Seal and Store:

- Seal the jar tightly with the lid.
- Store the jar in a cool, dark place for 4-6 weeks, shaking gently every few days.

5. Strain the Mixture:

- After 4-6 weeks, strain the mixture through cheesecloth or a fine strainer to remove the herbs.
- Transfer the strained liquid into amber glass dropper bottles for storage.

DOSAGE:

- Take 1-2 droppersful (approximately 1/4 to 1/2 teaspoon) of the tincture in a small amount of water about 30 minutes before bedtime.

POSSIBLE DRUG INTERACTIONS AND PRECAUTIONS

1. Lavender:

- **Interactions:** Lavender may enhance the effects of sedatives and depressants, including alcohol, benzodiazepines, and other central nervous system depressants.
- **Precautions:** Avoid using lavender in large amounts if pregnant or breastfeeding.

2. Hops:

- **Interactions:** Hops may interact with sedative medications and medications metabolized by the liver (e.g., cytochrome P450 substrates).
- **Precautions:** Use with caution if taking other sedatives or if you have a hormone-sensitive condition.

3. Chamomile:

- **Interactions:** Chamomile may interact with blood thinners (e.g., warfarin), antiplatelet drugs, and sedatives.
- **Precautions:** Avoid chamomile if you have allergies to plants in the Asteraceae family (e.g., ragweed, chrysanthemums, marigolds, daisies).

GENERAL ADVICE:

- Consult a healthcare professional before starting any new herbal remedies, especially if you are taking medications or have underlying health conditions.
- Start with a lower dosage to assess your tolerance to the herbs.
- Discontinue use if you experience any adverse reactions.

2.7 BOOSTING IMMUNITY WITH HERBS

In an era where wellness is paramount, fortifying your immune system naturally has never been more vital. Herbs like echinacea, elderberry, and astragalus not only offer an infusion of nature's best defenses but also bring centuries of traditional medicine to our modern lives. Echinacea, for instance, is celebrated for its ability to enhance the immune response. By increasing the number of white blood cells, which fight infections, echinacea can reduce the duration and severity of cold symptoms. Elderberry, rich in antioxidants and vitamins, has been scientifically shown to combat viruses and shorten flu duration. Astragalus, a staple in Traditional Chinese Medicine, fortifies the body against diseases by stimulating and increasing the immune system's overall function.

Creating herbal preparations such as syrups, teas, and capsules allows for daily incorporation of these immune-boosting herbs, making them a convenient addition to your wellness routine. For example, echinacea can be taken as a tea by steeping the roots and flowers in hot water, which helps extract its beneficial compounds. Elderberry syrup, a popular remedy during flu season, can be made by simmering the dried berries with water and honey, forming a thick, concentrated syrup that can be taken alone or mixed into beverages. Astragalus is often taken in capsule form, but it can also be added to soups, making it a warming, immune-enhancing addition to meals.

Integrating these immune herbs into your diet doesn't need to be complex. Simple recipes can effectively incorporate these power-houses into your daily meals. Imagine starting your day with a smoothie blended with a spoonful of elderberry syrup, or a lunch that includes a hearty chicken soup simmered with astragalus root. These small additions can significantly impact your immune health without altering your routine drastically. Additionally, echinacea can be brewed with peppermint and lemon for a refreshing iced tea that serves as a perfect afternoon pick-me-up while bolstering your immune defenses.

Maintaining robust immunity is not only about what you consume but also when and how you integrate these habits into your life. Herbal prevention tips can guide this process effectively. For instance, increasing your intake of immune-boosting herbs at the start of the cold and flu season can provide necessary support to fend off illnesses. Furthermore, lifestyle factors such as getting adequate sleep, managing stress, and maintaining a healthy diet all play critical roles in immune health. Herbs are a part of this holistic approach, working best in conjunction with other healthy habits to create a comprehensive defense system against pathogens.

By incorporating echinacea, elderberry, and astragalus into your daily routine, either through direct consumption or as part of your meals, you empower your body with nature's own protective mechanisms. These herbs offer a simple yet effective way to enhance your immune system, ensuring you are better equipped to face the challenges of different seasons and environments. As you make these natural remedies a staple in your wellness regimen, you'll not only feel better equipped to tackle illnesses but also enjoy the deeper vitality and health that comes from living in tune with nature's rhythms.

As we close this chapter on boosting immunity with herbs, remember the power that lies in these natural remedies. Integrating echinacea, elderberry, and astragalus into your daily practices doesn't just ward off illness—it enhances your overall vitality and connects you with the age-old wisdom of herbal medicine. These herbs are not just aids during illness but are powerful tools for maintaining long-term health and wellness. Moving forward, let these herbal solutions be a part of your journey towards a more resilient and vibrant life.

Echinacea Tincture Recipe

INGREDIENTS:

1. 1 cup dried echinacea root (or 1 1/2 cups fresh echinacea root)
2. 2 cups high-proof alcohol (such as vodka or brandy)
3. Quart-sized glass jar with a tight-fitting lid
4. Cheesecloth or fine strainer
5. Amber glass dropper bottles for storage

INSTRUCTIONS:

1. Prepare the Echinacea:

- If using fresh echinacea root, chop it finely.
- If using dried echinacea root, ensure it is broken into small pieces.

2. Combine in a Jar:

- Place the echinacea root into the quart-sized glass jar.

3. Add Alcohol:

- Pour the high-proof alcohol over the echinacea root, making sure it is fully submerged.

4. Seal and Store:

- Seal the jar tightly with the lid.
- Store the jar in a cool, dark place for 4-6 weeks. Shake the jar gently every few days to help the infusion process.

5. Strain the Mixture:

- After 4-6 weeks, strain the mixture through cheesecloth or a fine strainer to remove the echinacea root.
- Transfer the strained liquid into amber glass dropper bottles for storage.

DOSAGE:

- Take 1-2 droppersful (approximately 1/4 to 1/2 teaspoon) of the tincture up to three times a day, especially at the first sign of illness.

BENEFITS OF ECHINACEA TINCTURE

1. Boosts Immune System:

- Echinacea is well-known for its immune-boosting properties. It helps to stimulate the activity of immune cells, making the body more efficient at fighting off infections and viruses.

2. Reduces Duration of Colds:

- Regular use of echinacea tincture can help reduce the severity and duration of colds and respiratory infections.

3. Anti-inflammatory Properties:

- Echinacea has anti-inflammatory effects, which can help reduce inflammation in the body, providing relief from various inflammatory conditions.

4. Antioxidant Effects:

- The herb contains antioxidants that help protect cells from oxidative stress and damage caused by free radicals.

5. Wound Healing:

- Echinacea can promote wound healing and reduce the chances of infections in cuts and abrasions when applied topically.

6. May Help with Anxiety:

- Some studies suggest that echinacea can help reduce symptoms of anxiety due to its calming effects on the nervous system.

POSSIBLE DRUG INTERACTIONS AND PRECAUTIONS

1. Interactions:

- Echinacea may interact with immunosuppressant drugs, including corticosteroids and medications for autoimmune diseases.
- It may also interact with medications metabolized by the liver (e.g., cytochrome P450 substrates).

2. Precautions:

- Avoid using echinacea if you have an autoimmune disorder, as it may stimulate the immune system.
- People with allergies to plants in the Asteraceae family (e.g., ragweed, chrysanthemums, marigolds, daisies) should use echinacea with caution.

- Pregnant or breastfeeding women should consult a healthcare provider before using echinacea.

GENERAL ADVICE:

- Always consult with a healthcare professional before starting any new herbal remedies, especially if you are taking medications or have underlying health conditions.
- Start with a lower dosage to assess your tolerance to the herb.
- Discontinue use if you experience any adverse reactions.

Herbal Iced Tea Recipe with Echinacea, Peppermint, and Lemon

INGREDIENTS:

1. 2 tablespoons dried echinacea root
2. 1 tablespoon dried peppermint leaves
3. 1 lemon (sliced)
4. 4 cups water
5. Honey or your preferred sweetener (optional)
6. Ice cubes
7. Fresh mint leaves or lemon slices for garnish (optional)

INSTRUCTIONS:

1. Boil the Water:

- Bring 4 cups of water to a rolling boil in a pot.

2. Prepare the Herbs:

- Measure out 2 tablespoons of dried echinacea root and 1 tablespoon of dried peppermint leaves.

3. Steep the Herbs:

- Place the echinacea root and peppermint leaves in a heatproof container or teapot.
- Pour the boiling water over the herbs.
- Cover and let the mixture steep for 20-30 minutes to ensure a strong infusion.

4. Strain the Tea:

- After steeping, strain the tea into a large pitcher to remove the echinacea root and peppermint leaves.

5. Add Lemon:

- Add the slices of one lemon to the pitcher.
- Allow the tea to cool to room temperature.

6. Sweeten the Tea (Optional):

- If desired, add honey or your preferred sweetener to taste. Stir well to ensure the sweetener is fully dissolved.

7. Chill the Tea:

- Refrigerate the tea for at least 1-2 hours, or until it is well chilled.

8. Serve:

- Fill glasses with ice cubes and pour the chilled herbal tea over the ice.
- Garnish with fresh mint leaves or additional lemon slices if desired.

DOSAGE:

- Enjoy 1-2 cups of this refreshing iced tea daily for its immune-boosting and refreshing benefits.

BENEFITS OF ECHINACEA, PEPPERMINT, AND LEMON ICED TEA

1. Immune Support:

- Echinacea is known for its immune-boosting properties, which can help ward off colds and infections.

2. Digestive Aid:

- Peppermint helps soothe the digestive system, relieving symptoms like bloating, gas, and indigestion.

3. Refreshing and Hydrating:

- Lemon adds a refreshing citrus flavor and provides a good source of vitamin C, which is beneficial for the immune system and skin health.

4. Cooling Effect:

- This iced tea is perfect for hot days, offering a cooling and refreshing effect, thanks to the peppermint and lemon.

POSSIBLE DRUG INTERACTIONS AND PRECAUTIONS

1. Echinacea:

- **Interactions:** Echinacea may interact with immunosuppressant drugs, including corticosteroids and medications for autoimmune diseases.

- **Precautions:** Avoid using echinacea if you have an autoimmune disorder or allergies to plants in the Asteraceae family (e.g., ragweed, chrysanthemums, marigolds, daisies). Pregnant or breastfeeding women should consult a healthcare provider before use.

2. Peppermint:

- **Interactions:** Peppermint may interact with antacids and medications for gastroesophageal reflux disease (GERD).
- **Precautions:** Individuals with GERD or hiatal hernia should use peppermint with caution, as it may exacerbate symptoms.

GENERAL ADVICE:

- Always consult with a healthcare professional before starting any new herbal remedies, especially if you are taking medications or have underlying health conditions.
- Start with a lower dosage to assess your tolerance to the herbs.
- Discontinue use if you experience any adverse reactions.

Herbal Remedy Recipe for Elderberry Syrup

WHAT YOU NEED:

1. **Dried Elderberries**: 1 cup
2. **Water**: 4 cups
3. **Honey**: 1 cup (preferably raw, local honey)
4. **Cinnamon Sticks**: 2
5. **Fresh Ginger Root**: 1-inch piece (or 1 teaspoon ginger powder)
6. **Cloves**: 5-6 whole cloves (or 1/2 teaspoon ground cloves)
7. **Glass Jar**: For storing the syrup

STEPS TO PREPARE:

1. Prepare the Ingredients:

- Measure out 1 cup of dried elderberries.
- Peel and slice the ginger root.

2. Boil the Elderberries:

- In a saucepan, combine the dried elderberries, water, cinnamon sticks, ginger slices, and cloves.
- Bring the mixture to a boil.

3. Simmer the Mixture:

- Once boiling, reduce the heat to low and let it simmer for about 45 minutes to 1 hour, until the liquid has reduced by about half.

4. Mash the Berries:

- After simmering, use a spoon or potato masher to carefully mash the elderberries in the saucepan to release more juice.

5. Strain the Mixture:

- Place a fine strainer or cheesecloth over a clean bowl.
- Pour the mixture through the strainer to separate the liquid from the solids.
- Press down on the elderberry pulp to extract as much liquid as possible.

6. Add Honey:

- Allow the liquid to cool to lukewarm (not hot) to preserve the beneficial properties of the honey.
- Add 1 cup of honey to the strained liquid and stir well until fully dissolved.

7. Store the Syrup:

- Pour the elderberry syrup into a glass jar or bottle.
- Seal tightly and label with the date.

8. Refrigerate:

- Store the syrup in the refrigerator, where it will keep for about 2-3 months.

Dosage Instructions:

- **Adults**: Take 1 tablespoon daily for immune support. During illness, take 1 tablespoon every 2-3 hours.
- **Children**: Take 1 teaspoon daily for immune support. During illness, take 1 teaspoon every 2-3 hours. (Note: Do not give honey to children under 1 year old.)

Benefits of Elderberry Syrup:

1. Immune System Support:

- **Boosts Immunity**: Elderberries are rich in antioxidants and vitamins that enhance the immune system, making it easier for the body to fight off infections.
- **Antiviral Properties**: Elderberries have been shown to be effective against various strains of the flu virus, reducing the severity and duration of symptoms.

2. Anti-inflammatory Effects:

- **Reduces Inflammation**: Elderberries contain compounds that help reduce inflammation, which can alleviate symptoms of colds, flu, and other inflammatory conditions.

3. Antioxidant Properties:

- **Rich in Antioxidants**: Elderberries are packed with antioxidants that protect cells from damage caused by free radicals, contributing to overall health and wellness.

4. Respiratory Health:

- **Relieves Cold and Flu Symptoms**: Elderberry syrup can help soothe respiratory tract infections and relieve symptoms such as a sore throat, cough, and congestion.

5. Digestive Health:

- **Supports Digestive Health**: The high fiber content in elderberries aids in digestion and promotes a healthy gut.

This homemade elderberry syrup is a powerful and natural remedy to boost the immune system, fight off viral infections, and support overall health. It is especially beneficial during cold and flu season to help prevent and reduce the severity of illness.

Astragalus Herbal Remedy in Capsule Form

DOSAGE INFORMATION:

- **General Dosage:** The typical recommended dosage for astragalus in capsule form is between 250 to 500 mg, taken 1 to 3 times daily.

- **Standardized Extract:** If using a standardized extract (0.3% astragaloside IV), a common dosage is 200 to 400 mg, taken 1 to 2 times daily.
- **Consultation:** Dosage may vary based on individual health needs and conditions. It is advisable to consult with a healthcare provider for personalized dosing.

BENEFITS OF ASTRAGALUS:

1. Immune System Support:

- **Boosts Immunity:** Astragalus is known for its immune-boosting properties, helping to enhance the body's resistance to infections and illnesses.
- **Stimulates White Blood Cells:** It increases the production and activity of white blood cells, which are crucial for fighting off pathogens.

2. Antioxidant Properties:

- **Reduces Oxidative Stress:** Astragalus contains antioxidants that help protect cells from damage caused by free radicals, reducing oxidative stress and inflammation.

3. Anti-Inflammatory Effects:

- **Reduces Inflammation:** It has anti-inflammatory properties that can help reduce inflammation throughout the body, benefiting conditions such as arthritis and other inflammatory diseases.

4. Cardiovascular Health:

- **Heart Protection:** Astragalus is beneficial for heart health, helping to lower blood pressure, reduce cholesterol levels, and improve overall cardiovascular function.
- **Enhances Blood Flow:** It can improve blood flow and circulation, which is essential for maintaining heart health.

5. Adaptogenic Properties:

- **Stress Reduction:** As an adaptogen, astragalus helps the body adapt to stress and enhances resilience against physical, mental, and emotional stressors.
- **Supports Adrenal Function:** It supports adrenal gland function, which is crucial for managing stress and maintaining energy levels.

6. Kidney Health:

- **Protects Kidney Function:** Astragalus has been shown to support kidney function and may help protect against kidney damage and disease.

7. Anti-Aging Effects:

- **Promotes Longevity:** The herb is believed to have anti-aging effects, potentially extending lifespan and improving overall vitality.

POSSIBLE DRUG INTERACTIONS AND PRECAUTIONS:

1. Interactions:

- **Immunosuppressants:** Astragalus may interact with immunosuppressant drugs, such as those taken after organ transplants, potentially reducing their effectiveness.
- **Anticoagulants:** It may have an additive effect with anticoagulant medications (e.g., warfarin), increasing the risk of bleeding.
- **Blood Pressure Medications:** Astragalus can lower blood pressure, so it should be used cautiously with antihypertensive drugs to avoid hypotension.

2. Precautions:

- **Autoimmune Disorders:** People with autoimmune diseases should use astragalus with caution, as it can stimulate the immune system.
- **Pregnancy and Breastfeeding:** Pregnant or breastfeeding women should consult a healthcare provider before using astragalus.
- **Allergies:** Individuals with allergies to plants in the Fabaceae family should avoid astragalus.

GENERAL ADVICE:

- Always consult with a healthcare professional before starting any new herbal remedies, especially if you are taking medications or have underlying health conditions.
- Monitor for any adverse reactions and discontinue use if they occur.

WOMEN'S HEALTH AND HERBALISM

As the moon waxes and wanes, so too do the rhythms of a woman's body. It's a cyclical dance that, while beautiful, can often bring with it a host of discomforts and stresses, particularly during the premenstrual phase. You might find yourself grappling with cramps that throw off your day's rhythm or mood swings that make a roller coaster seem tame. But within the realm of nature's bounty lies a gentle yet powerful approach to easing these monthly trials. Herbal remedies, rooted in centuries of wisdom, offer more than just relief; they provide a pathway to harmonizing your body's natural rhythms with the nurturing touch of the earth.

3.1 HERBAL REMEDIES FOR PMS AND CRAMPS

Each month, many women experience the familiar pangs of premenstrual syndrome (PMS), which can manifest in ways as varied as the women it affects. The discomfort is not just physical; the emotional toll can be just as challenging. Fortunately, herbs like chaste berry, evening primrose oil, and cramp bark have been long celebrated for their efficacy in mitigating the less pleasant aspects of the menstrual cycle.

Chaste berry, often heralded as a woman's herb, works subtly to normalize and regulate hormone levels, particularly progesterone. This can alleviate symptoms like mood swings and breast tenderness. Evening primrose oil, rich in gamma-linolenic acid (GLA), a fatty acid, has been shown to help reduce both the physical and emotional symptoms of PMS, from bloating to irritability. Cramp bark, true to its name, offers potent relief for uterine cramps. By reducing muscle spasms and easing tension, it can transform a painful period into something more manageable.

Preparation Methods for Quick Relief

To harness these benefits, various preparation methods can be employed. For cramp bark, a simple tea can be quite effective. Just simmer one to two teaspoons of dried cramp bark in a cup of water for about 15 minutes, then strain and sip. The warmth of the tea not only aids in the absorption of the medicinal compounds but also provides soothing heat to the abdomen. For evening primrose oil, capsules are commonly available and provide a direct and measured dose of GLA. Chaste berry works well in both tinctures and capsules, often taken daily, starting from the middle of the menstrual cycle until it begins, to alleviate symptoms preemptively.

Integrative Herbal Strategies

Incorporating these herbs into a monthly regimen requires a proactive approach. Start with understanding your cycle and symptoms. Keeping a symptom diary can be immensely helpful in identifying patterns and pinpointing which days might benefit from specific herbal interventions. For instance, if you tend to experience severe cramps on the first day of your flow, planning to take cramp bark tea the day before and during can help manage the intensity. Similarly, integrating evening primrose oil capsules into your daily routine during the latter half of your cycle can help in smoothing emotional highs and lows.

Educational Insight on Menstrual Health

Understanding the ebb and flow of your menstrual cycle is not just about managing discomfort but recognizing it as a vital sign of your overall health. Hormonal fluctuations that dictate your cycle phases can impact everything from your mental clarity to your skin health. Herbs not only offer relief but also act as natural balancers, aligning your body's rhythms with the natural world. For instance, the regular use of chaste berry can enhance progesterone levels, which not only alleviates PMS but also promotes a healthy cycle length and ovulation pattern.

By embracing these herbal remedies, you're not just easing symptoms but actively participating in a tradition of women's herbal wisdom that stretches back through generations. Each cup of cramp bark tea, each capsule of evening primrose oil, becomes a thread in the fabric of knowledge that women have shared and passed down through the ages—herbal wisdom for menstrual health, honed by centuries of care, study, and understanding. As you integrate these practices into your life, you connect with a community of women worldwide who turn to the earth for healing, finding in its depths a wellspring of health and balance.

Cramp Bark Tea Recipe

INGREDIENTS:

1. 1 tablespoon dried cramp bark (Viburnum opulus)
2. 2 cups water
3. Honey or lemon (optional, for taste)

INSTRUCTIONS:

1. Boil the Water:

- Bring 2 cups of water to a rolling boil in a pot.

2. Prepare the Cramp Bark:

- Measure out 1 tablespoon of dried cramp bark.

3. Steep the Cramp Bark:

- Place the cramp bark in a teapot or a large mug.
- Pour the boiling water over the cramp bark.
- Cover and let the mixture steep for 15-20 minutes to ensure a strong infusion.

4. Strain the Tea:

- After steeping, strain the tea into another mug to remove the cramp bark.

5. Add Honey or Lemon (Optional):

- Stir in honey or add a slice of lemon if desired for additional flavor and sweetness.

DOSAGE:

- Drink 1-2 cups of cramp bark tea daily as needed for relief from muscle cramps or menstrual discomfort.

BENEFITS OF CRAMP BARK TEA

1. Relieves Muscle Cramps:

- Cramp bark is well-known for its ability to relax smooth muscle tissue, making it effective in alleviating muscle cramps and spasms.

2. Eases Menstrual Pain:

- The herb is commonly used to relieve menstrual cramps and discomfort by relaxing the uterine muscles and reducing spasms.

3. Anti-inflammatory Properties:

- Cramp bark contains anti-inflammatory compounds that can help reduce inflammation and pain associated with various conditions.

4. Reduces Nervous Tension:

- It has a mild sedative effect, which can help reduce nervous tension and promote relaxation.

5. Supports Digestive Health:

- The relaxing properties of cramp bark can also benefit the digestive system by alleviating cramps and spasms in the gastrointestinal tract.

6. Helps with Muscle Tension:

- It is useful for relieving general muscle tension, making it beneficial for conditions such as tension headaches and back pain.

POSSIBLE DRUG INTERACTIONS AND PRECAUTIONS

1. Interactions:

- **Antispasmodics and Sedatives:** Cramp bark may have additive effects with other antispasmodic or sedative medications, potentially enhancing their effects.
- **Blood Pressure Medications:** It may lower blood pressure, so use with caution if you are taking antihypertensive medications to avoid hypotension.

2. Precautions:

- **Pregnancy and Breastfeeding:** Pregnant or breastfeeding women should consult a healthcare provider before using cramp bark.
- **Kidney Stones:** Individuals with a history of kidney stones should use cramp bark with caution, as it contains oxalates which could potentially contribute to stone formation.
- **Allergies:** Those allergic to plants in the Viburnum family should avoid using cramp bark.

GENERAL ADVICE:

- Always consult with a healthcare professional before starting any new herbal remedies, especially if you are taking medications or have underlying health conditions.
- Monitor for any adverse reactions and discontinue use if they occur.

Primrose Oil in Capsule Form

DOSAGE INFORMATION:

- **General Dosage:** The typical recommended dosage for evening primrose oil (EPO) in capsule form is between 500 to 1,300 mg per day. It is often divided into 2-3 doses throughout the day.
- **Gamma-Linolenic Acid (GLA):** Standardized EPO supplements usually contain 8-10% gamma-linolenic acid (GLA). A common dosage is 240-320 mg of GLA per day.
- **Consultation:** Dosage may vary based on individual health needs and conditions. It is advisable to consult with a healthcare provider for personalized dosing.

BENEFITS OF PRIMROSE OIL:

1. **Supports Skin Health:**

- **Eczema and Psoriasis:** EPO is known to help manage symptoms of eczema and psoriasis by reducing inflammation and improving skin barrier function.
- **Acne:** It may help reduce acne flare-ups by balancing hormones and reducing skin inflammation.

2. **Hormonal Balance:**

- **Premenstrual Syndrome (PMS):** EPO is commonly used to alleviate symptoms of PMS, including breast tenderness, mood swings, and bloating.
- **Menopause:** It can help manage symptoms of menopause such as hot flashes and night sweats.

3. Anti-Inflammatory Properties:

- **Arthritis:** EPO has anti-inflammatory effects that can help reduce joint pain and stiffness associated with rheumatoid arthritis.
- **General Inflammation:** It may help reduce general inflammation in the body, providing relief for various inflammatory conditions.

4. Heart Health:

- **Cholesterol Levels:** EPO may help improve cholesterol levels by increasing HDL (good) cholesterol and reducing LDL (bad) cholesterol.
- **Blood Pressure:** It can help lower blood pressure, supporting overall cardiovascular health.

5. Nerve Health:

- **Neuropathy:** EPO may help manage symptoms of diabetic neuropathy, such as pain, tingling, and numbness in the limbs.

6. Hair and Nail Health:

- **Hair Growth:** It can promote hair growth and reduce hair loss, particularly in individuals with hormonal imbalances.
- **Nail Strength:** EPO can help improve nail strength and reduce brittleness.

POSSIBLE DRUG INTERACTIONS AND PRECAUTIONS

1. Interactions:

- **Anticoagulants and Antiplatelet Drugs:** EPO may increase the risk of bleeding, so it should be used cautiously with blood-thinning medications such as warfarin, aspirin, and clopidogrel.

- **Seizure Medications:** There are reports that EPO may lower the seizure threshold, so it should be used with caution in individuals taking anticonvulsants or with a history of seizures.
- **Blood Pressure Medications:** EPO can lower blood pressure, so use with caution if you are taking antihypertensive medications to avoid hypotension.

2. Precautions:

- **Pregnancy and Breastfeeding:** Pregnant or breastfeeding women should consult a healthcare provider before using EPO.
- **Surgery:** Discontinue use of EPO at least two weeks before scheduled surgery due to the increased risk of bleeding.
- **Allergies:** Individuals with allergies to plants in the Onagraceae family should use EPO with caution.

GENERAL ADVICE:

- Always consult with a healthcare professional before starting any new herbal remedies, especially if you are taking medications or have underlying health conditions.
- Monitor for any adverse reactions and discontinue use if they occur.

Herbal Remedy Recipe for Chasteberry Tincture

WHAT YOU NEED:

1. **Dried Chasteberries (Vitex agnus-castus)**: 1 part
2. **Alcohol**: Vodka or brandy, at least 80 proof (40% alcohol content)

3. **Glass Jar**: A clean, airtight glass container
4. **Cheesecloth or Strainer**: For filtering
5. **Dark Glass Dropper Bottles**: For storing the finished tincture
6. **Label and Pen**: For labeling the tincture

STEPS TO PREPARE:

1. Prepare the Chasteberries:

- Measure out the dried chasteberries. For example, if you use 1 cup of chasteberries, you'll need enough alcohol to cover them completely in the jar.

2. Fill the Jar:

- Place the dried chasteberries into the glass jar, filling it about halfway.

3. Add Alcohol:

- Pour the alcohol over the chasteberries, ensuring they are completely submerged. Leave about an inch of space at the top of the jar.

4. Seal and Shake:

- Seal the jar tightly with a lid.
- Shake the jar well to mix the chasteberries and alcohol.

5. Store and Shake:

- Place the jar in a cool, dark place.
- Shake the jar every day or every few days to keep the mixture well-blended.

- Let the tincture sit for at least 4-6 weeks. The longer it sits, the stronger it will be.

6. Strain the Tincture:

- After the waiting period, place cheesecloth or a fine strainer over a clean bowl.
- Pour the mixture through the cheesecloth to filter out the chasteberries.
- Squeeze the cheesecloth to extract as much liquid as possible.

7. Transfer to Dropper Bottles:

- Use a funnel to pour the strained liquid into dark glass dropper bottles.
- Label the bottles with the name of the tincture and the date.

DOSAGE INSTRUCTIONS:

- **Standard Dose**: Take 1-2 droppersful (1-2 ml) of the tincture diluted in a small amount of water or juice up to three times a day.
- **For Hormonal Balance**: Take 1-2 droppersful (1-2 ml) in the morning, preferably on an empty stomach, for best results.

BENEFITS OF CHASTEBERRY TINCTURE:

1. Hormonal Balance:

- **Regulates Menstrual Cycle**: Chasteberry is well-known for its ability to regulate the menstrual cycle and alleviate symptoms of PMS (premenstrual syndrome).
- **Reduces PMS Symptoms**: It helps reduce symptoms such as breast tenderness, bloating, mood swings, and irritability.

2. Supports Reproductive Health:

- **Enhances Fertility**: Chasteberry can help improve fertility by balancing hormones and promoting regular ovulation.
- **Eases Menopausal Symptoms**: It can help alleviate menopausal symptoms such as hot flashes, mood swings, and night sweats.

3. Prolactin Regulation:

- **Reduces Prolactin Levels**: Chasteberry has been shown to lower elevated prolactin levels, which can benefit women with conditions such as hyperprolactinemia or luteal phase defects.

4. Anti-inflammatory Properties:

- **Reduces Inflammation**: Chasteberry has anti-inflammatory properties that can help reduce inflammation and pain associated with menstrual cramps and other inflammatory conditions.

ADDITIONAL NOTES:

- **Consult a Healthcare Professional**: Before starting any new herbal remedy, especially for hormonal issues, consult with a healthcare professional, particularly if you are pregnant, nursing, or taking other medications.
- **Consistency is Key**: For best results, take chasteberry tincture consistently over a period of several months.

This chasteberry tincture is a natural and effective remedy for supporting hormonal balance, reproductive health, and overall well-being.

Chasteberry (Vitex agnus-castus) in Capsule Form

DOSAGE INFORMATION:

- **General Dosage:** The typical recommended dosage for chasteberry in capsule form is between 400 to 1,000 mg per day.
- **Standardized Extract:** If using a standardized extract (0.5% agnuside), a common dosage is 20 to 40 mg per day.
- **Duration:** It may take several weeks to a few months to notice the full benefits. Consistency is key for optimal results.
- **Consultation:** Dosage may vary based on individual health needs and conditions. It is advisable to consult with a healthcare provider for personalized dosing.

BENEFITS OF CHASTEBERRY:

1. **Hormonal Balance:**

- **Premenstrual Syndrome (PMS):** Chasteberry is commonly used to alleviate symptoms of PMS, including breast tenderness, irritability, mood swings, and bloating.
- **Menstrual Irregularities:** It helps regulate menstrual cycles and can be beneficial for women experiencing irregular periods or amenorrhea (absence of menstruation).

2. **Menopause:**

- **Symptom Relief:** Chasteberry may help reduce menopausal symptoms such as hot flashes, night sweats, and mood swings.

3. **Fertility Support:**

- **Ovulation:** Chasteberry can support ovulation and improve fertility in women with hormonal imbalances or luteal phase defects.

- **Prolactin Levels:** It helps normalize prolactin levels, which can be beneficial for women with hyperprolactinemia, a condition that can interfere with ovulation.

4. Acne:

- **Hormonal Acne:** Chasteberry may help reduce acne breakouts that are linked to hormonal fluctuations, particularly those occurring before menstruation.

5. Breast Health:

- **Fibrocystic Breasts:** It can alleviate symptoms of fibrocystic breast condition, such as breast pain and lumpiness, by regulating hormones.

6. Mood and Well-being:

- **Emotional Stability:** Chasteberry can help improve mood and emotional stability, particularly in women with PMS or menopause-related mood swings.

Possible Drug Interactions and Precautions

1. Interactions:

- **Hormone Therapy:** Chasteberry may interact with hormone replacement therapy (HRT) or oral contraceptives, potentially altering their effectiveness.
- **Dopamine-related Medications:** It may interfere with medications that affect dopamine levels, such as antipsychotics and medications for Parkinson's disease.

- **Progesterone:** Chasteberry's effects on hormone levels may interact with progesterone supplements.

2. Precautions:

- **Pregnancy and Breastfeeding:** Pregnant or breastfeeding women should consult a healthcare provider before using chasteberry, as its effects on pregnancy and lactation are not well-studied.
- **Hormone-sensitive Conditions:** Individuals with hormone-sensitive conditions, such as breast cancer, endometriosis, or uterine fibroids, should use chasteberry with caution.
- **Allergies:** Those allergic to plants in the Verbenaceae family should avoid using chasteberry.

GENERAL ADVICE:

- Always consult with a healthcare professional before starting any new herbal remedies, especially if you are taking medications or have underlying health conditions.
- Start with a lower dosage to assess your tolerance to the herb.
- Monitor for any adverse reactions and discontinue use if they occur.

3.2 NATURAL APPROACHES TO HORMONAL BALANCE

In the intricate dance of your body's systems, hormones play the lead role, orchestrating a wide array of functions from metabolism to mood, growth to reproduction. When this delicate balance is disrupted, it can ripple across your health, manifesting in ways as varied as persistent acne, mood swings, fatigue, or irregular menstrual cycles. Understanding the pivotal role of hormones is the first step in appreciating how vital maintaining this equilibrium is to your overall wellbeing.

Hormones, essentially chemical messengers produced by the endocrine glands, travel through your bloodstream, instructing tissues and organs on what to do. They help control many of your body's major processes, including metabolism and reproduction. When balanced, you likely feel energetic, stable, and healthy. However, when imbalances occur, it can feel like your body is out of control. This is where the power of herbs comes into play, offering a gentle yet effective means to support and restore hormonal balance naturally.

Herbs like maca root, licorice root, and holy basil have been revered through the ages for their ability to stabilize hormonal function and promote endocrine health. Maca root, often referred to as Peruvian ginseng, functions as an adaptogen, aiding in the normalization of hormone levels during stressful times. It's particularly noted for enhancing stamina and energy, attributes that are often compromised in states of hormonal imbalance. Licorice root, with its sweet, earthy flavor, extends beyond its culinary uses, acting profoundly on the endocrine system by mimicking the effects of adrenal hormones, which can help in maintaining an adequate hormonal response to stress. Holy basil, also known as Tulsi, is another adaptogen known for its wide-ranging benefits, including its ability to lower cortisol levels, which can significantly impact hormonal health.

Creating a daily regimen incorporating these herbs can help in managing hormonal fluctuations effectively. For instance, starting the day with a maca-infused smoothie can energize your mornings while stabilizing hormone levels. Incorporating a small amount of powdered maca root into your breakfast can set a positive tone for the day, ensuring your energy levels are balanced and your mood is stable. Licorice root can be brewed into a tea, perfect for after meals, not only aiding in digestion but also supporting adrenal function, crucial for maintaining hormonal balance. Holy basil works beautifully in both teas and as an extract, taken in the evening to help wind down the day with its stress-reducing properties, fostering a night of restful sleep, which itself is crucial for hormonal health.

Consider someone who struggles with chronic fatigue and erratic menstrual cycles. They would benefit from adding maca root to their morning routine and drinking licorice root tea post-lunch. There would be marked improvement in their energy levels and a regularization of their menstrual cycle within a few months. A person who faces severe pre-menopausal symptoms, including hot flashes and night sweats, would gain significant relief of symptoms from using holy basil extract in the evenings.

These examples underscore the potential of herbs in managing hormonal health, offering solutions that are not only effective but also align with a natural, holistic approach to wellness. As you consider integrating these herbs into your daily regimen, remember that each woman's body is unique, and what works for one may not work for another. It's about finding what works for you and adjusting your regimen as your body and its needs evolve. Listening to your body and responding with natural remedies can empower you to live a balanced, healthy life.

Maca Root Infused Smoothie Recipe

Ingredients:

1. 1 teaspoon maca root powder
2. 1 banana (fresh or frozen)
3. 1 cup unsweetened almond milk (or your preferred milk)
4. 1/2 cup Greek yogurt (optional for extra protein)
5. 1 tablespoon almond butter (or any nut butter)
6. 1 tablespoon honey or maple syrup (optional for sweetness)
7. 1/2 teaspoon cinnamon (optional for flavor)
8. A handful of ice cubes (if using fresh banana)
9. Fresh berries or a few spinach leaves (optional for extra nutrients)

INSTRUCTIONS:

1. Prepare the Ingredients:

- Peel the banana and measure out the rest of the ingredients.

2. Blend the Smoothie:

- Place the banana, almond milk, Greek yogurt (if using), almond butter, maca root powder, honey or maple syrup (if using), and cinnamon (if using) into a blender.
- Add ice cubes if you are using a fresh banana.

3. Blend Until Smooth:

- Blend all the ingredients on high speed until the mixture is smooth and creamy. Add more milk if the smoothie is too thick or more ice if it's too thin.

4. Serve:

- Pour the smoothie into a glass.
- Garnish with fresh berries or a sprinkle of cinnamon if desired.

5. Enjoy:

- Drink your maca root infused smoothie immediately for the best taste and nutrient intake.

BENEFITS OF MACA ROOT SMOOTHIE

1. Increased Energy Levels:

- **Natural Energizer:** Maca root is known for its ability to boost energy and stamina without the jitters associated with caffeine.

2. Hormonal Balance:

- **Supports Endocrine System:** Maca can help balance hormones, making it beneficial for both men and women dealing with hormonal imbalances.

3. Enhanced Mood and Mental Clarity:

- **Improves Mood:** Regular consumption of maca can help improve mood and reduce symptoms of anxiety and depression.
- **Boosts Cognitive Function:** It is believed to enhance mental clarity and improve focus.

4. Supports Sexual Health:

- **Libido Enhancer:** Maca root is known to enhance libido and sexual function in both men and women.
- **Improves Fertility:** It can support reproductive health and improve fertility.

5. Rich in Nutrients:

- **Vitamins and Minerals:** Maca is rich in essential vitamins and minerals, including vitamin C, copper, and iron.
- **Antioxidants:** It contains antioxidants that help protect cells from oxidative stress and inflammation.

6. Supports Physical Performance:

- **Improves Endurance:** Athletes often use maca to enhance endurance and performance.
- **Muscle Recovery:** It can aid in muscle recovery after intense exercise.

POSSIBLE DRUG INTERACTIONS AND PRECAUTIONS

1. Interactions:

- **Hormone-sensitive Conditions:** Maca may interact with medications for hormone-sensitive conditions. Consult with a healthcare provider if you have conditions like breast cancer, uterine cancer, ovarian cancer, endometriosis, or uterine fibroids.
- **Thyroid Medication:** Maca contains goitrogens, which could potentially interfere with thyroid function, especially in individuals with thyroid disorders.

2. Precautions:

- **Pregnancy and Breastfeeding:** Pregnant or breastfeeding women should consult a healthcare provider before using maca.
- **Dosage:** Start with a lower dosage to assess your tolerance to maca root. Gradually increase the amount as needed.
- **Allergies:** Ensure you do not have an allergy to maca or any of the other ingredients used in the smoothie.

Herbal Remedy Recipe for Licorice and Holy Basil Tea

What You Need:

1. **Dried Licorice Root**: 1 teaspoon
2. **Dried Holy Basil (Tulsi) Leaves**: 1 teaspoon
3. **Water**: 2 cups
4. **Honey or Lemon** (optional): For taste

Steps to Prepare:

1. Boil the Water:

- Pour 2 cups of water into a saucepan.
- Bring the water to a boil.

2. Add Licorice Root:

- Once the water is boiling, add the dried licorice root to the saucepan.
- Reduce the heat and let it simmer for about 10 minutes. Licorice root needs a longer simmering time to extract its beneficial compounds.

3. Add Holy Basil Leaves:

- After simmering the licorice root, add the dried holy basil leaves to the saucepan.
- Let it simmer for an additional 5-7 minutes. Holy basil does not require as long to infuse.

4. Remove from Heat:

- Turn off the heat and let the mixture steep for another 5 minutes to ensure all the herbs are fully infused.

5. Strain the Tea:

- Pour the mixture through a fine strainer or cheesecloth into a teapot or directly into cups to remove the herb pieces.

6. Add Honey or Lemon (Optional):

- If desired, add honey for sweetness or a slice of lemon for additional flavor and health benefits.

7. Serve:

- Pour the strained tea into a cup and enjoy.

TIPS:

- **Dosage**: Drink 1-2 cups daily, especially in the morning or early afternoon to help manage stress and support overall health.
- **Storage**: If you make a larger batch, store the tea in the refrigerator for up to 3 days. Reheat as needed.

BENEFITS OF LICORICE AND HOLY BASIL TEA:

1. Licorice Root:

- **Anti-inflammatory**: Licorice root has strong anti-inflammatory properties that can help reduce inflammation and soothe irritated tissues.
- **Digestive Health**: It helps soothe the digestive tract, reducing symptoms of indigestion, heartburn, and ulcers.
- **Immune Support**: Licorice root boosts the immune system, helping the body fight off infections.
- **Adrenal Support**: It helps support adrenal gland function, which can reduce stress and fatigue.

2. Holy Basil (Tulsi):

- **Adaptogenic Properties**: Holy basil is an adaptogen, which means it helps the body adapt to stress and promotes mental balance.
- **Antioxidant Effects**: It is rich in antioxidants, which help protect the body from damage by free radicals.
- **Anti-inflammatory**: Holy basil has anti-inflammatory properties that can help reduce inflammation and promote overall health.
- **Immune Boosting**: It supports the immune system, helping to protect against infections and diseases.
- **Respiratory Health**: Holy basil can help improve respiratory function and alleviate symptoms of asthma, bronchitis, and other respiratory conditions.

3. Combined Benefits:

- **Stress Reduction**: Both licorice root and holy basil have stress-reducing properties, making this tea an excellent choice for managing stress and anxiety.
- **Immune Support**: The combination of these two herbs provides a powerful boost to the immune system, helping to protect against illnesses.
- **Digestive Health**: This tea can help soothe the digestive tract, reduce inflammation, and improve overall digestive health.
- **Respiratory Support**: The tea can help improve respiratory function and alleviate symptoms of respiratory conditions.

This licorice and holy basil tea is a powerful herbal remedy that combines the benefits of both herbs to support stress management, immune health, digestive health, and overall well-being.

Herbal Remedy Recipe for Holy Basil Extract

WHAT YOU NEED:

1. **Dried Holy Basil (Tulsi) Leaves**: 1 part
2. **Alcohol**: Vodka or brandy, at least 80 proof (40% alcohol content)
3. **Glass Jar**: A clean, airtight glass container
4. **Cheesecloth or Strainer**: For filtering
5. **Dark Glass Dropper Bottles**: For storing the finished extract
6. **Label and Pen**: For labeling the extract

STEPS TO PREPARE:

1. Prepare the Holy Basil:

- Measure out the dried holy basil leaves. For example, if you use 1 cup of holy basil, you'll need enough alcohol to cover it completely in the jar.

2. Fill the Jar:

- Place the dried holy basil leaves into the glass jar, filling it about halfway.

3. Add Alcohol:

- Pour the alcohol over the holy basil leaves, ensuring they are completely submerged. Leave about an inch of space at the top of the jar.

4. Seal and Shake:

- Seal the jar tightly with a lid.
- Shake the jar well to mix the holy basil and alcohol.

5. Store and Shake:

- Place the jar in a cool, dark place.
- Shake the jar every day or every few days to keep the mixture well-blended.
- Let the extract sit for at least 4-6 weeks. The longer it sits, the stronger it will be.

6. Strain the Extract:

- After the waiting period, place cheesecloth or a fine strainer over a clean bowl.
- Pour the mixture through the cheesecloth to filter out the holy basil leaves.
- Squeeze the cheesecloth to extract as much liquid as possible.

7. Transfer to Dropper Bottles:

- Use a funnel to pour the strained liquid into dark glass dropper bottles.
- Label the bottles with the name of the extract and the date.

DOSAGE INSTRUCTIONS:

- **Standard Dose**: Take 1-2 droppersful (1-2 ml) of the extract diluted in a small amount of water or juice up to three times a day.
- **For Stress Relief**: Take 1-2 droppersful (1-2 ml) in the morning and evening to help manage stress and promote mental balance.

BENEFITS OF HOLY BASIL EXTRACT:

1. Adaptogenic Properties:

- **Stress Reduction**: Holy basil is an adaptogen, which helps the body adapt to stress and promotes mental balance.
- **Improves Mental Clarity**: It enhances cognitive function and helps improve focus and clarity.

2. Immune System Support:

- **Boosts Immunity**: Holy basil supports the immune system, helping to protect against infections and diseases.
- **Antimicrobial Properties**: It has antimicrobial properties that can help fight off harmful bacteria and viruses.

3. Anti-inflammatory Effects:

- **Reduces Inflammation**: Holy basil has strong anti-inflammatory properties that can help reduce inflammation and promote overall health.

4. Antioxidant Effects:

- **Rich in Antioxidants**: Holy basil is packed with antioxidants that protect cells from damage caused by free radicals.

5. Respiratory Health:

- **Supports Respiratory Function**: Holy basil can help improve respiratory function and alleviate symptoms of asthma, bronchitis, and other respiratory conditions.

ADDITIONAL NOTES:

- **Consult a Healthcare Professional**: Before starting any new herbal remedy, especially for specific health conditions, consult with a healthcare professional, particularly if you are pregnant, nursing, or taking other medications.
- **Consistency is Key**: For best results, take holy basil extract consistently over a period of several weeks to months.

This holy basil extract is a versatile and potent herbal remedy that offers a wide range of health benefits, including stress reduction, immune support, anti-inflammatory effects, and overall well-being.

3.3 NATURAL RELIEF OF ENDOMETRIOSIS

Endometriosis is a chronic condition characterized by the growth of endometrial tissue outside the uterus, leading to pain, inflammation, and sometimes infertility. Herbal remedies can play a supportive role in alleviating the symptoms of endometriosis, providing relief from pain and inflammation, and promoting overall reproductive health.

One effective herbal remedy for endometriosis is the use of Turmeric. Turmeric contains curcumin, a powerful anti-inflammatory compound that helps reduce inflammation and pain associated with endometriosis. Combining turmeric with other anti-inflammatory ingredients such as ginger, chamomile and red raspberry leaves into a tea can significantly alleviate the uncomfortable symptoms of endometriosis.

Vitex (Chasteberry) is a herb that supports hormonal balance by regulating the pituitary gland, which in turn can help alleviate the symptoms of endometriosis. It is especially useful for reducing menstrual pain and promoting regular cycles. Vitex is typically taken in capsule form, with a recommended dosage of 400 to 1,000 mg per day. However, it may take several months to notice its full benefits, so consistent use is important.

Evening Primrose Oil is rich in gamma-linolenic acid (GLA), an omega-6 fatty acid that has anti-inflammatory properties. Taking evening primrose oil supplements can help reduce menstrual cramps and inflammation associated with endometriosis. A common dosage is 500 to 1,300 mg per day, divided into two or three doses.

Milk Thistle supports liver health and can help the body process and eliminate excess estrogen, which is often elevated in women with endometriosis. Taking milk thistle in capsule form or as a tea can support hormonal balance and reduce symptoms. For tea, steep one teaspoon of dried milk thistle seeds in hot water for 10-15 minutes, strain, and drink.

While these herbal remedies can provide significant relief from endometriosis symptoms, it is essential to consult with a healthcare professional before starting any new treatment, especially if you are taking medications or have underlying health conditions. Combining these natural approaches with conventional treatments and lifestyle changes, such as maintaining a balanced diet, regular exercise, and stress management techniques, can offer a comprehensive strategy for managing endometriosis and improving overall quality of life.

Herbal Remedy Recipe for Endometriosis Management

INGREDIENTS:

1. **Ginger Root**: 1-inch piece (or 1 teaspoon dried ginger powder)
2. **Turmeric Powder**: 1/2 teaspoon
3. **Chamomile Flowers**: 1 teaspoon
4. **Red Raspberry Leaf**: 1 teaspoon
5. **Cramp Bark**: 1 teaspoon
6. **Water**: 4 cups
7. **Honey or Lemon** (optional): For taste

STEPS TO PREPARE:

1. Boil the Water:

- Pour 4 cups of water into a saucepan and bring it to a boil.

2. Prepare the Ingredients:

- Peel and slice the ginger root if using fresh ginger.

3. Combine and Simmer:

- Add the ginger, turmeric powder, chamomile flowers, red raspberry leaf, and cramp bark to the boiling water.
- Reduce the heat and let the mixture simmer for about 10-15 minutes.

4. Strain the Tea:

- After simmering, remove the saucepan from heat and let it cool slightly.
- Strain the tea through a fine strainer to remove the solids.

5. Add Honey or Lemon (Optional):

- If desired, add honey for sweetness or a slice of lemon for additional flavor and health benefits.

6. Serve:

- Pour the strained tea into a cup and enjoy.

DOSAGE:

- **For Regular Use**: Drink 1-2 cups daily to help manage symptoms of endometriosis.

BENEFITS OF THE INGREDIENTS:

1. Ginger:

- **Anti-inflammatory Properties**: Ginger contains compounds like gingerols that have strong anti-inflammatory effects, which can help reduce inflammation and pain associated with endometriosis.
- **Pain Relief**: Ginger is known for its ability to relieve pain, making it beneficial for menstrual pain and cramping.

2. Turmeric:

- **Reduces Inflammation**: Curcumin, the active compound in turmeric, has potent anti-inflammatory effects that can help alleviate pain and inflammation.
- **Antioxidant Properties**: Turmeric is rich in antioxidants that help protect cells from damage and support overall health.

3. Chamomile:

- **Calming Effects**: Chamomile is known for its calming and relaxing properties, which can help reduce stress and anxiety often associated with chronic pain conditions.
- **Anti-inflammatory**: Chamomile has anti-inflammatory properties that can help soothe inflamed tissues.

4. Red Raspberry Leaf:

- **Uterine Tonic**: Red raspberry leaf is traditionally used to tone the uterus and can help reduce menstrual cramps and heavy bleeding.
- **Anti-inflammatory**: It also has anti-inflammatory properties that can help reduce inflammation associated with endometriosis.

5. Cramp Bark:

- **Relieves Muscle Spasms**: Cramp bark is well-known for its ability to relieve muscle spasms and menstrual cramps, making it beneficial for managing pain associated with endometriosis.
- **Anti-inflammatory**: It also has anti-inflammatory properties that help reduce inflammation and pain.

This herbal tea blend combines ingredients known for their anti-inflammatory and pain-relieving properties, making it a beneficial addition to the management plan for endometriosis. Always consult with a healthcare provider before starting any new herbal remedy, especially if you have underlying health conditions or are taking other medications.

3.4 HERBS FOR HEALTHY PREGNANCY AND POSTPARTUM CARE

Navigating the journey of pregnancy and the postpartum period can be as challenging as it is joyous. During this time, your body under-goes significant changes that can bring about symptoms like nausea and fatigue, as well as the need for recovery support after childbirth. Fortunately, the natural world offers a variety of herbs that can provide gentle support during these transformative months. When choosing herbs for pregnancy and postpartum care, it's crucial to opt for those known for their safety and efficacy. For instance, ginger is renowned for its ability to alleviate morning sickness—a common discomfort in early pregnancy. A simple ginger tea can be made by steeping fresh ginger slices in boiling water, which can be sipped throughout the day to ease nausea. Another herb, lemon balm, offers a calming effect and can help reduce pregnancy-related anxiety and insomnia, making it a wonderful addition to your nighttime routine.

During pregnancy, fatigue is a prevalent issue as your body works harder to support the growing fetus. To combat this, consider incorporating peppermint into your daily regimen. Peppermint tea can invigorate your senses and boost your energy levels without the need for caffeine, making it a safe choice during pregnancy. Its refreshing flavor can also help ease digestive discomfort, which often accompanies pregnancy. Each of these herbs not only provides specific symptomatic relief but also contributes to a broader sense of well-being, allowing you to enjoy this special time with greater comfort and less stress.

Postpartum Recovery Herbs

After the arrival of your baby, the focus shifts to recovery and adjusting to life with a new member of the family. This period can be physically demanding and emotionally taxing, making support for recovery essential. Herbs such as raspberry leaf and nettle offer substantial benefits during the postpartum period. Raspberry leaf, often used during the final stages of pregnancy to prepare the uterus for labor, continues to be beneficial after childbirth. It helps tone the uterus and reduce bleeding, supporting the body's recovery. Nettle, rich in iron and vitamins, can aid in replenishing your body's energy levels and reducing fatigue, a common issue for new mothers.

To incorporate these herbs, a simple tea can be made by steeping dried raspberry leaves and nettle in boiling water. This herbal drink not only aids physical recovery but also provides a moment of peaceful respite in your new daily routine. For mothers who are breastfeeding, these herbs are considered safe and can support milk production, enhancing this new experience with your baby.

Preparation and Usage Tips

Using herbs effectively during pregnancy and postpartum requires careful preparation to ensure safety and maximize benefits. When preparing teas, it's important to use hot water, not boiling, to preserve the integrity of the herbs' beneficial properties. Steeping should be limited to about 10 minutes to avoid overly strong concoctions, which can be counterproductive, especially in pregnancy. If you choose to use tinctures, opt for alcohol-free versions to maintain safety during pregnancy and breastfeeding. Always start with small doses to observe how your body responds, and adjust accordingly.

Integrating Herbs with Prenatal Care

While herbs offer wonderful support during pregnancy and postpartum, they should be used in conjunction with traditional prenatal care. Discussing your herbal regimen with your healthcare provider is essential to ensure that it complements your overall care plan and doesn't interfere with any medical advice or treatments you may be receiving. This collaboration ensures that you benefit from both the wisdom of traditional herbal remedies and the advancements of modern medicine. For instance, while ginger is excellent for nausea, your doctor might also recommend B6 supplements, and using both in harmony can provide more comprehensive relief from morning sickness.

Moreover, educating yourself about the safe use of herbs during this time is crucial. Opt for sources that are reputable and specifically tailored to pregnancy and postpartum care, as general herbal information may not always take into account the unique considerations of these stages. By doing so, you ensure that you are using herbs not just effectively, but safely, protecting both your health and the health of your baby. This thoughtful approach to integrating herbal remedies provides a natural complement to your prenatal care, enriching your pregnancy and postpartum experience with the gentle power of nature.

Herbal Remedy Recipe for Ginger Tea

WHAT YOU NEED:

1. **Fresh Ginger Root**: 1-inch piece
2. **Water**: 2 cups
3. **Honey or Lemon** (optional): For taste

STEPS TO PREPARE:

1. Prepare the Ginger:

- Peel the ginger root and slice it into thin pieces.

2. Boil the Water:

- Pour 2 cups of water into a saucepan.
- Bring the water to a boil.

3. Add Ginger:

- Once the water is boiling, add the sliced ginger to the saucepan.
- Reduce the heat and let it simmer for about 10-15 minutes. The longer it simmers, the stronger the tea will be.

4. Remove from Heat:

- Turn off the heat and let the mixture steep for an additional 5 minutes.

5. Strain the Tea:

- Pour the mixture through a fine strainer or cheesecloth into a teapot or directly into cups to remove the ginger pieces.

6. Add Honey or Lemon (Optional):

- If desired, add honey for sweetness or a slice of lemon for additional flavor and health benefits.

7. Serve:

- Pour the strained tea into a cup and enjoy.

TIPS:

- **Dosage**: Drink 1-2 cups daily, especially in the morning or after meals to aid digestion and boost overall health.
- **Storage**: If you make a larger batch, store the tea in the refrigerator for up to 3 days. Reheat as needed.

BENEFITS OF GINGER TEA:

1. Digestive Health:

- **Aids Digestion**: Ginger tea helps stimulate digestion, relieve bloating, and reduce nausea. It's particularly effective for relieving morning sickness and motion sickness.
- **Reduces Indigestion**: It can help soothe an upset stomach and relieve symptoms of indigestion.

2. Anti-inflammatory Properties:

- **Reduces Inflammation**: Ginger contains potent anti-inflammatory compounds called gingerols that can help reduce inflammation and pain, especially in conditions like arthritis.

- **Eases Muscle Pain**: Regular consumption can help reduce exercise-induced muscle pain.

3. Immune System Support:

- **Boosts Immunity**: Ginger has antimicrobial and antioxidant properties that help boost the immune system and protect against infections.
- **Relieves Cold and Flu Symptoms**: It can help relieve congestion, sore throat, and other symptoms of colds and flu.

4. Antioxidant Effects:

- **Rich in Antioxidants**: Ginger is high in antioxidants, which help protect cells from damage caused by free radicals and support overall health.

5. Cardiovascular Health:

- **Lowers Blood Sugar Levels**: Some studies suggest that ginger can help lower blood sugar levels and improve heart health.
- **Improves Circulation**: It helps improve blood circulation, which can reduce the risk of cardiovascular diseases.

6. Respiratory Health:

- **Clears Respiratory Passages**: Ginger tea can help clear the respiratory passages and relieve symptoms of asthma and bronchitis.

This simple and effective ginger tea recipe offers a multitude of health benefits, making it a powerful natural remedy to support digestive health, reduce inflammation, boost immunity, and promote overall well-being.

Herbal Remedy Recipe for Lemon Balm Tea

WHAT YOU NEED:

1. **Dried Lemon Balm Leaves**: 1-2 teaspoons (or a handful of fresh lemon balm leaves)
2. **Water**: 1 cup (8 ounces)
3. **Honey or Lemon** (optional): For taste

STEPS TO PREPARE:

1. Boil the Water:

- Heat 1 cup of water until it reaches a rolling boil.

2. Prepare the Lemon Balm:

- If using fresh lemon balm leaves, rinse them thoroughly and gently crush to release the essential oils. If using dried leaves, measure out 1-2 teaspoons.

3. Steep the Tea:

- Place the lemon balm leaves into a teapot or cup.
- Pour the boiling water over the leaves.
- Cover and let the tea steep for 5-10 minutes. The longer it steeps, the stronger the flavor will be.

4. Strain the Tea:

- After steeping, strain the tea to remove the lemon balm leaves.

5. Add Honey or Lemon (Optional):

- If desired, add honey for sweetness or a slice of lemon for additional flavor and health benefits.

6. Serve:

- Pour the strained tea into a cup and enjoy.

TIPS:

- **Dosage**: Drink 1-3 cups daily to enjoy the full benefits of lemon balm tea.
- **Storage**: If you make a larger batch, store the tea in the refrigerator for up to 3 days. Reheat as needed.

BENEFITS OF LEMON BALM TEA:

1. Calming and Relaxing:

- **Reduces Anxiety**: Lemon balm has mild sedative properties that help reduce anxiety and promote relaxation.
- **Improves Sleep**: It can help improve sleep quality and is particularly useful for people suffering from insomnia.

2. Digestive Health:

- **Aids Digestion**: Lemon balm helps relieve indigestion, bloating, and gas. It can soothe the digestive tract and promote healthy digestion.
- **Reduces Nausea**: It can help alleviate nausea and motion sickness.

3. Cognitive Health:

- **Enhances Mood**: Lemon balm has mood-enhancing properties that can help reduce symptoms of depression and improve overall mood.
- **Boosts Cognitive Function**: It may improve focus, memory, and cognitive function, making it beneficial for mental clarity and alertness.

4. Antiviral and Antibacterial:

- **Fights Infections**: Lemon balm has antiviral and antibacterial properties that help protect against infections and support the immune system.

5. Anti-inflammatory Properties:

- **Reduces Inflammation**: Lemon balm contains compounds that help reduce inflammation and pain, making it useful for conditions like arthritis.

6. Menstrual Health:

- **Eases Menstrual Cramps**: Lemon balm can help alleviate menstrual cramps and other symptoms associated with menstruation.

This simple lemon balm tea recipe is a versatile and effective herbal remedy that offers a wide range of health benefits. It's particularly useful for promoting relaxation, improving sleep, aiding digestion, and supporting overall well-being.

Herbal Remedy Recipe for Peppermint Tea

WHAT YOU NEED:

1. **Dried Peppermint Leaves**: 1-2 teaspoons (or a handful of fresh peppermint leaves)
2. **Water**: 1 cup (8 ounces)
3. **Honey or Lemon** (optional): For taste

STEPS TO PREPARE:

1. Boil the Water:

- Heat 1 cup of water until it reaches a rolling boil.

2. Prepare the Peppermint:

- If using fresh peppermint leaves, rinse them thoroughly and gently crush to release the essential oils. If using dried leaves, measure out 1-2 teaspoons.

3. Steep the Tea:

- Place the peppermint leaves into a teapot or cup.
- Pour the boiling water over the leaves.
- Cover and let the tea steep for 5-10 minutes. The longer it steeps, the stronger the flavor will be.

4. Strain the Tea:

- After steeping, strain the tea to remove the peppermint leaves.

5. Add Honey or Lemon (Optional):

- If desired, add honey for sweetness or a slice of lemon for additional flavor and health benefits.

6. Serve:

- Pour the strained tea into a cup and enjoy.

TIPS:

- **Dosage**: Drink 1-3 cups daily to enjoy the full benefits of peppermint tea.
- **Storage**: If you make a larger batch, store the tea in the refrigerator for up to 3 days. Reheat as needed.

BENEFITS OF PEPPERMINT TEA:

1. Digestive Health:

- **Aids Digestion**: Peppermint tea helps relieve indigestion, bloating, and gas. It can soothe the digestive tract and promote healthy digestion.
- **Reduces Nausea**: It can help alleviate nausea and is particularly useful for motion sickness and morning sickness.

2. Respiratory Health:

- **Clears Respiratory Passages**: Peppermint tea has a cooling effect that can help clear the respiratory passages, making it useful for colds, coughs, and sinus congestion.
- **Eases Breathing**: It can help relax the muscles of the respiratory tract, making it easier to breathe.

3. Pain Relief:

- **Reduces Headaches**: The menthol in peppermint can help relieve headaches and migraines by relaxing the muscles and improving blood flow.
- **Relieves Muscle Pain**: Peppermint tea can help reduce muscle pain and tension due to its muscle-relaxing properties.

4. Stress and Mental Health:

- **Calming and Relaxing**: Peppermint tea has a soothing effect that can help reduce stress and promote relaxation.
- **Improves Focus**: It can enhance mental clarity and focus, making it beneficial for cognitive function.

5. Immune System Support:

- **Boosts Immunity**: Peppermint has antimicrobial properties that help boost the immune system and protect against infections.

6. Antioxidant Properties:

- **Rich in Antioxidants**: Peppermint is high in antioxidants, which help protect cells from damage caused by free radicals and support overall health.

This simple and effective peppermint tea recipe offers a multitude of health benefits, making it a powerful natural remedy to support digestive health, respiratory health, pain relief, stress reduction, and overall well-being.

Herbal Remedy Recipe for Raspberry Leaf and Nettle Tea

WHAT YOU NEED:

1. **Dried Raspberry Leaves**: 1 teaspoon
2. **Dried Nettle Leaves**: 1 teaspoon
3. **Water**: 1 cup (8 ounces)
4. **Honey or Lemon** (optional): For taste

STEPS TO PREPARE:

1. Boil the Water:

- Heat 1 cup of water until it reaches a rolling boil.

2. Prepare the Leaves:

- Measure out 1 teaspoon of dried raspberry leaves and 1 teaspoon of dried nettle leaves.

3. Steep the Tea:

- Place the dried raspberry leaves and dried nettle leaves into a teapot or cup.
- Pour the boiling water over the leaves.
- Cover and let the tea steep for 10-15 minutes to ensure the beneficial compounds are fully extracted.

4. Strain the Tea:

- After steeping, strain the tea to remove the leaves.

5. Add Honey or Lemon (Optional):

- If desired, add honey for sweetness or a slice of lemon for additional flavor and health benefits.

6. Serve:

- Pour the strained tea into a cup and enjoy.

TIPS:

- **Dosage**: Drink 1-3 cups daily to enjoy the full benefits of raspberry leaf and nettle tea.
- **Storage**: If you make a larger batch, store the tea in the refrigerator for up to 3 days. Reheat as needed.

BENEFITS OF RASPBERRY LEAF AND NETTLE TEA:

1. Raspberry Leaf:

- **Supports Reproductive Health**: Raspberry leaf is well-known for its benefits to female reproductive health, including regulating menstrual cycles and easing menstrual cramps.
- **Pregnancy Support**: It can help tone the uterus and prepare it for labor, making it a popular tea during pregnancy.
- **Rich in Nutrients**: Raspberry leaf is high in vitamins C, E, A, and B, as well as minerals like magnesium, potassium, and calcium.
- **Digestive Health**: It can help soothe the digestive tract, reducing symptoms of nausea and promoting healthy digestion.

2. Nettle:

- **Rich in Nutrients**: Nettle is packed with vitamins A, C, K, and several B vitamins, as well as minerals like iron, calcium, magnesium, potassium, and silica.
- **Anti-inflammatory Properties**: Nettle has strong anti-inflammatory properties that can help reduce inflammation and alleviate conditions like arthritis.
- **Supports Kidney Health**: It acts as a diuretic, promoting healthy kidney function and helping to flush out toxins from the body.
- **Allergy Relief**: Nettle can help reduce symptoms of allergies such as hay fever by acting as a natural antihistamine.
- **Energy Boost**: The high nutrient content in nettle can help boost energy levels and reduce fatigue.

3. Combined Benefits:

- **Overall Health Support**: This tea is a powerhouse of nutrients and can support overall health and wellness.
- **Women's Health**: The combination of raspberry leaf and nettle is particularly beneficial for women's health, supporting menstrual health, pregnancy, and postpartum recovery.
- **Immune Support**: Both herbs have immune-boosting properties, helping to protect against infections and support a healthy immune system.
- **Detoxification**: The tea promotes healthy digestion and kidney function, aiding in the body's natural detoxification processes.

This raspberry leaf and nettle tea is a versatile and effective herbal remedy that offers a wide range of health benefits, supporting reproductive health, immune function, and overall well-being.

3.5 MANAGING MENOPAUSE SYMPTOMS WITH HERBS

Navigating the waves of menopause can often feel like steering through uncharted waters, where sudden hot flashes or unexpected mood swings might rock the boat. However, turning to the natural world provides a compass in the form of herbal remedies that specifically target these symptoms, offering not just relief but a smoother sail through menopause. Herbs such as black cohosh, sage, and red clover have stood the test of time and scientific scrutiny, proving their worth in easing the often turbulent phase of menopause.

Black cohosh, in particular, has garnered acclaim for its effectiveness in reducing hot flashes, which are among the most common and uncomfortable symptoms of menopause. The root of this herb seems to have a regulating effect on estrogen levels, although its exact mechanism of action is still studied extensively. Many women have reported significant relief from the intensity and frequency of hot flashes and night sweats after incorporating black cohosh into their daily regimen. Sage, on the other hand, not only helps in reducing perspiration but is also beneficial for its calming properties, aiding in tempering mood swings and fostering a greater sense of well-being.

Incorporating these herbs into your life can be done gracefully through teas or dietary supplements. A soothing cup of tea made from sage leaves can be enjoyed in the evening to promote a good night's sleep, free from the interruptions of night sweats. Black cohosh is often taken in capsule form, but it can also be brewed into a tea. It's important to consult with a healthcare provider before starting any herbal treatment, especially since herbs like black cohosh can interact with other medications such as: Atorvastatin (Lipitor), Acetaminophen (Tylenol), Disulfiram (Antabuse), Leflunomide (Arava), Teriflunomide (Aubagio), Lomitapide (Juxapid) and Pexidartinib (Turalio). Additionally, black cohosh may interfere with medications metabolized by the CYP2D6 enzyme, potentially affecting their efficacy and safety. This includes drugs like venlafaxine (Effexor) and other antidepressants

The holistic management of menopause extends beyond herbal remedies, encapsulating diet, exercise, and overall lifestyle adjustments.
Integrating phytoestrogen-rich foods such as flax seeds, soy products,
and whole grains can help balance hormone levels naturally. Regular
physical activity, be it yoga, walking, or swimming, not only keeps
your body healthy but also boosts your mood and energy levels, coun-
tering some of the lethargy and emotional dips that can accompany
menopause.

Moreover, this period of change is significantly smoothed by the
support of a community—groups of women who are navigating the
same transitional waters. Sharing experiences and solutions, such as
which herbal remedies have eased certain symptoms, can be incredibly empowering. Online forums, local wellness groups, or even
informal gatherings with friends can provide this vital support.
Additionally, books and resources that delve into the specifics of
herbal treatments for menopause are invaluable. They offer insights
and detailed information that can help you make informed choices
about which herbs might work best for your individual symptoms.

By embracing a holistic approach that includes these supportive
herbs, dietary adjustments, regular physical activity, and leaning on
the strength of community, managing menopause can transform from
a daunting challenge into an empowered stage of life. This proactive
and nurturing approach not only alleviates the symptoms but also
enhances your overall well-being, allowing you to embrace this
natural phase of life with confidence and grace.

Black Cohosh in Capsule Form

DOSAGE INFORMATION:

- **General Dosage:** The typical recommended dosage for black
  cohosh in capsule form is between 20 to 80 mg per day, often
  divided into two doses.

- **Standardized Extract:** If using a standardized extract (containing 2.5% triterpene glycosides), a common dosage is 20 to 40 mg twice daily.
- **Duration:** It is generally recommended to use black cohosh for a period of up to six months. Longer-term use should be discussed with a healthcare provider.
- **Consultation:** Dosage may vary based on individual health needs and conditions. Consulting with a healthcare provider for personalized dosing is advisable.

BENEFITS OF BLACK COHOSH:

1. Menopause Symptom Relief:

- **Hot Flashes:** Black cohosh is widely used to alleviate hot flashes and night sweats, which are common symptoms of menopause.
- **Mood Swings:** It can help stabilize mood swings and reduce feelings of irritability and anxiety associated with menopause.
- **Sleep Disturbances:** The herb may improve sleep quality by reducing night sweats and promoting relaxation.

2. Menstrual Health:

- **Premenstrual Syndrome (PMS):** Black cohosh can help relieve symptoms of PMS, including cramps, breast tenderness, and mood swings.
- **Menstrual Irregularities:** It may assist in regulating menstrual cycles and alleviating menstrual pain.

3. Bone Health:

- **Osteoporosis Prevention:** Black cohosh may have a positive effect on bone health by mimicking estrogen and helping to maintain bone density, which is crucial for preventing osteoporosis.

4. Anti-Inflammatory Properties:

- **Reduces Inflammation:** The anti-inflammatory properties of black cohosh can help reduce inflammation and pain in conditions such as arthritis and muscle pain.

5. Digestive Health:

- **Alleviates Indigestion:** It can help soothe digestive issues like indigestion and bloating.

6. Cardiovascular Health:

- **Blood Pressure Regulation:** Black cohosh may assist in regulating blood pressure and supporting overall cardiovascular health.

POSSIBLE DRUG INTERACTIONS AND PRECAUTIONS

1. Interactions:

- **Hormone Replacement Therapy (HRT):** Black cohosh may interact with hormone replacement therapy, potentially enhancing or interfering with its effects.
- **Estrogen Medications:** It can interact with medications containing estrogen, affecting their efficacy.
- **Blood Pressure Medications:** Black cohosh may lower blood pressure, so use with caution if you are taking antihypertensive medications to avoid hypotension.
- **Liver Medications:** There is a potential risk of liver damage, so individuals taking medications that affect liver function should use black cohosh with caution.

2. Precautions:

- **Pregnancy and Breastfeeding:** Pregnant or breastfeeding women should avoid using black cohosh due to its potential effects on hormone levels and uterine contractions.
- **Liver Health:** Individuals with liver disorders should avoid using black cohosh, as it has been associated with rare cases of liver damage.
- **Hormone-sensitive Conditions:** Those with hormone-sensitive conditions, such as breast cancer, uterine cancer, or endometriosis, should use black cohosh with caution.

GENERAL ADVICE:

- Always consult with a healthcare professional before starting any new herbal remedies, especially if you are taking medications or have underlying health conditions.
- Monitor for any adverse reactions and discontinue use if they occur.
- Start with a lower dosage to assess your tolerance to the herb.

Herbal Remedy Recipe for Sage Tea

WHAT YOU NEED:

1. **Dried Sage Leaves**: 1 teaspoon (or 2-3 fresh sage leaves)
2. **Water**: 1 cup (8 ounces)
3. **Honey or Lemon** (optional): For taste

STEPS TO PREPARE:

1. Boil the Water:

- Heat 1 cup of water until it reaches a rolling boil.

2. Prepare the Sage Leaves:

- If using fresh sage leaves, rinse them thoroughly. If using dried sage, measure out 1 teaspoon.

3. Steep the Tea:

- Place the sage leaves into a teapot or cup.
- Pour the boiling water over the leaves.
- Cover and let the tea steep for 5-10 minutes. The longer it steeps, the stronger the flavor will be.

4. Strain the Tea:

- After steeping, strain the tea to remove the sage leaves.

5. Add Honey or Lemon (Optional):

- If desired, add honey for sweetness or a slice of lemon for additional flavor and health benefits.

6. Serve:

- Pour the strained tea into a cup and enjoy.

Tips:

- **Dosage**: Drink 1-2 cups daily to enjoy the full benefits of sage tea.
- **Storage**: If you make a larger batch, store the tea in the refrigerator for up to 3 days. Reheat as needed.

BENEFITS OF SAGE TEA:

1. Cognitive Health:

- **Improves Memory and Concentration**: Sage has been shown to enhance cognitive function, improving memory and concentration.
- **May Reduce Symptoms of Alzheimer's**: Some studies suggest that sage can help reduce symptoms of Alzheimer's disease by inhibiting the breakdown of acetylcholine, a neurotransmitter involved in memory and learning.

2. Digestive Health:

- **Aids Digestion**: Sage tea can help stimulate digestive enzymes, promoting healthy digestion and reducing symptoms like bloating and gas.

3. Anti-inflammatory Properties:

- **Reduces Inflammation**: Sage contains anti-inflammatory compounds that can help reduce inflammation in the body, making it beneficial for conditions like arthritis.

4. Immune System Support:

- **Boosts Immunity**: Sage has antimicrobial properties that help boost the immune system and protect against infections.
- **Soothes Sore Throats**: Sage tea can help soothe a sore throat and reduce symptoms of respiratory infections.

5. Menstrual Health:

- **Eases Menstrual Symptoms**: Sage can help alleviate

menstrual cramps and other symptoms associated with menstruation.

This sage tea recipe is a simple yet powerful herbal remedy that offers a variety of health benefits, including improved cognitive function, digestive health, reduced inflammation, immune support, and relief from menstrual symptoms.

3.6 NATURAL BEAUTY TREATMENTS FOR SKIN AND HAIR

In the tapestry of natural wellness, the radiance of healthy skin and the luster of vibrant hair are not just elements of beauty, but reflections of internal health. Turning to the earth's apothecary, herbs like calendula, chamomile, and aloe vera offer more than just aesthetic improvements—they provide a symbiotic relationship with your body, enhancing skin and hair health through their nurturing properties. Calendula, with its bright orange blossoms, is celebrated not only for its beauty but also for its potent healing capabilities. It's particularly effective in soothing irritated skin, healing wounds, and improving overall skin hydration and firmness. This makes it a perfect choice for those dealing with conditions like eczema or psoriasis, as well as those seeking a natural moisturizer.

Chamomile, another herb known for its calming effects when ingested as a tea, also has significant benefits for skin. Its anti-inflammatory properties help reduce redness and irritation, making it an excellent remedy for acne-prone skin. Additionally, chamomile's antioxidants protect the skin from free radical damage, promoting a youthful glow and delaying the signs of aging. Aloe vera, often dubbed the "plant of immortality," is a powerhouse of hydration. Known widely for its soothing effect on sunburns, aloe vera also deeply moisturizes the skin without leaving a greasy residue, making it ideal for oily skin types as well.

DIY Herbal Beauty Recipes

Creating your own herbal beauty treatments allows you to harness these benefits directly. For instance, a simple calendula face cream can be crafted by infusing oil with calendula petals, then blending the strained oil with beeswax to form a rich, healing cream. This can be applied nightly to help heal dry, irritated skin while reducing scars and fine lines. For those battling with sensitive or acne-prone skin, a chamomile toner can be made by steeping chamomile flowers in hot water, then adding witch hazel once cooled. Used after cleansing, this toner can help calm inflammation and prevent breakouts.

Aloe vera gel is incredibly versatile and can be used almost directly from the plant. For a soothing aloe mask, fresh aloe gel can be combined with honey and a pinch of turmeric to create a hydrating and antibacterial face mask, perfect for soothing inflamed skin and boosting radiance. These simple recipes not only bring the therapeutic properties of herbs into your skincare routine but also connect you to the rhythms of nature, transforming your beauty regimen into a ritual of self-care and environmental alignment.

Herbs for Hair Growth and Health

Just as herbs can enhance skin health, they also offer vital benefits for hair. Horsetail, rich in silica, helps to strengthen hair and improve its texture and sheen. Rosemary, another robust herb, stimulates the scalp, promoting hair growth and reducing hair loss. Its antiseptic properties also make it beneficial for scalp health, helping to alleviate dandruff and dryness. Lavender, renowned for its relaxing scent, is also great for hair health. It soothes the scalp and improves blood circulation, which in turn promotes hair growth. Furthermore, its antimicrobial properties help balance scalp oils.

To incorporate these herbs into your hair care routine, consider making a rosemary hair rinse by boiling rosemary leaves in water and using the strained liquid as a final rinse to stimulate hair follicles and add a natural shine to your hair. A lavender and horsetail scalp oil can be made by infusing the herbs in a carrier oil like coconut or almond for a few weeks, then applying the oil to the scalp before bedtime. This not only nourishes the scalp but also relaxes you, enhancing the overall health of your hair.

Integrating Beauty Routines

Integrating these herbal treatments into your daily beauty routine can enhance their effectiveness and make their use a seamless part of your lifestyle. For instance, calendula cream can be applied right after a shower when the skin is still slightly damp to lock in moisture. Chamomile toner can be used not just after washing your face but anytime during the day as a refreshing mist to calm and hydrate the skin. Similarly, making the rosemary rinse a part of your weekly hair care routine can gradually strengthen hair and reduce scalp issues.

These natural beauty treatments invite you to redefine your beauty routine as a nurturing practice, aligning skin and hair care with holistic health. As you blend, brew, and apply these herbal creations, you do more than care for your appearance—you connect with age-old traditions of herbal medicine and holistic health, crafting beauty rituals that nourish, heal, and celebrate the natural beauty of both the earth and your body.

Herbal Remedy Recipe for Calendula Face Cream with Beeswax

WHAT YOU NEED:

1. **Dried Calendula Flowers**: 1/2 cup
2. **Carrier Oil**: 1 cup (olive oil, almond oil, or jojoba oil)
3. **Beeswax**: 1/4 cup (grated or pellets)
4. **Shea Butter**: 1/4 cup
5. **Coconut Oil**: 1/4 cup

6. **Essential Oils**: 10-15 drops (optional, for fragrance and additional benefits; lavender or chamomile are good choices)
7. **Double Boiler**: Or a heatproof bowl and saucepan
8. **Cheesecloth or Strainer**: For filtering
9. **Glass Jar or Container**: For storing the finished cream

STEPS TO PREPARE:

1. Infuse the Oil with Calendula:

- Place the dried calendula flowers in a clean, dry glass jar.
- Pour the carrier oil over the flowers, ensuring they are completely submerged.
- Seal the jar tightly and place it in a sunny spot for 2-3 weeks, shaking occasionally. Alternatively, you can gently heat the jar in a double boiler for 2-3 hours.

2. Strain the Infused Oil:

- After infusing, strain the oil through cheesecloth or a fine strainer to remove the calendula flowers.
- Squeeze the cheesecloth to extract as much oil as possible.

3. Prepare the Double Boiler:

- Fill the bottom of the double boiler with water and bring it to a gentle simmer.
- Place the beeswax, shea butter, and coconut oil in the top of the double boiler.

4. Melt the Ingredients:

- Heat the mixture, stirring occasionally, until the beeswax, shea butter, and coconut oil are completely melted and well combined.

5. Add the Infused Oil:

- Once melted, slowly add the calendula-infused oil to the mixture, stirring constantly to combine.

6. Remove from Heat:

- Once everything is well combined, remove the mixture from the heat.

7. Add Essential Oils (Optional):

- If using essential oils, add them now and stir well to incorporate.

8. Cool and Whip:

- Allow the mixture to cool slightly, then use a hand mixer or whisk to whip the mixture until it reaches a creamy consistency.

9. Transfer to Containers:

- Spoon the finished face cream into glass jars or containers.
- Seal tightly and label with the contents and date.

STORAGE:

- Store the calendula face cream in a cool, dark place. It should last for several months if stored properly.

BENEFITS OF CALENDULA FACE CREAM:

1. Skin Healing:

- **Soothes Irritation**: Calendula has anti-inflammatory properties that can help soothe irritated skin and reduce redness.
- **Heals Minor Cuts and Wounds**: Its antiseptic and antimicrobial properties make it effective for healing minor cuts, scrapes, and wounds.

2. Moisturizing:

- **Deep Hydration**: The combination of oils and shea butter provides deep hydration, making the skin soft and supple.
- **Protects the Skin Barrier**: Beeswax helps create a protective barrier on the skin, locking in moisture and protecting against environmental pollutants.

3. Anti-Aging:

- **Rich in Antioxidants**: Calendula contains antioxidants that help fight free radicals, which can cause premature aging.
- **Promotes Collagen Production**: It may help stimulate collagen production, improving skin elasticity and reducing the appearance of fine lines and wrinkles.

4. Suitable for Sensitive Skin:

- **Gentle and Nourishing**: Calendula is gentle enough for sensitive skin and can help alleviate conditions like eczema and psoriasis.

This calendula face cream is a versatile and nourishing herbal remedy that provides numerous benefits for the skin, promoting healing, hydration, and overall skin health.

Herbal Remedy Recipe for Chamomile Toner with Witch Hazel

WHAT YOU NEED:

1. **Dried Chamomile Flowers**: 2 tablespoons (or 2 chamomile tea bags)
2. **Witch Hazel**: 1/2 cup (alcohol-free is preferred for sensitive skin)
3. **Distilled Water**: 1/2 cup
4. **Aloe Vera Gel**: 1 tablespoon (optional for extra soothing)
5. **Essential Oil**: 5-10 drops (optional; lavender or tea tree oil are good choices)
6. **Glass Jar or Bottle**: For storing the toner
7. **Fine Strainer or Cheesecloth**: For filtering

STEPS TO PREPARE:

1. Prepare the Chamomile Infusion:

- Boil 1/2 cup of distilled water.
- Place the dried chamomile flowers or tea bags in a bowl or teapot.
- Pour the boiling water over the chamomile and let it steep for about 10-15 minutes.
- Strain the chamomile infusion using a fine strainer or cheesecloth to remove the flowers or tea bags.

2. Combine Ingredients:

- In a clean glass jar or bottle, combine the chamomile infusion with 1/2 cup of witch hazel.

- Add 1 tablespoon of aloe vera gel if desired for extra soothing properties.
- If using, add 5-10 drops of your chosen essential oil for additional benefits and fragrance.

3. Mix Well:

- Shake the jar or bottle gently to mix all the ingredients thoroughly.

4. Cool and Store:

- Allow the toner to cool completely.
- Store the toner in a cool, dark place. It can be kept in the refrigerator for a refreshing effect and to extend its shelf life.

How to Use:

- **Application**: Apply the chamomile toner to your face using a cotton ball or pad after cleansing your skin. This helps remove any remaining impurities, tightens pores, and prepares your skin for moisturizing.
- **Frequency**: Use the toner twice daily, in the morning and evening, for best results.

Benefits of Chamomile Toner with Witch Hazel:

1. Chamomile:

- **Anti-inflammatory**: Chamomile has strong anti-inflammatory properties that can help reduce redness, irritation, and swelling in the skin.
- **Soothing**: It is known for its calming effects on the skin, making it excellent for sensitive or irritated skin.

- **Antioxidant**: Chamomile is rich in antioxidants which help protect the skin from damage by free radicals.

2. Witch Hazel:

- **Astringent**: Witch hazel is a natural astringent that helps tighten pores and control oil production, reducing the appearance of pores and preventing acne.
- **Anti-inflammatory**: It helps reduce inflammation and can soothe irritated skin, making it beneficial for conditions like eczema and psoriasis .
- **Antimicrobial**: Witch hazel has antimicrobial properties that help cleanse the skin and prevent bacterial infections .

3. Aloe Vera (Optional):

- **Hydrating**: Aloe vera provides deep hydration, making the skin soft and supple.
- **Soothing**: It has soothing properties that can help calm irritated skin and reduce redness.

4. Essential Oils (Optional):

- **Lavender Oil**: Known for its calming and antiseptic properties, it can help soothe and disinfect the skin.
- **Tea Tree Oil**: Has strong antibacterial and anti-inflammatory properties, making it excellent for acne-prone skin.

This chamomile toner with witch hazel is a gentle and effective herbal remedy that offers a range of benefits for all skin types, particularly sensitive and acne-prone skin.

Herbal Remedy Recipe for Rosemary Hair Rinse

WHAT YOU NEED:

1. **Fresh or Dried Rosemary Leaves**: 1-2 tablespoons (or a handful of fresh rosemary sprigs)
2. **Water**: 2 cups
3. **Optional Additions**: A few drops of essential oil (like rosemary or lavender) for added benefits and fragrance

STEPS TO PREPARE:

1. Boil the Water:

- Pour 2 cups of water into a saucepan and bring it to a boil.

2. Add Rosemary Leaves:

- Once the water is boiling, add the fresh or dried rosemary leaves to the saucepan.
- Reduce the heat and let the mixture simmer for 10-15 minutes to extract the beneficial compounds from the rosemary.

3. Cool and Strain:

- Remove the saucepan from the heat and allow the rosemary infusion to cool.
- Strain the mixture through a fine strainer or cheesecloth to remove the rosemary leaves.

4. Optional Additions:

- If desired, add a few drops of essential oil to the strained rosemary water for additional benefits and a pleasant scent.

5. Store:

- Pour the rosemary rinse into a clean bottle or jar.
- It can be stored in the refrigerator for up to one week.

HOW TO USE:

1. Wash Hair:

- Shampoo and condition your hair as usual.

2. Apply Rosemary Rinse:

- Pour the rosemary rinse over your hair, ensuring it covers your scalp and strands evenly.
- Massage it into your scalp for a few minutes.

3. Leave In or Rinse Out:

- You can choose to leave the rosemary rinse in your hair or rinse it out with cool water after a few minutes.

4. Dry and Style:

- Dry and style your hair as usual.

BENEFITS OF ROSEMARY HAIR RINSE:

1. Stimulates Hair Growth:

- **Improves Circulation**: Rosemary is known to improve blood circulation in the scalp, which can help stimulate hair follicles and promote hair growth.
- **Strengthens Hair**: It can help strengthen hair strands, reducing breakage and promoting thicker, healthier hair.

2. Reduces Dandruff and Scalp Irritation:

- **Antimicrobial Properties**: Rosemary has antimicrobial properties that can help reduce dandruff and soothe an itchy scalp.
- **Anti-inflammatory**: Its anti-inflammatory properties can help reduce scalp irritation and inflammation, promoting a healthier scalp environment.

3. Adds Shine and Softness:

- **Natural Conditioner**: Rosemary can act as a natural conditioner, adding shine and softness to your hair.
- **Reduces Frizz**: It can help tame frizz and improve the overall texture of your hair.

4. Prevents Premature Graying:

- **Antioxidant Properties**: The antioxidants in rosemary can help prevent premature graying by protecting hair follicles from damage.

This rosemary hair rinse is a simple yet powerful herbal remedy that can provide numerous benefits for your hair and scalp, promoting growth, reducing dandruff, and enhancing overall hair health.

Herbal Remedy Recipe for Lavender and Horsetail Scalp Oil Infused in Coconut or Almond Oil

WHAT YOU NEED:

1. **Dried Lavender Flowers:** 2 tablespoons
2. **Dried Horsetail (Equisetum arvense):** 2 tablespoons
3. **Carrier Oil:** 1 cup (coconut oil or almond oil)
4. **Glass Jar:** A clean, airtight glass container

5. **Cheesecloth or Fine Strainer:** For filtering

1. Prepare the Ingredients:

- Measure out 2 tablespoons of dried lavender flowers and 2 tablespoons of dried horsetail.
- Choose your carrier oil (coconut oil or almond oil).

2. Infuse the Oil:

- Place the dried lavender and horsetail into the glass jar.
- Pour the carrier oil over the herbs, ensuring they are completely submerged.
- Seal the jar tightly with a lid.

3. Heat the Mixture:

- There are two methods to infuse the oil:

  ○ Sun Method: Place the jar in a sunny spot for 2-4 weeks, shaking it gently every day to help mix the herbs and oil.
  ○ Double Boiler Method: Place the jar in a double boiler or a saucepan with water. Heat gently over low heat for 2-3 hours, ensuring the oil does not boil.

4. Strain the Oil:

- After the infusion period, strain the mixture through cheesecloth or a fine strainer into a clean bowl to remove the herb solids.
- Squeeze the cheesecloth to extract as much oil as possible.

5. Store the Infused Oil:

- Pour the strained oil into a clean glass bottle or jar.
- Label the bottle with the contents and date.

How to Use:

1. Application:

- Apply the infused oil to your scalp and hair, massaging it gently into your scalp for a few minutes.
- You can leave the oil on for at least 30 minutes, or for a more intensive treatment, leave it on overnight.

2. Rinse:

- Wash your hair with a mild shampoo to remove the oil. Repeat as needed to ensure all oil is washed out.

3. Frequency:

- Use this scalp treatment 1-2 times a week for best results.

Benefits of Lavender and Horsetail Scalp Oil:

1. Lavender:

- **Promotes Hair Growth:** Lavender oil can help improve blood circulation in the scalp, which promotes hair growth.
- **Reduces Dandruff and Itching:** It has antimicrobial properties that can help soothe the scalp and reduce dandruff and itching.
- **Calming and Relaxing:** Lavender is known for its calming effects, which can help reduce stress and promote overall well-being.

2. Horsetail:

- **Strengthens Hair:** Horsetail is rich in silica, which helps strengthen hair and reduce breakage.
- **Promotes Hair Growth:** It can improve blood circulation to the scalp, promoting healthy hair growth.
- **Reduces Hair Loss:** Horsetail contains antioxidants and anti-inflammatory compounds that can help reduce hair loss and support healthy hair.

3. Carrier Oils (Coconut Oil or Almond Oil):

- **Moisturizes and Nourishes:** Both coconut oil and almond oil are excellent for moisturizing and nourishing the scalp and hair, preventing dryness and breakage.
- **Improves Scalp Health:** These oils have anti-inflammatory and antimicrobial properties that can improve overall scalp health and reduce dandruff.

This lavender and horsetail scalp oil is a natural and effective herbal remedy that provides a range of benefits for your hair and scalp, promoting growth, reducing dandruff, and enhancing overall hair health.

3.7 HERBS FOR WEIGHT MANAGEMENT AND METABOLISM

In the pursuit of wellness, managing weight and enhancing metabolism are often at the forefront of many health goals. It's a dynamic balance that can significantly influence your energy levels, health, and overall quality of life. Thankfully, nature offers a palette of herbs that can naturally support these efforts. Herbs like green tea, cayenne pepper, and cinnamon are not only staples in the kitchen but are also celebrated for their metabolic boosting properties. Green tea, rich in antioxidants called catechins, particularly epigallocatechin gallate (EGCG), has been researched extensively for its ability to enhance metabolic rate and increase fat oxidation. A daily ritual of sipping green tea can subtly yet effectively boost your metabolism, providing a thermogenic effect that aids in weight management.

Cayenne pepper, with its active component capsaicin, adds more than just spice to your meals; it can also fire up your metabolism. Capsaicin has a thermogenic effect, meaning it causes the body to burn calories as heat, which can be particularly beneficial in weight management efforts. Incorporating cayenne pepper into your diet is as simple as sprinkling it on your morning eggs or mixing it into a homemade salad dressing for a spicy kick that boosts your metabolic rate. Cinnamon, another powerful herb, not only adds warmth and flavor but also helps in managing blood sugar levels, which plays a crucial role in weight control. Its influence on blood glucose levels helps minimize insulin spikes that can lead to cravings and overeating, making it a valuable addition to your diet.

Herbal Appetite Suppressants

In addition to metabolism boosters, certain herbs can help control appetite, a vital aspect of weight management. Fenugreek, for instance, is known for its fibrous, galactomannan content, which swells in the stomach and gives a feeling of fullness, reducing overeating tendencies. Incorporating fenugreek into your diet can be as simple as adding its seeds to curries or drinking a tea made from its leaves. Another herb, Gymnema sylvestre, famously known as the 'sugar destroyer,' temporarily decreases the ability to taste sweetness, which in turn can help curb sugar cravings. This herb can be taken in supplement form or as a tea, making it a practical choice for those looking to manage their sugar intake and overall appetite.

Incorporation into Daily Diet

Incorporating these herbs into your daily diet requires creativity and intention. Start by integrating green tea into your morning routine or after meals to enhance digestion and metabolism. Cayenne pepper can be added to soups, stews, or even smoothies, providing a spicy boost to your dishes while revving up your metabolism. Cinnamon can be sprinkled on breakfast cereals, added to your coffee, or used in baking, offering a sweet spice that helps control blood sugar levels throughout the day. By making these herbs part of your regular diet, you not only enhance flavor but also contribute to your health and weight management goals in significant ways.

Addressing Emotional Eating

Beyond physical hunger, emotional eating is a challenge many face, often sabotaging weight management efforts. Adaptogenic herbs like ashwagandha and Rhodiola can play a crucial role in managing this aspect by modulating stress responses, which are often the root cause of emotional eating. By enhancing resilience to stress, these herbs help stabilize mood swings and reduce stress-related cravings. Incorporating ashwagandha into your evening routine, for example, can help calm your mind and reduce the likelihood of stress-eating. Rhodiola, taken as a supplement in the morning, can increase your energy levels and mental clarity, helping you make mindful choices about your diet throughout the day.

By understanding and utilizing these herbs, you empower yourself with natural tools that support your weight management and metabolic health. These herbal allies offer more than just physical benefits; they enhance your overall well-being, helping you lead a balanced, healthier life. As you integrate these practices into your daily routine, remember that each step, each choice, brings you closer to your wellness goals, aligning your health with the natural rhythms and gifts of the earth.

This exploration of herbs for weight management and metabolism not only enriches your understanding but also equips you with practical tools to enhance your well-being. By embracing these natural solutions, you contribute to a holistic approach to health that resonates with your body's natural processes. As we transition from focusing on individual health challenges to exploring holistic wellness strategies in the following chapters, remember that each herb, each remedy, is a step towards a more vibrant, healthful life, deeply connected to the natural world.

Herbal Remedy Recipe for Fenugreek Tea

WHAT YOU NEED:

1. **Fenugreek Seeds**: 1 teaspoon
2. **Water**: 1 cup (8 ounces)
3. **Honey or Lemon** (optional): For taste

STEPS TO PREPARE:

1. Boil the Water:

- Pour 1 cup of water into a saucepan and bring it to a boil.

2. Prepare the Fenugreek Seeds:

- Lightly crush or grind the fenugreek seeds using a mortar and pestle to release their beneficial compounds.

3. Steep the Tea:

- Place the crushed fenugreek seeds into a teapot or cup.
- Pour the boiling water over the seeds.
- Cover and let the tea steep for 10-15 minutes. The longer it steeps, the stronger the flavor and benefits.

4. Strain the Tea:

- After steeping, strain the tea to remove the seeds.

5. Add Honey or Lemon (Optional):

- If desired, add honey for sweetness or a slice of lemon for additional flavor and health benefits.

6. Serve:

- Pour the strained tea into a cup and enjoy.

TIPS:

- **Dosage**: Drink 1-2 cups daily to enjoy the full benefits of fenugreek tea.
- **Storage**: If you make a larger batch, store the tea in the refrigerator for up to 3 days. Reheat as needed.

BENEFITS OF FENUGREEK TEA:

1. Digestive Health:

- **Aids Digestion**: Fenugreek tea helps stimulate digestion, relieve constipation, and reduce bloating and gas.
- **Soothes Inflammation**: It has anti-inflammatory properties that can help soothe gastrointestinal inflammation.

2. Blood Sugar Regulation:

- **Lowers Blood Sugar Levels**: Fenugreek is known for its ability to help lower blood sugar levels, making it beneficial for people with diabetes.

- **Improves Insulin Sensitivity**: It can enhance insulin sensitivity and reduce insulin resistance.

3. Women's Health:

- **Eases Menstrual Discomfort**: Fenugreek can help alleviate menstrual cramps and discomfort.
- **Supports Lactation**: It is known to promote milk production in breastfeeding mothers.

4. Heart Health:

- **Lowers Cholesterol Levels**: Regular consumption of fenugreek tea can help lower LDL (bad) cholesterol levels, promoting heart health.
- **Reduces Blood Pressure**: It may help in reducing blood pressure, contributing to cardiovascular health.

5. Anti-inflammatory and Antioxidant:

- **Reduces Inflammation**: Fenugreek has anti-inflammatory properties that can help reduce inflammation in the body, which is beneficial for conditions like arthritis.
- **Rich in Antioxidants**: It is high in antioxidants, which help protect cells from damage caused by free radicals.

6. Weight Management:

- **Promotes Weight Loss**: Fenugreek can help with weight management by reducing appetite and promoting a feeling of fullness.

This fenugreek tea recipe is a simple and effective herbal remedy that provides numerous health benefits, including improved digestion, blood sugar regulation, enhanced women's health, heart health support, anti-inflammatory effects, and weight management.

Herbal Remedy Recipe for Gymnema Sylvestre Tea

WHAT YOU NEED:

1. **Dried Gymnema Sylvestre Leaves**: 1 teaspoon
2. **Water**: 1 cup (8 ounces)
3. **Honey or Lemon** (optional): For taste

STEPS TO PREPARE:

1. Boil the Water:

- Pour 1 cup of water into a saucepan and bring it to a boil.

2. Prepare the Gymnema Leaves:

- Measure out 1 teaspoon of dried Gymnema sylvestre leaves.

3. Steep the Tea:

- Place the dried gymnema leaves into a teapot or cup.
- Pour the boiling water over the leaves.
- Cover and let the tea steep for 10-15 minutes to extract the beneficial compounds.

4. Strain the Tea:

- After steeping, strain the tea to remove the leaves.

5. Add Honey or Lemon (Optional):

- If desired, add honey for sweetness or a slice of lemon for additional flavor and health benefits.

6. Serve:

- Pour the strained tea into a cup and enjoy.

TIPS:

- **Dosage**: Drink 1-2 cups daily to enjoy the full benefits of Gymnema sylvestre tea.
- **Storage**: If you make a larger batch, store the tea in the refrigerator for up to 3 days. Reheat as needed.

BENEFITS OF GYMNEMA SYLVESTRE TEA:

1. Blood Sugar Regulation:

- **Lowers Blood Sugar Levels**: Gymnema sylvestre is known for its ability to help lower blood sugar levels, making it beneficial for people with diabetes. It works by reducing the absorption of sugar in the intestines and enhancing insulin production.
- **Improves Insulin Sensitivity**: It can enhance insulin sensitivity and reduce insulin resistance, helping to better control blood sugar levels.

2. Weight Management:

- **Reduces Sugar Cravings**: Gymnema sylvestre is often called the "sugar destroyer" because it can reduce the ability to taste sweetness, thus reducing sugar cravings and aiding in weight management.

3. Digestive Health:

- **Aids Digestion**: It has been used traditionally to aid digestion and reduce symptoms of indigestion and constipation.

4. Cholesterol and Heart Health:

- **Lowers Cholesterol Levels**: Regular consumption of gymnema can help lower LDL (bad) cholesterol and triglyceride levels, promoting heart health.
- **Reduces Cardiovascular Risk**: By improving lipid profiles and reducing blood sugar levels, gymnema can help reduce the risk of cardiovascular diseases.

5. Anti-inflammatory and Antioxidant:

- **Reduces Inflammation**: Gymnema has anti-inflammatory properties that can help reduce inflammation in the body, which is beneficial for conditions like arthritis.
- **Rich in Antioxidants**: It is high in antioxidants, which help protect cells from damage caused by free radicals and support overall health.

This gymnema sylvestre tea recipe is a simple and effective herbal remedy that provides numerous health benefits, including improved blood sugar regulation, weight management, digestive health, cholesterol control, and anti-inflammatory effects.

Dosage Recommendations for Cayenne Pepper, Cinnamon, Fenugreek, and Gymnema Sylvestre in Capsule Form

Cayenne Pepper:

- **Common Dosage**: 30-120 milligrams per day.
- **Usage**: Typically taken in divided doses throughout the day with meals to avoid stomach upset.
- **Purpose**: Often used for pain relief, digestive health, and improving circulation.

Cinnamon:

- **Common Dosage**: 500 milligrams to 1 gram per day.
- **Usage**: Can be taken all at once or divided into smaller doses throughout the day.
- **Purpose**: Known for its potential to lower blood sugar levels and improve heart health.

Fenugreek:

- **Common Dosage**: 500 milligrams to 1 gram per day.
- **Usage**: Usually taken before or with meals.
- **Purpose**: Often used to support lactation, improve digestion, and help manage blood sugar levels.

Gymnema Sylvestre:

- **Common Dosage**: 100 milligrams to 400 milligrams per day.
- **Usage**: Typically taken in divided doses with meals.
- **Purpose**: Known for its ability to help regulate blood sugar levels and reduce sugar cravings.

IMPORTANT CONSIDERATIONS:

- **Consultation**: Always consult with a healthcare professional before starting any new supplement, especially if you are pregnant, nursing, have underlying health conditions, or are taking other medications.
- **Start Low**: Begin with the lower end of the dosage range to see how your body reacts, then gradually increase if needed.
- **Consistency**: For best results, take the supplements consistently at the same time each day.

These dosage recommendations are general guidelines and may vary based on individual health needs and responses. Always follow the guidance of a healthcare provider for personalized advice.

HERBAL CARE FOR MENTAL WELLBEING

In the gentle quiet of morning, as the world stirs awake, imagine starting your day not with the harsh jolt of caffeine but with a soothing cup of tea made from herbs that naturally coax your body into balanced wakefulness. This isn't just a pleasant morning ritual; it's a profound way to harness the natural adaptogenic powers of herbs that have been used for centuries to combat stress and enhance mental clarity. In this chapter, we delve into the realm of adaptogens —nature's answer to modern stressors, offering a buffer against the pressures that can overwhelm our mental faculties and disrupt our physical health. Whether you're facing a looming deadline, managing household dynamics, or simply trying to keep pace with the fast-moving world, adaptogens provide a foundation of resilience that can transform your approach to life's challenges.

4.1 ADAPTOGENS FOR STRESS: NATURAL STRESS FIGHTERS

Introduction to Adaptogens

The term 'adaptogen' might sound modern, but these herbs have been a cornerstone of herbal medicine for thousands of years, particularly in Ayurvedic and Chinese practices. Adaptogens are a unique class of healing plants that promote hormone balance and protect the body from a wide array of diseases, including those caused by excessive stress. In times of increased stress and demand, adaptogens act almost like a thermostat. They 'adapt' their function according to your body's specific needs, helping to normalize your physiological functions. By supporting the adrenal glands, they counteract the adverse effects of stress and enable the body's cells to access more energy; they help eliminate toxic byproducts of the metabolic process and help the body to utilize oxygen more efficiently. On a day filled with back-to-back meetings or during a period of emotional upheaval, adaptogens work quietly and effectively to stabilize your mood and energy.

Key Adaptogenic Herbs

Among the pantheon of adaptogenic herbs, ashwagandha, rhodiola, and holy basil stand out for their robust effects on stress reduction. Ashwagandha, often called the 'strength of the stallion' because it traditionally has been used to strengthen the immune system after illness, is renowned for its ability to reduce anxiety and improve overall resilience to stress. Rhodiola rosea, often referred to as the 'golden root', is invaluable for improving concentration and diminishing fatigue, particularly in high-stress situations. Holy basil, also known as Tulsi, is not just a staple in Indian homes for its sacred nature but is also celebrated for its profound effects on mental balance and stress management.

Application and Dosage

Integrating these adaptogens into your daily routine requires some know-how, particularly regarding dosage and form. Ashwagandha is effective as a powdered root, usually taken in capsule form, with a general recommendation of about 300-500 mg twice daily, but it's wise to start at a lower dose to assess tolerance. Rhodiola is best taken in extract form, with a recommended dosage of 200-600 mg per day, ideally before meals to optimize absorption. Holy basil works beautifully both as a tea and in extract form; a cup of Tulsi tea can be soothing in the evening, while capsules can serve as a potent stress-reliever during a hectic day.

When overwhelmed with the merging demands of home and work life, incorporating a morning regimen of rhodiola extract, will show improvement in focus and a significant reduction in stress-induced fatigue. When dealing with the anxieties and stresses of everyday life, starting a routine that includes drinking holy basil tea each evening, will show a marked decrease in anxiety levels and an improved sense of calm.

These examples highlight not just the efficacy of adaptogens in managing stress but also their potential to enhance overall quality of life, enabling you to meet life's challenges not merely with endurance, but with grace and vitality. As you weave these miraculous herbs into the fabric of your daily routine, they quietly uplift your wellness journey, making resilience not just an occasional ally but a constant companion.

Herbal Remedy Recipe for Rhodiola Extract

WHAT YOU NEED:

1. **Dried Rhodiola Rosea Root**: 1 part (e.g., 1 cup)
2. **Alcohol**: Vodka or brandy, at least 80 proof (40% alcohol content)

3. **Glass Jar**: A clean, airtight glass container
4. **Cheesecloth or Fine Strainer**: For filtering
5. **Dark Glass Dropper Bottles**: For storing the finished extract
6. **Label and Pen**: For labeling the extract

STEPS TO PREPARE:

1. Prepare the Rhodiola Root:

- Measure out the dried Rhodiola root. For example, if you are using 1 cup of dried Rhodiola root, you will need enough alcohol to cover it completely in the jar.

2. Fill the Jar:

- Place the dried Rhodiola root into the glass jar, filling it about halfway.

3. Add Alcohol:

- Pour the alcohol over the Rhodiola root, ensuring it is completely submerged. Leave about an inch of space at the top of the jar.

4. Seal and Shake:

- Seal the jar tightly with a lid.
- Shake the jar well to mix the Rhodiola root and alcohol.

5. Store and Shake:

- Place the jar in a cool, dark place.
- Shake the jar every day or every few days to keep the mixture well-blended.

- Let the extract sit for at least 4-6 weeks. The longer it sits, the stronger it will be.

6. Strain the Extract:

- After the waiting period, place cheesecloth or a fine strainer over a clean bowl.
- Pour the mixture through the cheesecloth to filter out the Rhodiola root solids.
- Squeeze the cheesecloth to extract as much liquid as possible.

7. Transfer to Dropper Bottles:

- Use a funnel to pour the strained liquid into dark glass dropper bottles.
- Label the bottles with the name of the extract and the date.

DOSAGE INSTRUCTIONS:

- **Standard Dose**: Take 1-2 droppersful (1-2 ml) of the extract diluted in a small amount of water or juice up to twice a day.
- **For Stress and Fatigue**: Take 1-2 droppersful (1-2 ml) in the morning and early afternoon to help manage stress and combat fatigue.

BENEFITS OF RHODIOLA EXTRACT:

1. Stress Reduction:

- **Adaptogenic Properties**: Rhodiola is an adaptogen, which helps the body adapt to stress and reduces fatigue and anxiety.
- **Improves Mood**: It can help improve mood and alleviate symptoms of depression by balancing neurotransmitters in the brain.

2. Enhances Cognitive Function:

- **Boosts Mental Performance**: Rhodiola has been shown to enhance mental performance, improve focus, and reduce mental fatigue.
- **Memory Enhancement**: It can help improve memory and cognitive function by protecting brain cells from damage.

3. Physical Performance:

- **Increases Stamina**: Rhodiola can enhance physical endurance and reduce fatigue, making it beneficial for athletes and those with physically demanding lifestyles.
- **Reduces Muscle Damage**: It can help reduce muscle damage and inflammation caused by intense physical activity.

4. Immune Support:

- **Boosts Immunity**: Rhodiola can strengthen the immune system by enhancing the body's resistance to infections.

5. Heart Health:

- **Protects the Heart**: It has cardioprotective effects, helping to reduce the risk of heart disease by improving heart function and reducing stress-related damage.

This Rhodiola extract recipe is a potent herbal remedy that provides a wide range of health benefits, including stress reduction, enhanced cognitive function, improved physical performance, immune support, and heart health protection. Always consult with a healthcare provider before starting any new herbal remedy.

4.2 HERBS FOR ANXIETY: GENTLE ALTERNATIVES TO MEDICATION

In the quiet moments of self-reflection or during the rush of daily tasks, feelings of anxiety can surface, bringing with them a sense of unease that might seem overwhelming at times. While traditional medications have long been the cornerstone of treating anxiety, a growing number of individuals are seeking gentler, more natural alternatives. Herbs like lemon balm, passionflower, and kava hold a storied history in traditional medicine for their calming effects and are re-emerging as beneficial anxiolytics that can be woven into your daily routines to help manage anxiety without the harsh side effects often associated with pharmaceuticals.

Lemon balm, with its mild lemon scent and flavor, acts as a natural sedative, gently soothing the nervous system. This herb increases the activity of gamma-aminobutyric acid (GABA) in the brain, a neurotransmitter that helps regulate nerve cells and calms anxiety. Passionflower, another powerful herb, boosts GABA levels in the brain, which helps lower the brain activity that causes anxiety. It's particularly useful for those who experience anxiety alongside insomnia, as it aids in sleep without inducing lethargy. Kava, known for its ceremonial use in the Pacific Islands, contains kavalactones, compounds that have been shown to possess sedative properties and are effective in calming anxiety, promoting a state of relaxed focus without impairing cognitive function.

Safety and Efficacy

When incorporating these herbs into your life, understanding their safety profiles is crucial. Lemon balm is generally safe for most people and can be taken regularly without the risk of dependency or severe side effects. However, it should be used with caution if you are on thyroid medication, as it can potentially interfere with thyroid hormone levels. Passionflower is also safe for most adults when used in moderation. It's important to note that while it is helpful for short-term management of anxiety, it should not be used concurrently with sedative medications without supervision from a healthcare provider. Kava, while effective, requires careful consideration; it should not be used by people with liver disease or those taking medications that affect liver function, and it should always be taken under the guidance of a healthcare professional due to concerns about its effects on the liver.

Integrative Treatment Plans

To fully benefit from these herbal remedies, integrating them into a broader treatment plan that includes lifestyle adjustments and psychological therapies can be incredibly effective. Incorporating routine exercise, a balanced diet, adequate sleep, and mindfulness practices like meditation can significantly enhance the efficacy of these herbs. For instance, pairing the daily intake of passionflower tea with mindfulness exercises can help create a deeper sense of calm and manage anxiety more effectively. Additionally, cognitive-behavioral therapy (CBT) and other forms of psychological counseling can complement the use of these herbs, addressing the root causes of anxiety and providing strategies to cope with it.

Personalization of Herbal Treatments

Tailoring these herbal treatments to your specific needs is key to their effectiveness. Start by identifying the type and triggers of your anxiety. For situational anxiety, such as anxiety before public speaking or flying, kava might be particularly beneficial due to its fast-acting, short-term calming effects. For ongoing, generalized anxiety, a combination of lemon balm and passionflower might be more effective, providing a sustained decrease in anxiety levels throughout the day. The dosages should be adjusted based on your experience with the herbs and their effects on your body. Starting with lower doses and gradually adjusting based on your response can help manage anxiety safely without overwhelming your system. For example, incorporating a cup of lemon balm tea in your morning routine and a passionflower capsule at night can balance the therapeutic effects throughout the day and night. Refer to section 3.4 on Healthy Pregnancy and Postpartum Care for a Lemon Balm Tea recipe.

As you explore these gentle herbal alternatives, remember that the goal is to find a harmonious balance that suits your lifestyle and personal health profile. Each herb offers a unique bouquet of benefits, and when used thoughtfully, they can provide a natural and effective way to manage anxiety, enhancing your overall quality of life.

Passionflower in Capsule Form

DOSAGE INFORMATION:

- **General Dosage:** The typical recommended dosage for passionflower in capsule form is between 250 to 500 mg, taken one to three times daily.
- **Standardized Extract:** If using a standardized extract, a common dosage is 200 to 400 mg per day, divided into two to three doses.
- **Duration:** Passionflower can be taken consistently for several weeks. Long-term use should be discussed with a healthcare provider.
- **Consultation:** Dosage may vary based on individual health needs and conditions. It is advisable to consult with a healthcare provider for personalized dosing.

BENEFITS OF PASSIONFLOWER:

1. Anxiety Relief:

- **Calming Effect:** Passionflower is known for its calming properties, which can help reduce symptoms of anxiety and promote relaxation.

- **Supports Emotional Balance:** It may help manage stress and improve overall emotional well-being.

2. Insomnia and Sleep Disorders:

- **Improves Sleep Quality:** Passionflower can help improve sleep quality and duration, making it beneficial for those with insomnia or other sleep disorders.
- **Promotes Relaxation:** It aids in calming the mind and body, making it easier to fall asleep and stay asleep.

3. Nervous System Support:

- **Reduces Nervous Tension:** The herb is effective in reducing nervous tension and restlessness, providing a sense of calm and peace.
- **Helps with Withdrawal Symptoms:** Passionflower may be beneficial for individuals experiencing withdrawal symptoms from substances such as nicotine, caffeine, or alcohol.

4. Pain Relief:

- **Analgesic Properties:** Passionflower has mild analgesic properties that can help alleviate minor aches and pains, including headaches and muscle cramps.

5. Supports Digestive Health:

- **Relieves Gastrointestinal Issues:** It can help soothe gastrointestinal issues such as indigestion, irritable bowel syndrome (IBS), and stomach cramps.

6. Menopausal Symptoms:

- **Eases Menopausal Discomfort:** Passionflower may help alleviate symptoms of menopause, such as hot flashes, mood swings, and sleep disturbances.

POSSIBLE DRUG INTERACTIONS AND PRECAUTIONS

1. Interactions:

- **Sedatives:** Passionflower may enhance the effects of sedative medications, including benzodiazepines, barbiturates, and sleep aids.
- **Antidepressants:** It can interact with certain antidepressants, particularly monoamine oxidase inhibitors (MAOIs).
- **Blood Thinners:** Passionflower may interact with anticoagulant medications, increasing the risk of bleeding.
- **Anticonvulsants:** It can potentially interact with anticonvulsant medications, altering their effectiveness.

2. Precautions:

- **Pregnancy and Breastfeeding:** Pregnant or breastfeeding women should consult a healthcare provider before using passionflower due to its potential effects on the fetus and milk production.
- **Surgery:** Discontinue use of passionflower at least two weeks before scheduled surgery due to its sedative effects.
- **Liver Health:** Individuals with liver disorders should use passionflower with caution, as its safety in liver-compromised individuals is not well-studied.

4.3 MOOD-ENHANCING HERBS: A NATURAL UPLIFT

In the ebb and flow of daily life, maintaining a consistently positive mood can sometimes feel elusive, particularly during times of stress or seasonal changes that impact our emotional well-being. However, nature offers a bouquet of mood-enhancing herbs that act as natural uplifters, gently supporting your emotional health. St. John's Wort, saffron, and chamomile are among these cherished natural allies, each bringing a unique set of benefits that can help elevate your mood and restore a sense of joy and calm to your daily life.

St. John's Wort is perhaps one of the most well-known herbs for boosting mood. Traditionally used for its positive impact on emotional well-being, it influences neurotransmitters in the brain such as serotonin and dopamine, which are crucial for maintaining a positive mood. The active compounds in St. John's Wort, notably hypericin and hyperforin, are thought to inhibit the reuptake of serotonin, thereby increasing its availability in the brain. This action can help alleviate mild to moderate depression and promote a more cheerful mood. Saffron, another powerful herb, has been studied for its potential antidepressant properties. Research suggests that saffron's bioactive compounds, such as crocin and safranal, modulate the levels of serotonin, much like conventional antidepressants, but without the side effects often associated with these medications. This makes saffron an excellent option for those seeking a natural mood enhancer. Chamomile, widely regarded for its calming effects, also plays a subtle role in mood enhancement. It contains apigenin, a compound that binds to certain receptors in the brain which may help promote relaxation and reduce irritability.

Incorporating these herbs into your daily routine can be a delightful and effective way to enhance your mood. Starting your day with a cup of St. John's Wort tea can set a positive tone for the hours ahead. For a mid-day boost, a small dose of saffron in a glass of warm milk or a saffron-infused smoothie can provide a quick uplift. Chamomile tea in the evening serves as a perfect wind-down drink, soothing your nerves and setting the stage for a restful night, which in itself is beneficial for maintaining a good mood the following day.

While these herbs offer significant benefits, it's important to approach their use with mindfulness, particularly regarding their interactions with other medications and their overall safety profile. St. John's Wort, for instance, is known to interact with a variety of pharmaceuticals, including antidepressants, birth control pills, and blood thinners, potentially diminishing their effectiveness. Therefore, it is crucial to consult with a healthcare provider before starting any regimen that includes St. John's Wort, especially if you are currently taking other medications. Saffron, while generally safe in culinary doses, should be used cautiously in medicinal amounts as high doses can be toxic. Always ensure that you are using high-quality, pure saffron to avoid contaminants that can cause adverse effects. Chamomile, generally safe for most people, can cause allergic reactions in individuals sensitive to plants in the daisy family. As with any herbal treatment, starting with smaller doses and gradually adjusting based on your body's response can help minimize risks and enhance the therapeutic benefits of these mood-enhancing herbs.

As you weave these natural mood enhancers into the fabric of your daily life, they not only act as catalysts for emotional uplift but also enrich your connection to the natural world, reminding you of the gentle power of plants to heal and harmonize. Whether sipped as a warm tea or taken as a supplement, these herbs offer a natural, gentle way to support your emotional health, making your days brighter and your spirits lighter.

Herbal Remedy Recipe for St. John's Wort Tea

WHAT YOU NEED:

1. **Dried St. John's Wort**: 1-2 teaspoons (or 1 St. John's Wort tea bag)
2. **Water**: 1 cup (8 ounces)

3. **Honey or Lemon** (optional): For taste

STEPS TO PREPARE:

1. Boil the Water:

- Pour 1 cup of water into a saucepan and bring it to a boil.

2. Prepare the St. John's Wort:

- If using dried St. John's Wort, measure out 1-2 teaspoons. If using a tea bag, it's ready to use.

3. Steep the Tea:

- Place the dried St. John's Wort or tea bag into a teapot or cup.
- Pour the boiling water over the herb.
- Cover and let the tea steep for 5-10 minutes to extract the beneficial compounds.

4. Strain the Tea:

- If using loose dried St. John's Wort, strain the tea to remove the herb. If using a tea bag, simply remove the bag.

5. Add Honey or Lemon (Optional):

- If desired, add honey for sweetness or a slice of lemon for additional flavor and health benefits.

6. Serve:

- Pour the strained tea into a cup and enjoy.

TIPS:

- **Dosage**: Drink 1-2 cups daily to enjoy the full benefits of St. John's Wort tea.
- **Storage**: If you make a larger batch, store the tea in the refrigerator for up to 3 days. Reheat as needed.

BENEFITS OF ST. JOHN'S WORT TEA:

1. Mood and Mental Health:

- **Antidepressant Properties**: St. John's Wort is well-known for its antidepressant effects. It is commonly used to alleviate symptoms of mild to moderate depression by increasing levels of neurotransmitters such as serotonin.
- **Reduces Anxiety**: It can help reduce anxiety and promote a sense of calm and well-being.

2. Sleep Aid:

- **Improves Sleep**: St. John's Wort can help improve sleep quality and reduce symptoms of insomnia.

3. Anti-inflammatory:

- **Reduces Inflammation**: It has anti-inflammatory properties that can help reduce inflammation in the body, which is beneficial for conditions like arthritis.

4. Antimicrobial:

- **Fights Infections**: St. John's Wort has antimicrobial properties that can help protect against bacterial and viral infections.

5. Wound Healing:

- **Promotes Healing**: When applied topically, it can help heal wounds, burns, and bruises due to its antimicrobial and anti-inflammatory properties.

6. Digestive Health:

- **Aids Digestion**: It can help soothe the digestive tract and alleviate symptoms of indigestion and stomach discomfort.

This St. John's Wort tea recipe is a simple and effective herbal remedy that provides numerous health benefits, including improved mood and mental health, better sleep, reduced inflammation, antimicrobial properties, and digestive health support. Always consult with a healthcare provider before starting any new herbal remedy.

DOSAGE AMOUNT FOR ST. JOHN'S WORT IN CAPSULE FORM

When taking St. John's Wort in capsule form, the standard dosage generally recommended is:

- **300 milligrams** of extract, taken **three times a day**.

This dosage is based on the standardized extract containing 0.3% hypericin, which is one of the active compounds in St. John's Wort.

IMPORTANT CONSIDERATIONS:

1. **Start Low**: If you are new to taking St. John's Wort, it might be beneficial to start with a lower dose and gradually increase to the recommended dosage to see how your body reacts.
2. **Consistency**: For best results, take the capsules consistently at the same time each day.
3. **Consult a Healthcare Provider**: Always consult with a healthcare provider before starting any new supplement,

especially if you are taking other medications, as St. John's Wort can interact with various drugs, including antidepressants, birth control pills, blood thinners, and others.

POTENTIAL INTERACTIONS:

- St. John's Wort can interact with various medications by inducing the cytochrome P450 enzymes (CYP3A4, CYP2C9, CYP2D6) and P-glycoprotein, which can reduce the effectiveness of these medications.
- **Medications to be cautious with include**:

  - Antidepressants
  - Birth control pills
  - Blood thinners (like warfarin)
  - Immunosuppressants
  - Antiviral drugs for HIV
  - Chemotherapy drugs
  - Antiepileptic drugs

MONITORING AND ADJUSTMENTS:

- **Monitor Symptoms**: Pay attention to how you feel while taking St. John's Wort, and if you notice any adverse effects or interactions with other medications, consult your healthcare provider immediately.
- **Adjust Dosage if Necessary**: Depending on your response, your healthcare provider may adjust your dosage.

These references provide comprehensive information about the usage, benefits, and precautions when taking St. John's Wort. Always follow the advice of a healthcare provider for personalized guidance.

Herbal Remedy Recipe for Saffron Infused Smoothie

INGREDIENTS:

1. **Saffron Threads**: A pinch (about 5-10 threads)
2. **Milk**: 1 cup (can substitute with almond milk or any other plant-based milk)
3. **Banana**: 1 (ripe)
4. **Greek Yogurt**: 1/2 cup (can substitute with plant-based yogurt for a dairy-free option)
5. **Honey**: 1 tablespoon (optional, for sweetness)
6. **Almonds**: 1 tablespoon (optional, for added texture and nutrients)
7. **Cardamom Powder**: 1/4 teaspoon (optional, for additional flavor)
8. **Ice Cubes**: A few (optional, for a colder smoothie)

STEPS TO PREPARE:

1. Infuse the Saffron:

- Soak the saffron threads in 2 tablespoons of warm milk for about 10-15 minutes to release their color and flavor.

2. Blend Ingredients:

- In a blender, add the soaked saffron and milk, banana, Greek yogurt, honey, almonds, cardamom powder, and ice cubes.
- Blend until smooth and creamy.

3. Serve:

- Pour the smoothie into a glass and enjoy immediately.

TIPS:

- **Adjust Sweetness**: If you prefer a sweeter smoothie, add more honey or use a sweeter fruit.
- **Texture Variation**: For a thicker smoothie, add more yogurt. For a thinner consistency, add more milk.

BENEFITS OF SAFFRON INFUSED SMOOTHIE:

1. Saffron:

- **Mood Enhancement**: Saffron is known for its antidepressant properties, helping to improve mood and reduce symptoms of depression and anxiety.
- **Antioxidant Properties**: It is rich in antioxidants like crocin, crocetin, and safranal, which help protect cells from oxidative stress and reduce inflammation.
- **Cognitive Function**: Saffron may improve cognitive function and memory, making it beneficial for mental clarity and focus.
- **Heart Health**: It can help lower blood pressure and cholesterol levels, promoting cardiovascular health.

2. Banana:

- **Energy Boost**: Bananas provide a quick source of energy due to their natural sugars and carbohydrates.
- **Digestive Health**: Rich in dietary fiber, bananas help promote healthy digestion and regular bowel movements.

3. Greek Yogurt:

- **Protein-Rich**: Provides a good amount of protein, essential for muscle repair and growth.
- **Probiotics**: Contains beneficial probiotics that support gut health and boost the immune system.

4. Almonds:

- **Nutrient Dense**: Almonds are packed with healthy fats, protein, vitamins, and minerals.
- **Heart Health**: They can help lower cholesterol levels and reduce the risk of heart disease.

5. Honey:

- **Natural Sweetener**: A healthier alternative to refined sugar, providing natural sweetness.
- **Antibacterial Properties**: Honey has antibacterial properties that can help boost the

DOSAGE FOR SAFFRON IN CAPSULE FORM

When taking saffron in capsule form, the typical recommended dosage ranges from 30 mg to 200 mg per day. The specific dosage may vary based on the intended use and the formulation of the supplement.

Common Dosage Guidelines:

1. **General Wellness and Mood Improvement:**
2. **Standard Dose**: 30 mg to 50 mg per day.
3. **Usage**: Usually taken in one or two divided doses.
4. **Depression and Anxiety:**
5. **Standard Dose**: 30 mg to 100 mg per day.
6. **Usage**: Often taken in two divided doses of 15 mg to 50 mg each.
7. **Premenstrual Syndrome (PMS):**
8. **Standard Dose**: 30 mg per day.
9. **Usage**: Typically taken in one or two divided doses.

IMPORTANT CONSIDERATIONS:

1. **Consult a Healthcare Provider**: Always consult with a healthcare provider before starting any new supplement, especially if you are pregnant, nursing, have underlying health conditions, or are taking other medications.
2. **Quality and Standardization**: Ensure you are using a high-quality saffron supplement that is standardized to contain active compounds like safranal and crocin.
3. **Start Low and Monitor**: Start with the lower end of the dosage range to see how your body reacts, then gradually increase if needed and as advised by a healthcare provider.
4. **Consistency**: For best results, take the supplement consistently at the same time each day.

POTENTIAL BENEFITS OF SAFFRON:

1. **Mood Enhancement**: Saffron has been shown to help improve mood and reduce symptoms of depression and anxiety by increasing levels of neurotransmitters like serotonin.
2. **Antioxidant Properties**: It is rich in antioxidants, which help protect cells from oxidative stress and reduce inflammation.
3. **Cognitive Function**: Saffron may improve cognitive function and memory, making it beneficial for mental clarity and focus.
4. **Heart Health**: It can help lower blood pressure and cholesterol levels, promoting cardiovascular health.
5. **Premenstrual Syndrome (PMS)**: Saffron has been found to alleviate symptoms of PMS, such as mood swings and cramps.

These dosage recommendations are general guidelines and may vary based on individual health needs and responses. Always follow the advice of a healthcare provider for personalized guidance.

4.4 HERBAL THERAPIES FOR DEPRESSION

Depression, a cloak that dims life's vibrancy, can often leave one navigating through a haze of sadness and disinterest. While there are many conventional treatments available, an increasing number of individuals are turning toward more natural options to manage symptoms of mild to moderate depression. Herbs like turmeric, lavender, and ginkgo biloba are not just culinary delights or fragrant additions to gardens and homes; they are also potent herbal remedies with the potential to lift moods and brighten days. Turmeric, often hailed for its anti-inflammatory properties, contains curcumin, a compound that has shown promise in various studies for its ability to enhance mood by reducing inflammation, which is often increased in individuals with depression. Lavender, on the other hand, is widely recognized for its calming aroma but is also effective in alleviating depression symptoms by reducing anxiety and improving sleep quality, thus addressing some of the common co-occurring symptoms of depression. Ginkgo biloba, a plant with ancient roots, has been studied for its potential to improve cognitive function and overall mood by increasing blood flow to the brain, thus potentially alleviating some of the cognitive symptoms associated with depression.

These herbs have not just been chosen at random but are backed by scientific research that underscores their efficacy. Studies have shown that curcumin can boost brain-derived neurotrophic factor (BDNF) levels, which are often low in individuals with depression. This effect is akin to that of some antidepressant medications, offering a natural alternative with fewer side effects. Lavender oil, particularly in its silexan form, has been compared to antidepressants like paroxetine in clinical studies and found to be effective in alleviating anxiety and depression with minimal side effects. Ginkgo biloba's ability to enhance memory and cognitive function also plays a crucial role in its antidepressant effects, as cognitive decline is often a concern in those suffering from long-term depression.

Combining these herbs can often lead to enhanced therapeutic outcomes. For instance, integrating turmeric in your diet along with directed use of lavender oil for relaxation and mood stabilization can create a synergistic effect, enhancing overall well-being. Adding ginkgo biloba to this regimen can aid in maintaining cognitive function and energy, often affected by depressive states. This holistic approach not only addresses the symptoms but also contributes to a general upliftment in mental health.

Long-term use of these herbal therapies requires careful consideration and monitoring. It's important to note that while these herbs are natural, they are not without potential side effects or interactions with other medications. For instance, ginkgo biloba can interact with anticoagulants and isn't recommended for those on blood thinners. Similarly, high doses of turmeric can cause gastrointestinal discomfort in some individuals. Regular consultations with healthcare providers, ideally those knowledgeable about both herbal and conventional therapies, are crucial. They can help monitor the effectiveness of the herbal regimen and make adjustments as needed. Keeping a journal of your mood and any side effects can be beneficial in tracking what works and what doesn't, providing valuable information that can aid in tailoring your treatment plan.

This approach not only empowers you with choices but also aligns your treatment with a more natural, holistic path. It's about finding balance, enhancing your body's healing capabilities, and gradually restoring your mental landscape to one of vibrancy and hope. As you consider these options, remember that each step taken is part of a larger commitment to your health and well-being, reflecting a choice to nurture yourself with nature's profound gifts.

Turmeric Tea Recipe

INGREDIENTS:

1. 1 teaspoon ground turmeric (or 1-inch piece of fresh turmeric root, grated)
2. 1/2 teaspoon ground ginger (or 1/2-inch piece of fresh ginger, grated)
3. 1 tablespoon lemon juice
4. 1 tablespoon honey or maple syrup (optional, for taste)
5. 1 cup boiling water
6. Pinch of black pepper (enhances absorption of turmeric)

INSTRUCTIONS:

1. Prepare the Ingredients:

- If using fresh turmeric and ginger, grate them.
- Measure out the ground turmeric, ground ginger, lemon juice, honey (if using), and black pepper.

2. Boil the Water:

- Bring 1 cup of water to a rolling boil.

3. Combine in a Cup:

- Place the turmeric, ginger, and black pepper in a mug.

4. Add Boiling Water:

- Pour the boiling water over the turmeric and ginger mixture.

5. Stir Well:

- Stir the mixture thoroughly to ensure the turmeric and ginger are well combined.

6. Add Lemon and Honey:

- Add the lemon juice and honey (if using). Stir again to mix everything evenly.

7. Steep:

- Allow the tea to steep for about 5-10 minutes.

8. Strain and Serve:

- If you used fresh turmeric and ginger, strain the tea to remove the solid pieces.
- Enjoy your turmeric tea warm.

BENEFITS OF TURMERIC TEA:

1. Anti-Inflammatory Properties:

- **Curcumin:** The active ingredient in turmeric, curcumin, has powerful anti-inflammatory effects, helping to reduce inflammation and pain in the body. It is beneficial for conditions like arthritis and inflammatory bowel disease.

2. Antioxidant Effects:

- **Free Radical Protection:** Turmeric is rich in antioxidants, which help neutralize harmful free radicals and protect cells from damage. This can contribute to overall health and disease prevention.

3. Boosts Immune System:

- **Immune Support:** Regular consumption of turmeric can enhance the immune system, making the body more resilient against infections and illnesses.

4. Digestive Health:

- **Digestive Aid:** Turmeric stimulates bile production, which aids in the digestion of fats and improves overall digestion. It can help alleviate symptoms of indigestion, bloating, and gas.

5. Heart Health:

- **Cardiovascular Benefits:** Turmeric can help improve heart health by reducing cholesterol levels, preventing the oxidation of LDL cholesterol, and improving blood vessel function.

6. Anti-Cancer Properties:

- **Cancer Prevention:** Some studies suggest that curcumin can help prevent the growth and spread of cancer cells, making it a potential complementary treatment in cancer therapy.

7. Supports Brain Health:

- **Cognitive Function:** Curcumin may help improve brain function and lower the risk of brain diseases by increasing levels of brain-derived neurotrophic factor (BDNF), which supports the growth of new neurons and synaptic connections.

8. Mood and Mental Health:

- **Reduces Depression Symptoms:** Curcumin has been shown to have potential antidepressant effects by boosting the levels of serotonin and dopamine, the "feel-good" neurotransmitters in the brain.

POSSIBLE DRUG INTERACTIONS AND PRECAUTIONS

1. Interactions:

- **Blood Thinners:** Turmeric may increase the risk of bleeding when taken with anticoagulant and antiplatelet medications, such as warfarin, aspirin, and clopidogrel.
- **Diabetes Medications:** It can enhance the effects of diabetes medications, potentially leading to hypoglycemia (low blood sugar).
- **Stomach Acid Reducers:** Turmeric may interfere with medications that reduce stomach acid, such as omeprazole and ranitidine.

2. Precautions:

- **Pregnancy and Breastfeeding:** Pregnant or breastfeeding women should consult a healthcare provider before using turmeric in medicinal amounts.
- **Gallbladder Issues:** Individuals with gallstones or bile duct obstruction should avoid turmeric, as it can stimulate bile production.
- **Surgery:** Discontinue use of turmeric at least two weeks before scheduled surgery due to its blood-thinning properties.

GENERAL ADVICE:

- Always consult with a healthcare professional before starting any new herbal remedies, especially if you are taking medications or have underlying health conditions.
- Start with a lower dosage to assess your tolerance to turmeric.
- Monitor for any adverse reactions and discontinue use if they occur.

Lavender Oil Recipe and Benefits

Simple Lavender Oil Infusion

INGREDIENTS:

1. 1 cup dried lavender flowers (or fresh lavender flowers)
2. 1 cup carrier oil (such as olive oil, almond oil, or jojoba oil)
3. Glass jar with a tight-fitting lid
4. Cheesecloth or fine strainer
5. Dark glass bottle for storage

INSTRUCTIONS:

1. Prepare the Lavender:

- If using fresh lavender, ensure it is completely dry to prevent mold growth. You can dry lavender by hanging it upside down in a cool, dark place for a few days.

2. Combine Ingredients:

- Place the dried lavender flowers into the glass jar.
- Pour the carrier oil over the lavender, ensuring the flowers are fully submerged.

3. Infuse the Oil:

- Seal the jar tightly with the lid.
- Place the jar in a sunny windowsill or another warm spot for 2-4 weeks. Shake the jar gently every few days to help the infusion process.

4. Strain the Oil:

- After 2-4 weeks, strain the oil through cheesecloth or a fine strainer into a clean bowl to remove the lavender flowers.
- Transfer the strained oil into a dark glass bottle for storage.

5. Store:

- Store the lavender-infused oil in a cool, dark place. Properly stored, it can last for up to a year.

BENEFITS OF LAVENDER OIL

1. Promotes Relaxation and Reduces Anxiety:

- **Calming Effect:** Lavender oil is well-known for its calming and relaxing properties, making it effective in reducing anxiety, stress, and promoting a sense of calm.
- **Improves Mood:** The soothing aroma of lavender oil can help improve mood and alleviate symptoms of depression.

2. Improves Sleep Quality:

- **Sleep Aid:** Lavender oil is commonly used as a natural remedy for insomnia and other sleep disorders. Its calming effects help promote better sleep quality and duration.

3. Relieves Pain:

- **Pain Relief:** Lavender oil has analgesic properties that can help alleviate various types of pain, including headaches, muscle aches, and joint pain.
- **Migraine Relief:** Applying diluted lavender oil to the temples and inhaling its aroma can help reduce the severity of migraine attacks.

4. Supports Skin Health:

- **Antiseptic and Anti-inflammatory:** Lavender oil's antiseptic and anti-inflammatory properties make it beneficial for treating minor cuts, burns, and insect bites. It can also help reduce inflammation and promote faster healing.
- **Acne Treatment:** Its antimicrobial properties help combat acne-causing bacteria, making it effective in treating and preventing acne.

5. Improves Digestive Health:

- **Digestive Aid:** Lavender oil can help alleviate digestive issues such as bloating, gas, and indigestion. Massaging diluted lavender oil onto the abdomen can provide relief from these symptoms.

6. Hair and Scalp Health:

- **Promotes Hair Growth:** Lavender oil can stimulate hair growth and improve scalp health. It helps increase circulation to the scalp, promoting hair growth and reducing hair loss.
- **Dandruff Treatment:** Its antimicrobial properties can help combat dandruff and other scalp infections.

7. Supports Respiratory Health:

- **Respiratory Relief:** Inhaling lavender oil can help alleviate respiratory issues such as colds, flu, and sinus congestion. It helps clear airways and reduce inflammation in the respiratory tract.

POSSIBLE DRUG INTERACTIONS AND PRECAUTIONS

1. Interactions:

- **Sedatives:** Lavender oil may enhance the effects of sedative medications, including benzodiazepines, barbiturates, and sleep aids.
- **Antidepressants:** It can interact with certain antidepressants, particularly monoamine oxidase inhibitors (MAOIs).
- **Blood Pressure Medications:** Lavender oil can lower blood pressure, so use with caution if you are taking antihypertensive medications to avoid hypotension.

2. Precautions:

- **Pregnancy and Breastfeeding:** Pregnant or breastfeeding women should consult a healthcare provider before using lavender oil.
- **Allergic Reactions:** Perform a patch test before using lavender oil topically to ensure you do not have an allergic reaction.
- **Children and Pets:** Use lavender oil with caution around young children and pets, as it can be toxic in large quantities.

GENERAL ADVICE:

- Always consult with a healthcare professional before starting any new herbal remedies, especially if you are taking medications or have underlying health conditions.
- Start with a lower concentration to assess your tolerance to lavender oil.
- Monitor for any adverse reactions and discontinue use if they occur.

Herbal Remedy Recipe for Ginkgo Biloba Tea

WHAT YOU NEED:

1. **Dried Ginkgo Biloba Leaves**: 1 teaspoon
2. **Water**: 1 cup (8 ounces)
3. **Honey or Lemon** (optional): For taste

STEPS TO PREPARE:

1. Boil the Water:

- Pour 1 cup of water into a saucepan and bring it to a boil.

2. Prepare the Ginkgo Leaves:

- Measure out 1 teaspoon of dried Ginkgo biloba leaves.

3. Steep the Tea:

- Place the dried ginkgo leaves into a teapot or cup.
- Pour the boiling water over the leaves.
- Cover and let the tea steep for 5-10 minutes to extract the beneficial compounds.

4. Strain the Tea:

- After steeping, strain the tea to remove the leaves.

5. Add Honey or Lemon (Optional):

- If desired, add honey for sweetness or a slice of lemon for additional flavor and health benefits.

6. Serve:

- Pour the strained tea into a cup and enjoy.

TIPS:

- **Dosage**: Drink 1-2 cups daily to enjoy the full benefits of Ginkgo biloba tea.
- **Storage**: If you make a larger batch, store the tea in the refrigerator for up to 3 days. Reheat as needed.

BENEFITS OF GINKGO BILOBA TEA:

1. Cognitive Health:

- **Improves Memory and Focus**: Ginkgo biloba is known for its ability to enhance memory and cognitive function by increasing blood flow to the brain.
- **Reduces Symptoms of Dementia and Alzheimer's**: It has been used to reduce symptoms of cognitive disorders such as dementia and Alzheimer's disease.

2. Antioxidant Properties:

- **Rich in Antioxidants**: Ginkgo biloba contains powerful antioxidants that help protect cells from oxidative damage caused by free radicals.

3. Circulatory Health:

- **Improves Blood Circulation**: Ginkgo biloba improves blood flow and circulation, which can benefit cardiovascular health and help alleviate symptoms of poor circulation such as cold hands and feet.

4. Anxiety Reduction:

- **Reduces Anxiety**: Some studies suggest that Ginkgo biloba can help reduce anxiety symptoms due to its potential ability to modulate the body's stress response.

5. Anti-inflammatory:

- **Reduces Inflammation**: Ginkgo biloba has anti-inflammatory properties that can help reduce inflammation throughout the body, benefiting conditions like arthritis.

DOSAGE FOR GINKGO BILOBA IN CAPSULE FORM:

Common Dosage Guidelines:

- **Standard Dose**: 120 mg to 240 mg per day.
- **Usage**: Typically taken in two or three divided doses throughout the day.

SPECIFIC USES:

1. **Cognitive Enhancement and Memory Improvement:**
2. **Standard Dose**: 120 mg to 240 mg per day.
3. **Usage**: Taken in divided doses, usually in the morning and afternoon.
4. **Anxiety Reduction:**
5. **Standard Dose**: 120 mg to 240 mg per day.
6. **Usage**: Taken in divided doses.
7. **Improving Circulation:**
8. **Standard Dose**: 120 mg to 240 mg per day.
9. **Usage**: Taken in divided doses.

IMPORTANT CONSIDERATIONS:

- **Consult a Healthcare Provider**: Always consult with a healthcare provider before starting any new supplement, especially if you are pregnant, nursing, have underlying health conditions, or are taking other medications.
- **Start Low and Monitor**: Start with the lower end of the dosage range to see how your body reacts, then gradually increase if needed and as advised by a healthcare provider.
- **Consistency**: For best results, take the supplement consistently at the same time each day.

These dosage recommendations are general guidelines and may vary based on individual health needs and responses. Always follow the advice of a healthcare provider for personalized guidance.

4.5 IMPROVING FOCUS AND COGNITIVE FUNCTION WITH HERBS

In the bustling rhythm of daily life, maintaining sharp cognitive function and focus can be as crucial for a high-performing student as it is for a managing professional or an active senior. The natural pharmacy offers a treasury of herbs known to enhance mental clarity and support brain health, among which bacopa, gotu kola, and rosemary are standout performers. These herbs are not just aids for memory recall or momentary concentration; they offer long-term improvements in cognitive function, making them invaluable in today's fast-paced world.

Bacopa monnieri, often referred to simply as Bacopa, is a herb that has been used in Ayurvedic medicine for centuries, primarily for enhancing cognitive abilities and reducing anxiety. It is well-regarded for its ability to improve both the retention of new information and the speed at which it is recalled. This makes Bacopa particularly beneficial for students who are studying for exams or professionals learning new skills. The active compounds in Bacopa, known as bacosides, are thought to repair damaged neurons and promote new nerve growth, which directly enhances neuron communication and brain function.

Gotu kola, another revered herb, is often called the "herb of longevity" in Ayurveda and traditional Chinese medicine. It is praised for its ability to improve circulation and, by extension, enhance brain function and memory. Gotu kola has been shown to increase levels of antioxidants in the brain, which helps protect neurons from environmental stressors. This herb is particularly beneficial for the elderly, as it not only boosts cognitive function but also improves vitality and reduces fatigue, contributing to an overall sense of well-being.

Rosemary, while commonly known for its culinary uses, also boasts potent nootropic properties. The aroma of rosemary alone has been shown in studies to enhance memory performance. The active ingredient in rosemary, 1,8-cineole, affects the neurotransmitters in the brain, increasing alertness and improving memory consolidation. For professionals juggling multiple tasks or seniors aiming to preserve and enhance their cognitive function, incorporating rosemary into their diet or simply inhaling its scent can provide a significant cognitive boost.

Preparation and Usage Tips

To maximize the cognitive benefits of these herbs, proper preparation and usage are key. Bacopa is best taken in extract form, with a typical dosage ranging from 300 to 450 mg daily. It can be taken with a meal to enhance absorption. Gotu kola can be consumed as a tea or in capsules. For tea, steeping 1-2 teaspoons of dried gotu kola in boiling water for 10-15 minutes is recommended. Drinking 1-2 cups daily can significantly enhance its efficacy. Rosemary can be used both in culinary contexts and for its aromatic benefits. Adding fresh rosemary to dishes can help enhance flavor and cognitive function, while keeping a sprig of rosemary on your desk and inhaling its scent intermittently can help maintain alertness during long working hours.

Integrating Cognitive Herbs with Diet

Enhancing the effectiveness of these cognitive herbs can also be achieved by integrating them with certain foods that support brain health. For instance, pairing rosemary with fatty fish, which are high in omega-3 fatty acids, can enhance its neuroprotective effects. Omega-3s are crucial for brain health, promoting brain cell membrane flexibility and improving communication between neurons. Similarly, combining bacopa or gotu kola with antioxidant-rich berries like blueberries can amplify their cognitive-enhancing effects. Berries are rich in flavonoids that may slow down memory decline and improve communication between brain cells.

Incorporating these cognitive herbs into your daily routine can transform your approach to mental clarity and focus. Whether you're a student preparing for exams, a professional keen on maintaining productivity, or a senior invested in sustaining mental agility, these herbs offer a natural, effective solution to enhancing cognitive function. By understanding and utilizing bacopa, gotu kola, and rosemary, not only do you invest in your current cognitive needs but also in a long-term strategy for maintaining brain health and vitality.

Herbal Remedy Recipe for Bacopa Extract

WHAT YOU NEED:

1. **Dried Bacopa Monnieri (Brahmi) Leaves**: 1 part
2. **Alcohol**: Vodka or brandy, at least 80 proof (40% alcohol content)
3. **Glass Jar**: A clean, airtight glass container
4. **Cheesecloth or Fine Strainer**: For filtering
5. **Dark Glass Dropper Bottles**: For storing the finished extract
6. **Label and Pen**: For labeling the extract

STEPS TO PREPARE:

1. Prepare the Bacopa Leaves:

- Measure out the dried Bacopa monnieri leaves. For example, if you use 1 cup of dried Bacopa leaves, you will need enough alcohol to cover them completely in the jar.

2. Fill the Jar:

- Place the dried Bacopa leaves into the glass jar, filling it about halfway.

3. Add Alcohol:

- Pour the alcohol over the Bacopa leaves, ensuring they are completely submerged. Leave about an inch of space at the top of the jar.

4. Seal and Shake:

- Seal the jar tightly with a lid.
- Shake the jar well to mix the Bacopa leaves and alcohol.

5. Store and Shake:

- Place the jar in a cool, dark place.
- Shake the jar every day or every few days to keep the mixture well-blended.
- Let the extract sit for at least 4-6 weeks. The longer it sits, the stronger it will be.

6. Strain the Extract:

- After the waiting period, place cheesecloth or a fine strainer over a clean bowl.
- Pour the mixture through the cheesecloth to filter out the Bacopa leaves.
- Squeeze the cheesecloth to extract as much liquid as possible.

7. Transfer to Dropper Bottles:

- Use a funnel to pour the strained liquid into dark glass dropper bottles.
- Label the bottles with the name of the extract and the date.

DOSAGE INSTRUCTIONS:

- **Standard Dose**: Take 1-2 droppersful (1-2 ml) of the extract diluted in a small amount of water or juice up to twice a day.
- **For Cognitive Enhancement**: Take 1-2 droppersful (1-2 ml) in the morning and early afternoon to help improve memory and cognitive function.

BENEFITS OF BACOPA EXTRACT:

1. Cognitive Enhancement:

- **Improves Memory**: Bacopa is known for its ability to enhance memory and improve cognitive function by promoting communication between neurons and protecting brain cells from damage.
- **Reduces Anxiety and Stress**: Bacopa has adaptogenic properties that help reduce anxiety and stress by modulating the body's stress response and promoting relaxation.

2. Antioxidant Properties:

- **Rich in Antioxidants**: Bacopa contains powerful antioxidants that help protect cells from oxidative damage caused by free radicals.

3. Anti-inflammatory:

- **Reduces Inflammation**: Bacopa has anti-inflammatory properties that can help reduce inflammation in the body, benefiting conditions like arthritis.

4. Neuroprotective:

- **Protects Brain Cells**: Bacopa helps protect brain cells from damage and supports the repair of damaged neurons, which can improve overall brain health.

5. Enhances Learning:

- **Improves Learning Ability**: Bacopa can enhance learning ability and information retention, making it beneficial for students and those engaged in mentally demanding tasks.

This Bacopa extract recipe is a potent herbal remedy that provides a wide range of health benefits, including cognitive enhancement, stress reduction, antioxidant protection, anti-inflammatory effects, and overall brain health support. Always consult with a healthcare provider before starting any new herbal remedy.

4.6 MINDFULNESS AND HERBS: A HOLISTIC APPROACH TO MENTAL HEALTH

In the serene embrace of mindfulness, where each moment is observed and appreciated in its fullness, the addition of certain calming herbs can significantly enhance the experience, creating a deeper sense of relaxation and focus. Among these, CBD, valerian, and hops are particularly notable for their synergistic effects with mindfulness practices. CBD, derived from the hemp plant, is renowned for its ability to reduce anxiety and stress without the psychoactive effects associated with its cousin THC. Its use in mindfulness practices can help quiet the mind, making it easier to achieve a meditative state. Valerian root, a herb long used for its sedative qualities, can also enhance mindfulness by soothing nervous tension and promoting relaxation, thereby deepening meditation sessions. Hops, commonly associated with brewing beer, contain compounds that naturally relax the body and mind, aiding in the practice of mindfulness by fostering a calm internal environment.

Integrating these herbs into your mindfulness routine can be both simple and transformative. For instance, starting your meditation or yoga session with a cup of tea infused with CBD oil or valerian can prepare your mind and body for a deeper experience. You might also consider using a pillow filled with dried hops as a supportive prop during meditation or as a comforting addition to your space, releasing its calming scent as you dive deeper into mindfulness. The routine use of these herbs, aligned with regular mindfulness practice, can significantly enhance your mental clarity and emotional balance, helping you to navigate daily stresses with greater ease and resilience.

This holistic approach to mental health is not merely anecdotal; it is supported by numerous personal stories from individuals who have found profound relief and heightened awareness through the combined power of herbs and mindfulness. By integrating CBD oil into a nightly meditation session can significantly alleviate anxiety. Studies have shown that incorporating valerian root into a bedtime routine, and engaging in guided mindfulness exercises, proved greatly beneficial for individuals struggling with PTSD. Following those practices have also shown notable improvements in sleep quality and overall well-being.

Incorporating calming herbs into your mindfulness practice offers a gentle yet powerful tool to enhance your mental health and emotional resilience. As you continue to explore this path, remember that each herb and each moment of mindfulness adds a layer of depth to your journey toward holistic well-being. By embracing these natural allies, you not only enrich your personal health regimen but also tap into the timeless wisdom of herbal medicine, woven seamlessly with the practice of mindfulness to support a balanced, serene life.

Herbal Remedy Recipe for Tea Infused with CBD Oil or Valerian Oil

INGREDIENTS:

1. **Dried Herbal Tea Leaves**: Choose your favorite herbal tea (e.g., chamomile, peppermint, or green tea) - 1 teaspoon or 1 tea bag.
2. **Water**: 1 cup (8 ounces).
3. **CBD Oil or Valerian Oil**: 1-2 drops.
4. **Honey or Lemon** (optional): For taste.

STEPS TO PREPARE:

1. Boil the Water:

- Pour 1 cup of water into a saucepan and bring it to a boil.

2. Prepare the Tea:

- Place the dried herbal tea leaves or tea bag into a teapot or cup.

3. Steep the Tea:

- Pour the boiling water over the tea leaves or tea bag.
- Cover and let the tea steep for 5-10 minutes.

4. Add CBD Oil or Valerian Oil:

- After the tea has steeped and slightly cooled, add 1-2 drops of CBD oil or valerian oil.
- Stir well to ensure the oil is evenly distributed.

5. Add Honey or Lemon (Optional):

- If desired, add honey for sweetness or a slice of lemon for additional flavor and health benefits.

6. Serve:

- Pour the tea into a cup and enjoy.

TIPS:

- **Dosage**: Start with 1 drop of CBD or valerian oil and increase gradually if needed, based on individual tolerance and desired effect.
- **Avoid Boiling**: Do not add CBD or valerian oil to boiling water as high temperatures can degrade the oil's beneficial compounds.

BENEFITS OF CBD OIL INFUSED TEA:

1. Pain Relief:

- **Reduces Chronic Pain**: CBD has analgesic properties that can help reduce chronic pain and inflammation.

2. Anxiety and Stress Reduction:

- **Calms Anxiety**: CBD is known for its anxiolytic effects, helping to reduce anxiety and promote a sense of calm.
- **Improves Sleep**: It can help improve sleep quality and reduce insomnia by promoting relaxation.

3. Anti-inflammatory:

- **Reduces Inflammation**: CBD has anti-inflammatory properties that can help alleviate inflammatory conditions like arthritis.

BENEFITS OF VALERIAN OIL INFUSED TEA:

1. Sleep Aid:

- **Improves Sleep Quality**: Valerian oil is commonly used to promote better sleep and reduce the time it takes to fall asleep.

2. Anxiety Reduction:

- **Calms Anxiety**: Valerian oil has sedative properties that can help reduce anxiety and promote relaxation.

3. Muscle Relaxation:

- **Relieves Muscle Tension**: It can help relieve muscle tension and spasms, promoting overall relaxation.

This tea recipe with CBD oil or valerian oil offers a range of health benefits, including pain relief, anxiety reduction, improved sleep quality, and muscle relaxation. Always consult with a healthcare provider before starting any new herbal remedy, especially if you are taking other medications or have underlying health conditions.

MAKE A DIFFERENCE WITH YOUR REVIEW

UNLOCK THE POWER OF GENEROSITY

"Money can't buy happiness, but giving it away can."

— FREDDIE MERCURY

People who give without expectation live longer, happier lives and feel more fulfilled. If we've got a shot at that during our time together, let's go for it.

To make that happen, I have a question for you...

Would you help someone you've never met, even if you never got credit for it?

Who is this person you ask? They are like you. Or, at least, like you used to be. They might be less experienced, wanting to make a difference, and needing help, but not sure where to look.

Our mission is to make herbal remedies accessible to everyone. Everything I do stems from that mission. And the only way for me to accomplish that mission is by reaching...well...everyone.

This is where you come in. Most people do, in fact, judge a book by its cover (and its reviews). So here's my ask on behalf of a struggling person you've never met:

Please help by leaving this book a review.

Your gift costs no money and takes less than 60 seconds to make real, but it can change someone's life forever. Your review could help...

...one more small business provide for their community. ...one more person support their family. ...one more employee get meaningful work. ...one more person transform their life. ...one more dream come true.

To get that 'feel good' feeling and help this person for real, all you have to do is...and it takes less than 60 seconds... leave a review.

Simply scan the QR code below to leave your review:

http://www.amazon.com/review/review-your-purchases/?asin=B0DCCJX6DT

If you feel good about helping a faceless person, you are my kind of person. Welcome to the club. You're one of us.

I'm that much more excited to help you achieve wellness, beauty, and stress relief faster and easier than you can possibly imagine. You'll love the tips and strategies I'm about to share in the coming chapters.

Thank you from the bottom of my heart. Now, back to our regularly scheduled programming.

HERBAL REMEDIES FOR THE FAMILY

❧

Imagine a household where the gentle hum of daily life is supported not just by love and laughter, but also by the nurturing power of nature's bounty. In this chapter, we explore how herbal remedies can be woven into the fabric of family life, offering natural solutions that cater not only to adults but also to the youngest members of the household. Here, the focus shifts to creating a healthful, holistic environment where even children can benefit from the gentle effects of herbal treatments, seamlessly integrating these natural wonders into their routines from a tender age.

5.1 SAFE HERBS FOR CHILDREN: WHAT YOU NEED TO KNOW

Choosing Child-Friendly Herbs

When it comes to treating little ones, safety is paramount. Herbs like chamomile and lavender are not only safe for children but are also effective in treating common childhood ailments such as colds and minor scrapes. Chamomile, known for its soothing properties, can be a gentle remedy for a child's upset stomach or an aid to help them relax before bedtime. Its mild flavor and calming effects make it a favorite among herbal remedies for children. Lavender, renowned for its soothing aroma, is excellent for treating minor scrapes and burns due to its natural antiseptic properties. It can also be used in a diffuser in the child's room to promote a calming atmosphere and support restful sleep.

Dosage Guidelines for Children

When administering herbal remedies to children, understanding the correct dosage is crucial. The general rule of thumb is to adjust the adult dosage according to the child's weight. Typically, if using a formula based on an adult weight of 150 pounds, you would calculate the child's dose proportionally based on their actual weight. For instance, for a child weighing 50 pounds, you would use one-third of the adult dose. However, it is always recommended to consult with a pediatrician or a qualified herbalist before giving herbs to children to ensure safety and efficacy.

Incorporating Herbs into Children's Diets

Introducing herbs into children's diets can be both fun and creative. Herbal teas can be a delightful way for children to enjoy the benefits of herbs. For example, a lukewarm chamomile tea with a bit of honey can be a comforting drink for children, especially during colder months. Another way to incorporate herbs is by adding them to foods they already enjoy. For instance, finely chopped fresh mint or basil can be sprinkled over fruits or homemade pizzas, adding a fresh flavor that kids love while boosting their antioxidant intake.

Educational Activities for Kids

Engaging children with herbs can also be educational. Simple activities like making herbal sachets with lavender or creating small herb gardens can teach children about the uses and benefits of herbs. These activities not only provide practical knowledge but also foster a deeper connection with nature. Children can learn how to care for plants and understand the basics of herbal medicine, empowering them with knowledge they can carry into adulthood. This hands-on approach can make the learning process enjoyable and memorable, instilling a sense of wonder and respect for the natural world.

Herbal Remedy Recipe for Chamomile Tea for Children

WHAT YOU NEED:

1. **Dried Chamomile Flowers**: 1 teaspoon (or 1 chamomile tea bag)
2. **Water**: 1 cup (8 ounces)
3. **Honey** (optional, for children over 1 year old): For taste

STEPS TO PREPARE:

1. Boil the Water:

- Pour 1 cup of water into a saucepan and bring it to a boil.

2. Prepare the Chamomile:

- Place the dried chamomile flowers or tea bag into a teapot or cup.

3. Steep the Tea:

- Pour the boiling water over the chamomile flowers or tea bag.
- Cover and let the tea steep for 5-10 minutes.

4. Strain the Tea:

- After steeping, strain the tea to remove the chamomile flowers if using loose leaves. If using a tea bag, simply remove the bag.

5. Add Honey (Optional):

- If desired and if the child is over 1 year old, add a small amount of honey to sweeten the tea.

6. Cool the Tea:

- Allow the tea to cool to a safe temperature before serving it to the child.

7. Serve:

- Pour the tea into a child-friendly cup and let them enjoy.

TIPS:

- **Dosage**: Start with 1/2 cup and see how the child responds. Chamomile tea can be given 1-2 times daily if well-tolerated.
- **Avoid Honey for Infants**: Do not give honey to children under 1 year old due to the risk of botulism.

BENEFITS OF CHAMOMILE TEA FOR CHILDREN:

1. Calming and Relaxing:

- **Reduces Anxiety**: Chamomile has mild sedative properties that can help reduce anxiety and promote relaxation in children.
- **Improves Sleep**: It is known to help improve sleep quality and can be particularly useful for children who have trouble falling asleep.

2. Digestive Health:

- **Aids Digestion**: Chamomile tea can help soothe the digestive tract, reducing symptoms of indigestion, bloating, and gas.
- **Relieves Colic and Upset Stomach**: It has been traditionally used to relieve colic and stomach aches in children.

3. Anti-inflammatory and Antioxidant:

- **Reduces Inflammation**: Chamomile has anti-inflammatory properties that can help reduce inflammation and soothe irritated skin and tissues.
- **Rich in Antioxidants**: It contains antioxidants that help protect cells from damage caused by free radicals.

4. Immune Support:

- **Boosts Immunity**: Chamomile can help support the immune system and may reduce the severity and duration of colds and other infections.

This chamomile tea recipe is a gentle and effective herbal remedy that provides numerous benefits for children, including promoting relaxation, improving sleep, aiding digestion, and supporting overall health. Always consult with a healthcare provider before giving any new herbal remedy to a child.

5.2 HERBAL FIRST AID FOR HOME USE

Creating an herbal first aid kit is akin to planting a garden of safety and relief right in your own home. Essential to any household, especially for those preferring natural remedies, a well-stocked herbal first aid kit addresses a variety of acute conditions, from minor cuts and burns to bruises and skin irritations. Key components should include calendula, known for its exceptional healing properties, arnica, a must-have for bruises and muscle soreness, and aloe vera, the go-to remedy for burns and skin hydration. Calendula, with its potent anti-inflammatory and antimicrobial properties, can be used as an ointment or a lotion to speed up the healing of cuts and soothe irritated skin. Arnica serves as a miraculous healer for those unexpected bruises or sprains, available in both cream and gel forms, it helps to reduce swelling and pain, promoting faster recovery. Aloe vera, often celebrated for its cooling and soothing effects, is perfect for treating burns; its gel can be applied directly from the plant to the affected area, offering immediate relief and aiding in the healing process.

In the event of minor household injuries, having these remedies at your disposal allows for quick and effective treatment, which can make all the difference in recovery times and comfort. For instance, when dealing with a kitchen burn, applying aloe vera gel immediately can significantly reduce the severity of the burn and soothe the pain. For cuts, washing the wound with clean water followed by the application of calendula cream can prevent infection and support the skin's healing process. In cases of bruises or muscle aches from minor falls or bumps, arnica gel can be applied to the affected area to diminish bruising and relieve pain.

Common Herbal Remedies for Acute Conditions

Incorporating herbal remedies into your home care practice not only enriches your ability to manage common ailments but also aligns with a holistic approach to health. Beyond the basics of the first aid kit, several other herbs can be pivotal in treating acute conditions effectively. For instance, witch hazel is excellent for its astringent properties, making it ideal for treating insect bites or soothing hemorrhoids. Its ability to reduce inflammation and calm irritation makes it a versatile addition to your herbal arsenal. Another invaluable herb is echinacea, which can be used to boost the immune system at the first sign of a cold or flu, potentially reducing the illness's duration and severity.

For each condition, specific herbs can be prepared in various forms to maximize their healing properties. Learning how to prepare these remedies ensures that you are ready to handle common health issues that may arise. For example, creating a witch hazel compress involves soaking a clean cloth in witch hazel extract and applying it to the affected area, providing relief from itching or swelling. Similarly, echinacea can be taken as a tincture or tea at the onset of cold symptoms, enhancing the body's natural immune response.

Step-by-Step Treatment Guides

Effectively using herbal remedies requires knowledge not only of the herbs themselves but also of how to apply them safely and effectively. Detailed step-by-step guides can demystify the process, making herbal treatment accessible even for those new to herbal medicine. For instance, to use calendula for wound care, begin by cleaning the area with mild soap and water. Apply calendula salve directly to the wound, then cover it with a clean bandage to protect it while it heals. Change the bandage daily, applying new salve each time, until the wound has healed. This method ensures that the healing properties of calendula are maximized, promoting faster recovery without the use of synthetic chemicals.

Herbal Remedy Recipe for Calendula Ointment

WHAT YOU NEED:

1. **Dried Calendula Flowers**: 1 cup
2. **Carrier Oil**: 1 cup (olive oil, almond oil, or coconut oil)
3. **Beeswax**: 1/4 cup (grated or pellets)
4. **Shea Butter**: 1/4 cup (optional for added moisturizing benefits)
5. **Essential Oils**: 10-15 drops (optional, for fragrance and additional benefits; lavender or tea tree oil are good choices)
6. **Double Boiler**: Or a heatproof bowl and saucepan
7. **Cheesecloth or Fine Strainer**: For filtering
8. **Glass Jar or Container**: For storing the finished ointment

STEPS TO PREPARE:

1. Infuse the Oil with Calendula:

- Place the dried calendula flowers in a clean, dry glass jar.
- Pour the carrier oil over the flowers, ensuring they are completely submerged.
- Seal the jar tightly and place it in a sunny spot for 2-3 weeks, shaking occasionally. Alternatively, you can gently heat the jar in a double boiler for 2-3 hours.

2. Strain the Infused Oil:

- After infusing, strain the oil through cheesecloth or a fine strainer to remove the calendula flowers.
- Squeeze the cheesecloth to extract as much oil as possible.

3. Prepare the Double Boiler:

- Fill the bottom of the double boiler with water and bring it to a gentle simmer.
- Place the beeswax and shea butter (if using) in the top of the double boiler.

4. Melt the Ingredients:

- Heat the mixture, stirring occasionally, until the beeswax and shea butter are completely melted and well combined.

5. Add the Infused Oil:

- Once melted, slowly add the calendula-infused oil to the mixture, stirring constantly to combine.

6. Remove from Heat:

- Once everything is well combined, remove the mixture from the heat.

7. Add Essential Oils (Optional):

- If using essential oils, add them now and stir well to incorporate.

8. Cool and Store:

- Allow the mixture to cool slightly, then pour it into glass jars or containers.
- Seal tightly and label with the contents and date.

STORAGE:

- Store the calendula ointment in a cool, dark place. It should last for several months if stored properly.

BENEFITS OF CALENDULA OINTMENT:

1. Skin Healing:

- **Soothes Irritation**: Calendula has anti-inflammatory properties that can help soothe irritated skin and reduce redness.
- **Heals Minor Cuts and Wounds**: Its antiseptic and antimicrobial properties make it effective for healing minor cuts, scrapes, and wounds.

2. Moisturizing:

- **Deep Hydration**: The combination of oils and shea butter provides deep hydration, making the skin soft and supple.
- **Protects the Skin Barrier**: Beeswax helps create a protective barrier on the skin, locking in moisture and protecting against environmental pollutants.

3. Anti-aging:

- **Rich in Antioxidants**: Calendula contains antioxidants that help fight free radicals, which can cause premature aging.
- **Promotes Collagen Production**: It may help stimulate collagen production, improving skin elasticity and reducing the appearance of fine lines and wrinkles.

4. Suitable for Sensitive Skin:

- **Gentle and Nourishing**: Calendula is gentle enough for sensitive skin and can help alleviate conditions like eczema and psoriasis.

This calendula ointment is a versatile and nourishing herbal remedy that provides numerous benefits for the skin, promoting healing, hydration, and overall skin health.

Herbal Remedy Recipe for Arnica Ointment

WHAT YOU NEED:

1. **Dried Arnica Flowers**: 1/2 cup
2. **Carrier Oil**: 1 cup (olive oil, almond oil, or sunflower oil)
3. **Beeswax**: 1/4 cup (grated or pellets)
4. **Essential Oils**: 10-15 drops (optional; lavender or eucalyptus oil are good choices for added benefits and fragrance)
5. **Double Boiler**: Or a heatproof bowl and saucepan
6. **Cheesecloth or Fine Strainer**: For filtering
7. **Glass Jar or Container**: For storing the finished ointment

STEPS TO PREPARE:

1. Infuse the Oil with Arnica:

- Place the dried arnica flowers in a clean, dry glass jar.
- Pour the carrier oil over the flowers, ensuring they are completely submerged.
- Seal the jar tightly and place it in a sunny spot for 2-3 weeks, shaking occasionally. Alternatively, you can gently heat the jar in a double boiler for 2-3 hours.

2. Strain the Infused Oil:

- After infusing, strain the oil through cheesecloth or a fine strainer to remove the arnica flowers.
- Squeeze the cheesecloth to extract as much oil as possible.

3. Prepare the Double Boiler:

- Fill the bottom of the double boiler with water and bring it to a gentle simmer.
- Place the beeswax in the top of the double boiler.

4. Melt the Beeswax:

- Heat the beeswax, stirring occasionally, until it is completely melted.

5. Add the Infused Oil:

- Once the beeswax is melted, slowly add the arnica-infused oil to the mixture, stirring constantly to combine.

6. Remove from Heat:

- Once everything is well combined, remove the mixture from the heat.

7. Add Essential Oils (Optional):

- If using essential oils, add them now and stir well to incorporate.

8. Cool and Store:

- Allow the mixture to cool slightly, then pour it into glass jars or containers.
- Seal tightly and label with the contents and date.

STORAGE:

- Store the arnica ointment in a cool, dark place. It should last for several months if stored properly.

BENEFITS OF ARNICA OINTMENT:

1. Pain Relief:

- **Reduces Pain and Swelling**: Arnica is well-known for its ability to reduce pain and swelling associated with bruises, sprains, muscle aches, and arthritis.
- **Soothes Sore Muscles**: It can help relieve muscle soreness and stiffness after physical activity or injury.

2. Anti-inflammatory:

- **Reduces Inflammation**: Arnica contains helenalin, a compound with strong anti-inflammatory properties that help reduce inflammation and promote healing.

3. Bruise Healing:

- **Speeds Up Healing**: Arnica ointment can help speed up the healing process of bruises by stimulating the flow of white blood cells, which process congested blood and disperse trapped fluids from the injured area.

4. Skin Health:

- **Promotes Skin Health**: The anti-inflammatory and antimicrobial properties of arnica can help with various skin conditions and promote overall skin health.

SAFETY CONSIDERATIONS:

- **External Use Only**: Arnica should only be used externally and should not be applied to broken skin or open wounds.
- **Allergic Reactions**: Some people may be allergic to arnica. Conduct a patch test before using the ointment extensively.

This arnica ointment recipe is a versatile and effective herbal remedy that provides numerous benefits for pain relief, inflammation reduction, and skin health. Always consult with a healthcare provider before using new herbal remedies, especially if you have any existing health conditions.

Herbal Remedy Recipe for Echinacea Tincture

WHAT YOU NEED:

1. **Dried Echinacea Root**: 1 part
2. **Alcohol**: Vodka or brandy, at least 80 proof (40% alcohol content)
3. **Glass Jar**: A clean, airtight glass container
4. **Cheesecloth or Fine Strainer**: For filtering
5. **Dark Glass Dropper Bottles**: For storing the finished tincture
6. **Label and Pen**: For labeling the tincture

Steps to Prepare:

1. Prepare the Echinacea Root:

- Measure out the dried echinacea root. For example, if you use 1 cup of dried echinacea root, you will need enough alcohol to cover it completely in the jar.

2. Fill the Jar:

- Place the dried echinacea root into the glass jar, filling it about halfway.

3. Add Alcohol:

- Pour the alcohol over the echinacea root, ensuring it is completely submerged. Leave about an inch of space at the top of the jar.

4. Seal and Shake:

- Seal the jar tightly with a lid.
- Shake the jar well to mix the echinacea root and alcohol.

5. Store and Shake:

- Place the jar in a cool, dark place.
- Shake the jar every day or every few days to keep the mixture well-blended.
- Let the tincture sit for at least 4-6 weeks. The longer it sits, the stronger it will be.

6. Strain the Tincture:

- After the waiting period, place cheesecloth or a fine strainer over a clean bowl.
- Pour the mixture through the cheesecloth to filter out the echinacea root.
- Squeeze the cheesecloth to extract as much liquid as possible.

7. Transfer to Dropper Bottles:

- Use a funnel to pour the strained liquid into dark glass dropper bottles.
- Label the bottles with the name of the tincture and the date.

DOSAGE INSTRUCTIONS:

- **Standard Dose**: Take 1-2 droppersful (1-2 ml) of the tincture diluted in a small amount of water or juice up to three times a day.
- **Immune Boosting**: Take 1-2 droppersful (1-2 ml) at the first sign of a cold or flu and continue for a few days.

BENEFITS OF ECHINACEA TINCTURE:

1. Immune System Support:

- **Boosts Immunity**: Echinacea is well-known for its ability to enhance the immune system, making it easier for the body to fight off infections, particularly the common cold and flu.
- **Antiviral and Antibacterial**: Echinacea has antiviral and antibacterial properties that can help prevent and reduce the severity of infections.

2. Anti-inflammatory Properties:

- **Reduces Inflammation**: Echinacea contains compounds that help reduce inflammation, which can alleviate symptoms of various inflammatory conditions.

3. Antioxidant Effects:

- **Rich in Antioxidants**: Echinacea is packed with antioxidants that help protect cells from damage caused by free radicals, contributing to overall health and wellness.

4. Respiratory Health:

- **Relieves Respiratory Issues**: Echinacea tincture can help soothe respiratory tract infections and relieve symptoms such as a sore throat, cough, and congestion.

This echinacea tincture recipe is a powerful and natural herbal remedy that supports the immune system, reduces inflammation, and promotes overall health. Always consult with a healthcare provider before starting any new herbal remedy.

5.3 ELDERLY CARE: SUPPORTING HEALTH WITH HERBS

As we gracefully navigate the latter chapters of life, maintaining health and independence becomes a priority, and herbal remedies can play a crucial role in this process. Common age-related conditions such as joint pain, memory decline, and circulatory issues often become more prevalent, but the gentle power of herbs offers a beacon of hope and relief. For instance, herbs like ginger and turmeric are celebrated not only for their culinary uses but also for their potent anti-inflammatory properties, making them excellent choices for managing joint pain and arthritis. Ginger contains gingerol, which helps reduce inflammation and can alleviate pain, while turmeric's curcumin has strong anti-inflammatory effects that rival over-the-counter remedies without the side effects.

Memory decline, another concern among the elderly, can be addressed with herbs like ginkgo biloba, which is renowned for its ability to enhance brain function and improve memory and concentration. Its active components improve blood circulation, particularly to the brain, supporting cognitive functions that tend to decline with age. For circulatory health, hawthorn is an invaluable herb. It is extensively used to support heart health, enhancing blood flow, and strengthening the heart's pumping ability, which can be particularly beneficial for those dealing with blood pressure issues or mild heart problems.

Integrating Herbs with Conventional Medications

When incorporating herbal remedies into the health regimen of elderly individuals, it's essential to ensure these natural solutions harmonize with existing medical treatments. Many seniors take a range of prescription medications, and certain herbs can interact with these drugs. It is crucial to consult healthcare providers before combining herbs with conventional medications. For example, while ginkgo biloba is fantastic for memory, it can interfere with blood thinners. A healthcare provider can offer guidance on safe use and appropriate dosages, ensuring that the benefits of herbal treatments are enjoyed without compromising safety.

Adaptive Techniques for Elderly

Adapting herbal intake to match the unique needs of the elderly can significantly enhance their efficacy and ease of use. As swallowing pills can sometimes be challenging, creating tinctures or teas from herbs offers a practical alternative. These methods allow for the easy adjustment of dosages and personalized blends to suit individual needs. For instance, a simple tea made from hawthorn berries can be a delightful way to incorporate this heart-healthy herb into daily routines. Likewise, turmeric can be integrated into meals, like soups or stews, or taken as a golden milk preparation, a warm and soothing beverage that combines turmeric with milk and a hint of black pepper to enhance absorption.

Supporting Independence and Wellness

Herbs do more than address specific health issues; they enhance overall wellness and can help seniors maintain their independence. By reducing discomfort from ailments like joint pain or improving circulation, seniors can enjoy a more active lifestyle. Furthermore, engaging with herbs, whether through growing them at home or preparing herbal remedies, can also provide a sense of purpose and joy. Activities such as tending to a small herb garden can be a rewarding hobby that keeps one physically active and mentally engaged. Moreover, the routine of preparing and using herbal remedies can enhance a senior's daily life, offering not just health benefits but also a routine that supports independence and a higher quality of life.

Incorporating herbal remedies into the care routine for the elderly is about creating a supportive environment that respects their needs and challenges. It's about enhancing their quality of life, not just adding years to it. With careful consideration and creative adaptation, herbs can be a wonderful addition to the holistic care of seniors, helping them live fuller, more vibrant lives.

Herbal Remedy Recipe for Hawthorn Berry Tea

WHAT YOU NEED:

1. **Dried Hawthorn Berries**: 1-2 teaspoons
2. **Water**: 1 cup (8 ounces)
3. **Honey or Lemon** (optional): For taste

Steps to Prepare:

1. Boil the Water:

- Pour 1 cup of water into a saucepan and bring it to a boil.

2. Prepare the Hawthorn Berries:

- Measure out 1-2 teaspoons of dried hawthorn berries.

3. Steep the Tea:

- Place the dried hawthorn berries into a teapot or cup.
- Pour the boiling water over the berries.
- Cover and let the tea steep for 10-15 minutes to extract the beneficial compounds.

4. Strain the Tea:

- After steeping, strain the tea to remove the berries.

5. Add Honey or Lemon (Optional):

- If desired, add honey for sweetness or a slice of lemon for additional flavor and health benefits.

6. Serve:

- Pour the strained tea into a cup and enjoy.

Tips:

- **Dosage**: Drink 1-2 cups daily to enjoy the full benefits of hawthorn berry tea.

- **Storage**: If you make a larger batch, store the tea in the refrigerator for up to 3 days. Reheat as needed.

BENEFITS OF HAWTHORN BERRY TEA:

1. Cardiovascular Health:

- **Supports Heart Health**: Hawthorn berries are well-known for their positive effects on heart health. They can help improve blood flow, strengthen the heart muscle, and reduce the risk of heart-related issues.
- **Lowers Blood Pressure**: Hawthorn berry tea may help lower blood pressure by dilating blood vessels and improving circulation.
- **Reduces Cholesterol Levels**: It can help reduce LDL (bad) cholesterol and triglyceride levels, promoting overall cardiovascular health.

2. Antioxidant Properties:

- **Rich in Antioxidants**: Hawthorn berries contain powerful antioxidants, such as flavonoids and oligomeric procyanidins, which help protect cells from oxidative stress and reduce inflammation.

3. Digestive Health:

- **Aids Digestion**: Hawthorn berry tea can help improve digestion by increasing the production of digestive enzymes and alleviating symptoms like indigestion and bloating.

4. Anxiety and Stress Relief:

- **Calms the Nervous System**: Hawthorn has mild sedative

properties that can help reduce anxiety and promote relaxation, making it useful for managing stress.

5. Anti-inflammatory:

- **Reduces Inflammation**: The anti-inflammatory properties of hawthorn berries can help reduce inflammation in the body, which is beneficial for conditions like arthritis.

This hawthorn berry tea recipe is a simple and effective herbal remedy that provides numerous health benefits, including supporting cardiovascular health, improving digestion, reducing inflammation, and promoting relaxation. Always consult with a healthcare provider before starting any new herbal remedy.

5.4 HERBAL PET CARE: NATURAL REMEDIES FOR YOUR PETS

The love we share with our pets is immeasurable, and naturally, we strive to care for them in the best ways possible. Integrating herbal remedies into your pet's care regimen offers a gentle, effective method to enhance their well-being, addressing issues from anxiety to digestive health, and even flea prevention. Safe herbs like valerian root, which is renowned for its calming effects, can be particularly beneficial for pets suffering from anxiety, especially during stressful situations like thunderstorms or fireworks. Slippery elm bark, on the other hand, is excellent for digestive health, soothing the stomach and intestines to ease discomfort from ailments like indigestion or constipation in pets.

When considering the use of herbs for flea prevention, neem is a standout choice. This potent plant repels pests naturally, making it an excellent addition to your pet's grooming routine. You can create a neem leaf rinse by steeping the leaves in hot water, then cooling and applying the strained liquid to your pet's coat after shampooing. Not only does this rinse help ward off fleas, but it also leaves the fur soft and shiny, enhancing your pet's natural defenses against skin irritations.

Preparation and Dosage for Pets

Preparing and administering herbal remedies to pets requires careful consideration to ensure efficacy and safety. The form and dosage of the herb will depend significantly on the type and size of the animal. For instance, a calming tea made from valerian root can be added to your pet's water bowl, but the amount should be adjusted based on the pet's weight and size. A general guideline is to start with a minimal dose and observe the pet's response, gradually adjusting as needed. This cautious approach helps prevent any adverse reactions and ensures the herb's benefits are delivered safely.

For digestive issues, slippery elm bark can be administered in powder form, mixed into your pet's food. The typical dosage is about one-quarter teaspoon per 10 pounds of body weight, mixed into their meal once daily. This herb forms a gel-like substance when mixed with water, which coats the lining of the intestines, providing relief from irritation and mild stomach upset.

Integrating Herbal Remedies with Veterinary Care

While herbal remedies offer wonderful benefits, they should not replace professional veterinary care but rather complement it. Always consult with a veterinarian before introducing any new herbal treatment to your pet's regimen. This is crucial not only to avoid any potential interactions with existing medications but also to ensure that the health issue is correctly diagnosed and treated. Veterinarians who are knowledgeable about herbal medicine can provide valuable guidance on effective herbs and appropriate dosages, tailored to your pet's specific health needs.

Case Studies

Pets who suffer from chronic anxiety, particularly during thunderstorms, saw remarkable benefit from a small amount of valerian root extract in their water bowl before thunderstorms. Valerian root extract alleviates the anxiety without the lethargy typically induced by conventional anxiety medications. Another example would be administering slippery elm bark for a pet with recurring digestive issues. Mixing slippery elm bark into their food daily, provides the gentle relief needed, and allows them to enjoy meals without discomfort.

These examples highlight not only the effectiveness of herbal remedies in addressing specific health challenges but also the broader impact they can have on enhancing the well-being of our beloved pets. As we continue to explore and understand the benefits of natural treatments, the integration of herbs into pet care opens up a realm of possibilities for improving their health in a gentle, natural way.

Herbal Remedy Recipe for Neem Rinse for Pets

WHAT YOU NEED:

1. **Dried Neem Leaves**: 1 cup (or 2 tablespoons of neem leaf powder)
2. **Water**: 4 cups
3. **Apple Cider Vinegar**: 1/4 cup (optional, for added antibacterial properties)
4. **Essential Oils**: 5-10 drops (optional, for fragrance and added benefits; lavender or tea tree oil are good choices)
5. **Spray Bottle or Container**: For applying the rinse

STEPS TO PREPARE:

1. Boil the Water:

- Pour 4 cups of water into a saucepan and bring it to a boil.

2. Add Neem Leaves:

- Add the dried neem leaves (or neem leaf powder) to the boiling water.
- Reduce the heat and let it simmer for about 10-15 minutes.

3. Cool and Strain:

- Remove the saucepan from heat and allow the mixture to cool completely.
- Strain the liquid through a fine strainer or cheesecloth to remove the neem leaves.

4. Add Optional Ingredients:

- If desired, add 1/4 cup of apple cider vinegar to the strained liquid for additional antibacterial properties.
- Add 5-10 drops of essential oils for fragrance and additional benefits.

5. Transfer to Spray Bottle:

- Pour the neem rinse into a spray bottle or container for easy application.

HOW TO USE:

- **Application**: After bathing your pet, apply the neem rinse all over their coat, avoiding the eyes and mouth. Gently massage it into the skin.
- **Leave-In**: You can leave the rinse on without rinsing it off, allowing it to dry naturally.

BENEFITS OF NEEM RINSE FOR PETS:

1. Flea and Tick Control:

- **Natural Insect Repellent**: Neem has insecticidal properties that help repel and kill fleas, ticks, and other parasites.
- **Soothes Irritation**: It helps soothe irritation caused by flea bites and other skin conditions.

2. Skin Health:

- **Antibacterial and Antifungal**: Neem has strong antibacterial and antifungal properties that help prevent and treat skin infections, hot spots, and other dermatological issues.
- **Reduces Inflammation**: Its anti-inflammatory properties can help reduce redness, swelling, and itching.

3. Overall Coat Health:

- **Promotes a Healthy Coat**: Regular use of neem rinse can help promote a healthy, shiny coat by improving skin health and reducing dandruff and dry skin.

This neem rinse is a natural and effective remedy for maintaining your pet's skin and coat health, providing protection against parasites, and soothing skin irritations. Always consult with a veterinarian before starting any new herbal remedy for your pet.

Herbal Remedy Recipe for Valerian Root Tea for Dogs

WHAT YOU NEED:

1. **Dried Valerian Root**: 1 teaspoon
2. **Water**: 1 cup (8 ounces)
3. **Honey** (optional): For taste

STEPS TO PREPARE:

1. Boil the Water:

- Pour 1 cup of water into a saucepan and bring it to a boil.

2. Prepare the Valerian Root:

- Measure out 1 teaspoon of dried valerian root.

3. Steep the Tea:

- Place the dried valerian root into a teapot or cup.
- Pour the boiling water over the valerian root.
- Cover and let the tea steep for 10-15 minutes.

4. Strain the Tea:

- After steeping, strain the tea to remove the valerian root.

5. Cool the Tea:

- Allow the tea to cool completely before adding it to your dog's water bowl.

DOSAGE INSTRUCTIONS AND RATIO CHART:

Valerian root is generally safe for dogs when used in appropriate amounts. However, it's important to start with a small dose to see how your dog reacts. Here is a suggested dosage based on your dog's weight:

Dog's Weight	Valerian Tea Dosage
Up to 10 lbs	1/2 teaspoon
10-20 lbs	1 teaspoon
20-50 lbs	1 tablespoon
Over 50 lbs	2 tablespoons

- **Mix with Water**: Add the appropriate amount of cooled valerian tea to your dog's water bowl. Make sure the tea is well diluted with their regular water.
- **Monitor**: Observe your dog for any adverse reactions. If your dog shows any signs of discomfort, discontinue use and consult with your veterinarian.

BENEFITS OF VALERIAN ROOT FOR DOGS:

1. Calming and Anxiety Relief:

- **Reduces Anxiety**: Valerian root is known for its calming properties, helping to reduce anxiety and stress in dogs.
- **Promotes Relaxation**: It can help promote relaxation and reduce hyperactivity, making it beneficial for dogs with anxiety disorders or those experiencing stressful situations.

2. Sleep Aid:

- **Improves Sleep**: Valerian root can help improve sleep quality and duration, making it useful for dogs with insomnia or other sleep disturbances.

3. Pain Relief:

- **Eases Discomfort**: It has mild analgesic properties that can help reduce pain and discomfort from conditions like arthritis or muscle pain.

Valerian root tea can be a beneficial herbal remedy for dogs when used correctly. Always consult with a veterinarian before starting any new herbal treatment for your pet, especially if your dog has underlying health conditions or is taking other medications.

5.5 BUILDING A FAMILY HERB GARDEN: TIPS AND TRICKS

Creating a family herb garden is a delightful way to bring the natural world closer to home, offering a vibrant array of benefits from the practical to the profound. Whether you have a sprawling backyard or a modest balcony space, starting your own herb garden is a journey that can deepen your family's connection to nature, enhance your cooking, and even bolster your home health remedies. The first step is planning, which involves assessing the space available, understanding your climate, and evaluating the soil quality. If you're working with limited space, consider container gardening, which can be incredibly versatile and just as rewarding. For those with more room, raised beds or in-ground planting might be the best route. Each option has its advantages and can be adapted according to your living situation.

The climate in your region will significantly influence what you can grow. Herbs like basil and cilantro thrive in warmer climates and need plenty of sunlight, while others such as parsley and mint prefer cooler, partially shaded areas. Understanding these needs will help you choose the right spot for your garden and ensure your herbs grow healthy and strong. Soil quality is equally important; most herbs thrive in well-draining soil with a neutral to slightly alkaline pH.

Before planting, it's beneficial to test your soil and amend it with organic matter like compost to improve its structure and fertility.

Choosing Herbs for the Family

Selecting the right herbs to grow should reflect the needs and preferences of your family. Start with the herbs you commonly use in your cooking or remedies. Basil, mint, rosemary, and thyme are all versatile and easy to grow, making them excellent choices for beginners. If your family enjoys herbal teas, consider planting chamomile or lemon balm, which are not only easy to cultivate but also have calming properties. For those interested in natural remedies, echinacea and calendula are valuable additions for their immune-boosting and skin-healing benefits, respectively.

Growing these herbs not only provides fresh, flavorful ingredients for your meals but also ensures you have a supply of natural remedies right at your fingertips. Imagine the convenience of plucking fresh mint for a stomach-soothing tea or harvesting chamomile flowers to prepare a calming bedtime infusion. The practical benefits are matched by the educational opportunities these activities offer to your family, especially children, who can learn about the growth cycles of plants and the uses of various herbs.

Gardening as a Family Activity

Gardening can be a wonderful way to spend quality time together as a family, fostering teamwork and teaching valuable skills. Children, in particular, benefit from the hands-on experience, gaining knowledge about biology and ecology in a fun, engaging way. Tasks like planting seeds, watering, and harvesting can be adapted to suit different age groups, giving everyone a role to play. Moreover, the sense of responsibility and accomplishment that comes from caring for a garden can boost confidence and instill a sense of pride in children.

To make gardening even more engaging, consider creating themed plots such as a pizza garden planted with tomatoes, basil, and oregano, or a tea garden featuring a variety of mints and chamomile. These themed gardens can make the experience more relatable and exciting for children, providing a tangible connection between the garden and its uses in everyday life.

Sustainable Gardening Practices

Adopting sustainable practices in your family herb garden not only protects the environment but also teaches your children the importance of ecological responsibility. One fundamental practice is composting, which recycles kitchen and garden waste into rich soil that can greatly enhance the growth of your herbs. Composting reduces landfill waste and teaches children about the lifecycle of organic matter, turning disposal habits into ecological contributions.

Another key practice is natural pest control. Instead of relying on chemical pesticides, which can harm the beneficial insects that your garden needs to thrive, explore organic options. Introducing ladybugs can naturally keep aphid populations in check, while planting marigolds can deter pests with their strong scent. These methods protect your herbs from pests while maintaining the ecological balance in your garden.

By integrating these sustainable practices, your herb garden becomes a dynamic classroom not only for growing food but also for imparting lessons about environmental stewardship. It becomes a place where each family member can learn, contribute, and watch the fruits of their labor flourish under their care.

5.6 EDUCATING YOUR FAMILY ON HERBAL REMEDIES

Navigating the world of herbal remedies offers a unique opportunity to integrate nature's wisdom into your family's lifestyle, enriching your home with practices that foster well-being and connection to the natural world. Engaging with your local community through workshops and classes focused on herbal remedies not only enhances your knowledge but also connects you with like-minded individuals who share your interest in natural health. Many communities offer workshops at local health food stores, botanical gardens, or through community colleges that are family-friendly and provide hands-on learning experiences. These classes often cover a range of topics from basic herb gardening to making your own herbal remedies, which can be a delightful way to spend quality time with your family while learning valuable skills.

Creating an herbal learning environment at home can transform your living space into a vibrant hub of health and education. Start by designating a special place in your home where herbal activities can take place. This could be a kitchen corner with herbs and spices within easy reach or a special cabinet filled with teas, tinctures, and dried herbs. Encourage family members to participate in preparing herbal remedies and experimenting with creating their own. For instance, making a simple herbal salve together can be an enjoyable and educational activity that shows the practical benefits of herbs.

Documenting and sharing your family's herbal remedy experiences can further enrich your journey. Keeping a journal or blog allows you to track what works and what doesn't, providing a valuable resource that you can look back on and share with others. Encourage each family member to contribute, whether by writing about an herb they researched or drawing a picture of a plant they found in the garden. Sharing these experiences on social media or family blogs can also inspire others to explore herbal remedies, creating a ripple effect that promotes community learning and support.

By integrating these educational resources, engaging in community learning, and creating an interactive herbal environment at home, you weave a tapeboard of knowledge and practice that will serve your family for years to come. This approach not only enhances your family's health naturally but also fosters a deeper connection with the environment and each other through shared learning experiences.

As this chapter closes, we reflect on the integration of herbal remedies into family life, highlighting the importance of education, community engagement, and the joy of shared learning. These themes weave through the narrative of nurturing a naturally healthy family, setting the stage for the next chapter where we will explore advanced herbal applications, deepening our understanding and skills in herbal medicine. This transition from foundational practices to more complex applications marks a progression in our herbal journey, promising new insights and inspirations for enhancing our health and well-being with the healing power of herbs.

ADVANCED HERBAL APPLICATIONS

Imagine transforming simple herbs into powerful remedies that can soothe, heal, and rejuvenate. This chapter unravels the art of herbal extractions, a process that might seem complex but is steeped in tradition and simplicity. Here, you'll learn to craft your own tinctures, salves, and essential oils, harnessing the essence of plants in your very own kitchen. This is not just about creating herbal products; it's about embracing a role as a creator, where each jar and bottle is infused with not just botanicals but your personal touch and intention.

6.1 MASTERING HERBAL EXTRACTIONS: TINCTURES, SALVES, AND OILS

Overview of Extraction Methods

The essence of herbal extraction lies in its ability to pull the beneficial compounds out of the plant materials, and there are several methods to achieve this, each suitable for different types of herbs and desired outcomes. Maceration, percolation, and distillation are three core techniques that any herbal enthusiast should become familiar with.

Maceration involves soaking the plant in a solvent such as alcohol or vinegar to extract the active compounds. This method is ideal for herbs that are more delicate and do not require heat to release their beneficial properties. It's akin to steeping tea, only over a longer period, and it allows for the full strength of the herb to infuse into the liquid.

Percolation, on the other hand, is more complex and faster than maceration. It's akin to making coffee in a percolator, where the solvent passes through a compacted bed of herb grounds, extracting its constituents quickly and efficiently. This method is particularly useful when working with harder, denser materials that might resist maceration.

Distillation, used primarily for making essential oils, involves steaming the plant materials. The steam carries the aromatic compounds to a cooling chamber, where they recondense into a liquid. This method captures the volatile oils that are responsible for the plant's fragrance and many therapeutic properties.

Step-by-Step Extraction Processes

Creating tinctures, salves, and essential oils at home can be deeply rewarding. For tinctures, begin by finely chopping or grinding your dried herbs to increase the surface area. Place these in a clean jar, and cover with a solvent like alcohol, ensuring the herbs are completely submerged. Seal the jar and store it in a cool, dark place, shaking it daily for about four to six weeks before straining the liquid through a fine-mesh sieve or cheesecloth.

For salves, the process starts similarly by infusing herbs into a carrier oil via slow heating. Once the oil has absorbed the plant's properties, it's strained and then blended with beeswax, which is melted together until a thick, consistent cream forms upon cooling.

Essential oils are best extracted through steam distillation, which might require specific equipment. You'll need a distillation kit, which includes a boiler to generate steam that passes through the plant material, capturing the essential oils as vapor. This vapor then condenses back into liquid in a cooling chamber.

Optimizing Extraction for Maximum Potency

The potency of herbal extracts is influenced by several factors, including the solvent used, the herb-to-solvent ratio, and the extraction time. Higher-proof alcohol, for example, will extract more constituents than lower-proof alternatives but may also capture more unwanted substances, affecting the flavor and therapeutic quality. The ratio of herb to solvent can vary depending on the specific herb and the desired strength of the extract, but a general guideline is one part herb to four parts solvent by weight for fresh herbs, and one part herb to five parts solvent for dried herbs.

Extraction time also plays a critical role; too short may yield a weak extract, while too long can result in a bitter or otherwise unpleasant product. Monitoring and adjusting based on these variables are key to creating effective herbal extracts.

Quality Control in Herbal Extractions

Assessing the quality of your homemade extracts is crucial for ensuring their effectiveness and safety. Always start with high-quality, organic herbs to reduce the risk of contaminants. After extraction, evaluate the color, smell, and texture. Any signs of mold, unusual odors, or discoloration could indicate spoilage or contamination. Keeping detailed records of your processes, ingredients, and results can help troubleshoot issues and refine your techniques over time.

Creating your own herbal extracts offers not only a way to personalize your health and wellness regimen but also connects you more deeply with the healing powers of nature. As you experiment and learn, you'll gain not only tinctures, salves, and oils but also an invaluable understanding of the plants that support your health. Each drop and dollop carries the essence of the earth, crafted by your own hands, bringing nature's healing right into your home.

6.2 ADVANCED BLENDING TECHNIQUES FOR PERSONALIZED REMEDIES

When you step into the world of herbal blending, you embrace the role of both healer and artisan, crafting concoctions that soothe, invigorate, and heal. Understanding the foundational principles of herbal blending is crucial—it's about more than mixing a few herbs together; it's about weaving a tapestry of flavors, benefits, and energies to address specific health needs. Each herb carries its own set of properties, categorized into herbal actions such as carminative (which can help relieve gas), demulcent (soothing), or astringent (tightening and toning). Knowing these actions allows you to predict how herbs might interact within a blend. For instance, pairing the soothing effects of marshmallow root with the digestive support of ginger creates a blend that not only enhances digestion but also soothes the digestive tract.

Synergy is another pillar of herbal blending where the combined effect of the herbs is greater than the sum of their individual effects. This concept is beautifully illustrated in traditional remedies like the Ayurvedic Triphala, a blend of three fruits that together enhance detoxification and rejuvenation more effectively than when used separately. Understanding contraindications is equally crucial to ensure safety in herbal blends. For example, while ephedra is a powerful stimulant, it can be dangerous when combined with caffeine-rich herbs like guarana because the combined effect on the heart can be too stimulating.

Creating custom herbal blends starts with a clear understanding of the individual's health profile and goals. The process is deeply personal and begins with a consultation to understand the specific ailments or wellness goals the blend aims to address. This could range from managing chronic pain, supporting sleep, enhancing digestion, or boosting immune function. Once the goals are set, selecting herbs that align with these targets involves considering not only the herbs' medicinal properties but also their energetics—whether they are warming or cooling, drying or moistening—which should complement the person's constitution and current state.

For instance, if creating a blend for someone with inflammatory conditions who runs cold and dry, choosing warming and moistening herbs like ginger and licorice can balance their inherent dryness while combating inflammation. The process includes meticulous measuring and perhaps several iterations to perfect the blend. Each herb is added in specific ratios, often starting with small scale batches to test the effects, ensuring each herb is present in a therapeutic but safe amount.

Balancing the flavors of a blend is essential for ensuring that the remedies are not only effective but also enjoyable to take. This involves a keen understanding of the taste profiles of each herb—bitter, sweet, sour, salty, pungent, and astringent—and how these can be layered to create a harmonious final product. For instance, the bitterness of dandelion root can be balanced with the sweetness of licorice and the pungency of ginger, creating a blend that is easier on the palate while still being highly effective.

Case Studies on Successful Blends

The real-world application of these blending techniques is evident in numerous case studies that highlight both the process and outcomes of personalized herbal blends. One case involved a middle-aged individual dealing with chronic insomnia and anxiety. Their blend included chamomile and lavender for their calming properties, ashwagandha for its ability to regulate stress hormones, and a small amount of licorice to harmonize the blend and add a touch of sweetness to improve the taste. Over several weeks, they reported a significant improvement in sleep quality and a reduction in anxiety levels, illustrating how a well-crafted herbal blend can effectively address multiple, interconnected health issues.

Another case involved a retired veteran who suffered from joint pain and stiffness due to arthritis. Their blend focused on anti-inflammatory herbs like turmeric and boswellia, combined with cayenne for its pain-relieving properties and hawthorn berry to support circulation. The careful balance of these herbs addressed not only the symptoms of pain and inflammation but also supported overall circulatory health, which is crucial in managing arthritis. They experienced enhanced mobility and a noticeable reduction in pain, highlighting how targeted herbal blends can offer relief and improve quality of life.

These case studies demonstrate the efficacy of personalized herbal blends and underscore the importance of a thoughtful, informed approach to herbal blending. By considering an individual's unique health needs, the synergistic potential of the chosen herbs, and the balance of flavors, herbalists can create powerful, personalized remedies that resonate with the needs of those they serve. As you explore the art and science of herbal blending, remember that each herb has its story and each blend reflects the person it is created for. This personalized approach is what makes herbal blending both a craft and a deeply rewarding part of the healing arts.

6.3 THE SCIENCE BEHIND HERBAL EFFICACY: STUDIES AND RESEARCH

As you delve deeper into the realm of herbal medicine, it becomes essential to understand not only the traditional uses of herbs but also the scientific evidence supporting their efficacy. Recent studies have brought to light fascinating insights into how herbs can positively impact health, from reducing inflammation to enhancing cognitive function. A notable example is the research conducted on turmeric, specifically its active compound curcumin, which has been widely studied for its anti-inflammatory and antioxidant properties. Clinical trials have shown that curcumin can significantly decrease markers of inflammation in conditions like arthritis, and it's comparable to some anti-inflammatory drugs, without the side effects. These findings are not just isolated to turmeric; numerous studies on herbs like lavender have demonstrated its efficacy in reducing anxiety through its interaction with the neurotransmitter GABA, much like certain anti-anxiety medications.

Understanding how these herbs interact with the body, a concept known as pharmacodynamics, can provide deeper insight into why certain herbs are effective for specific conditions. For instance, the reason behind the calming effects of lavender on the nervous system involves its compounds binding to GABA receptors, which reduce nerve activity, helping to calm the mind and body. Similarly, the pharmacokinetics, or how the body processes these herbs, from absorption to metabolism and excretion, is crucial for maximizing their benefits. For example, the bioavailability of curcumin is relatively low, but when combined with piperine, found in black pepper, its absorption by the body can increase by 2000%, enhancing its effectiveness.

Evaluating the quality of herbal research is as important as understanding the herbs themselves. Factors like study design, sample size, and potential biases can greatly influence the reliability of the findings. Randomized controlled trials (RCTs), considered the gold standard in clinical research, offer the most reliable evidence due to their design, which minimizes bias. However, many herbal studies may rely on smaller sample sizes or observational models, which can introduce variables that affect the outcomes. As a discerning practitioner or learner, critically assessing these studies involves examining how the research was conducted, the size of the study population, the treatment duration, and whether the findings have been replicated in other studies.

Bridging the gap between traditional knowledge and modern scientific research offers a comprehensive understanding of herbal actions. While traditional uses provide a historical basis for the use of certain herbs, modern research often validates these practices with scientific evidence, explaining the mechanisms behind the herbs' effects. This synergy between old and new enriches our understanding and application of herbal remedies, ensuring they are used safely and effectively. For instance, the traditional use of chamomile for sleep and relaxation has been supported by research identifying its sedative compounds, which interact with brain receptors to help decrease anxiety and initiate sleep. This merging of knowledge not only bolsters the credibility of herbal medicine but also enhances its integration into contemporary health practices, allowing for a holistic approach that respects and utilizes the best of both worlds.

6.4 DEVELOPING THERAPEUTIC HERBAL FORMULAS

Creating effective herbal formulas is an intricate process that blends science with tradition, demanding a deep understanding of each herb's properties and how they interact within the body. When developing therapeutic herbal formulas, one of the first steps involves selecting herbs that complement each other. This synergy is crucial because the interaction between different herbs can enhance the overall effectiveness of the formula. For example, when addressing inflammatory conditions such as arthritis, incorporating anti-inflammatory herbs like turmeric or ginger with herbs that support circulation and detoxification like ginkgo or milk thistle can enhance the formula's efficacy. This is because while turmeric reduces inflammation, ginkgo improves blood circulation, helping the body to remove toxins and deliver nutrients more efficiently, which is essential in managing arthritis.

Determining the correct dosages of each herb is equally vital. This requires not only a thorough understanding of the herbs' effects individually but also their potential interactions. Dosages must be precise to ensure safety and effectiveness. Over-dosing can lead to adverse effects, while under-dosing might render the formula ineffective. The process often starts with conservative doses, followed by adjustments based on the individual's response. For instance, in a formula designed for diabetes management, herbs like cinnamon and fenugreek, which are known to help regulate blood sugar levels, must be dosed carefully to avoid potential complications, especially if the individual is also on conventional blood sugar medications.

The development of herbal formulas for chronic conditions like diabetes, arthritis, and chronic fatigue syndrome offers a glimpse into the potential of herbs to provide relief and manage symptoms. For diabetes, an effective formula might include herbs such as gymnema, known for its ability to reduce sugar cravings and help with blood sugar control, and bitter melon, which has insulin-like properties. When combined with lifestyle changes, such a formula can significantly aid in managing blood sugar levels. For chronic fatigue syndrome, a condition often marked by persistent tiredness and low energy, adaptogenic herbs like ashwagandha and rhodiola can be invaluable. These herbs help enhance energy production at a cellular level and improve the body's response to stress, which can be a contributing factor to fatigue.

Adjusting and refining these formulas is a continual process, guided by feedback from those using them. This iterative process allows for the customization of the formula to meet individual needs more effectively. For instance, if a patient reports that a formula designed to alleviate arthritis symptoms is causing mild digestive upset, herbs like peppermint or ginger might be added to soothe the digestive system without detracting from the formula's overall purpose.

Documentation plays a critical role in the development and refinement of herbal formulas. Keeping detailed records of each formula—the herbs used, their sources, dosages, and the client's responses—enables the practitioner to replicate successful formulas and adjust less effective ones. Documentation also provides valuable data that can contribute to the broader field of herbal medicine, supporting further research and development. For instance, detailed records of a formula used to manage arthritis can provide insights into which herb combinations are most effective, information that can benefit others with similar conditions.

In essence, developing therapeutic herbal formulas is both an art and a science. It requires a nuanced understanding of herbal properties, a careful balancing of dosages, and a commitment to ongoing evaluation and adjustment based on real-world results. This approach not only enhances the effectiveness of the treatments provided but also ensures they are tailored to meet the unique needs and conditions of each individual, offering a more personalized and responsive approach to health care.

6.5 PRESERVATION AND STORAGE OF HERBAL PRODUCTS

Preserving the potency and freshness of herbal products is as crucial as the initial preparation. After all, what good is a meticulously crafted herbal remedy if it doesn't retain its therapeutic properties over time? Let's explore some of the most effective ways to ensure that your herbal creations remain as beneficial as the day they were made.

Drying is one of the most ancient and widely used methods for preserving herbs. It involves removing moisture from the herbs, which helps to prevent the growth of bacteria and mold. The key to effective drying is to ensure that it is done slowly and at low temperatures, which helps to preserve the essential oils and active compounds in the herbs. A food dehydrator can be a valuable tool here, as it allows you to control the temperature and ensure even drying. However, if you don't have a dehydrator, spreading the herbs out in a warm, airy room away from direct sunlight can also be effective. Once dried, the herbs should be stored in airtight containers away from light and heat to maintain their potency.

Freezing is another viable option, especially for preserving the freshness of herbs that don't dry well, such as basil or chives. By chopping the fresh herbs and sealing them in an airtight bag or container, you can capture their vibrant flavor and medicinal qualities. Some herbs can even be frozen into ice cube trays with water or oil, making them easy to pop out and use in cooking or as a quick addition to a tea or tincture.

For those herbal preparations that involve oils or water, such as tinctures or extracts, the use of natural preservatives can be necessary to extend their shelf life. Ingredients like alcohol in tinctures naturally preserve the concoction, allowing them to be stored for several years without spoiling. Vinegar, too, is an excellent preservative for herbal extracts, imparting not only preservation qualities but also adding a zesty flavor profile that can enhance the herb's natural flavors.

Storing herbal remedies correctly is equally critical to maintaining their effectiveness. Tinctures should be kept in cool, dark places, ideally in amber or blue glass bottles to protect them from light, which can degrade their quality. Dried herbs, on the other hand, are best stored in tightly sealed containers in a cool, dark cupboard. They should be kept whole for as long as possible, as grinding or powdering increases the surface area exposed to air, which can lead to a quicker degradation of essential oils and active ingredients. Ointments and salves should be stored in opaque, airtight containers to prevent exposure to air and light, both of which can cause the oils to go rancid.

The impact of packaging materials on the quality of herbal products cannot be overstated. Eco-friendly options not only support sustainability but also contribute to the overall safety and efficacy of the herbal products. Glass, for instance, is an excellent choice for storing tinctures and dried herbs as it is inert and does not leach chemicals into the product. It can also be reused and recycled, reducing its environmental impact. For those who need lighter, more durable materials, especially when mobility is a factor, aluminum containers can be a good choice for salves and creams as they are also impermeable to light and air.

Monitoring and maintaining the quality of stored herbal products is a continuous process. Regular checks for signs of spoilage such as mold, unusual odors, or discoloration are essential. Keeping a log of when each product was made and noting any changes over time can help in determining their longevity and when they might need to be discarded. This proactive approach not only ensures the safety and effectiveness of the herbal remedies but also helps in refining preservation techniques for future batches.

By understanding and implementing these preservation and storage techniques, you can ensure that your herbal remedies continue to provide their maximum therapeutic benefits long after they have been crafted. This not only maximizes the value of your efforts but also deepens your connection to the age-old practices of herbal medicine, bridging the gap between past wisdom and modern application.

6.6 INNOVATIONS IN HERBAL THERAPY AND FUTURE TRENDS

As we embrace the dynamic interface between tradition and modernity, herbal medicine is experiencing a renaissance, propelled by cutting-edge technological advancements and a shift towards personalized, sustainable healthcare practices. One of the most significant technological strides has been in the realm of extraction techniques. Innovations such as supercritical fluid extraction, which uses supercritical CO_2, have revolutionized the purity and efficiency of extracting bioactive compounds from herbs. This method not only ensures a cleaner extract by avoiding toxic solvents but also preserves the integrity of the delicate phytochemicals, resulting in products that are both potent and environmentally friendly.

Precision dosing is another area where technology is making a substantial impact. With the advent of digital droppers and microencapsulation techniques, it is now possible to deliver exact dosages of herbal extracts, enhancing their efficacy and reducing the risk of side effects. This precision allows practitioners to tailor treatments to individual needs with unprecedented accuracy, ushering in a new era of personalized medicine in the herbal domain. Moreover, the integration of Artificial Intelligence (AI) and machine learning in formulating herbal remedies is beginning to transform how formulations are developed. AI algorithms can analyze vast amounts of data on herb interactions and health outcomes to predict which combinations of herbs will be most effective for specific conditions, making the practice of herbal blending more scientifically driven and personalized.

Sustainability in herbal practice has also taken center stage as both consumers and practitioners increasingly prioritize environmental impact in their healthcare choices. Ethical wildcrafting and sustainable cultivation practices are becoming the norm, ensuring that herbal remedies are produced responsibly. Ethical wildcrafting involves harvesting herbs in a way that does not deplete natural populations or harm the environment, while sustainable cultivation focuses on using organic farming practices that maintain soil health and biodiversity. These practices not only protect the planet but also ensure the long-term availability of medicinal plants, securing the future of herbal medicine.

Looking ahead, the future of herbal research promises to further validate and expand the use of herbs in healthcare. Areas like psychoneuroimmunology, which explores the link between mental states, nervous system function, and immune response, are ripe for exploration with herbal therapies. Research into the gut-brain axis and the role of herbal remedies in influencing gut microbiota also holds tremendous potential. These studies could revolutionize our understanding of how herbs can be used to treat complex, chronic conditions by addressing underlying physiological processes.

The fusion of advanced extraction methods, precision dosing, AI, and a strong commitment to sustainability marks a new frontier in herbal therapy. It reflects a deeper understanding of the intricate dance between human health and the natural world, and a step towards more personalized, effective, and conscientious healthcare solutions. As we continue to explore these exciting developments, the next chapter will delve into the global reach of herbal medicine, exploring its role in public health and its integration into mainstream healthcare systems around the world. This exploration will not only highlight the universal relevance of herbal medicine but also its potential to shape the future of global health practices.

INTEGRATING HERBALISM INTO DAILY LIFE

Imagine beginning and ending your day enveloped in nature's essence, transforming ordinary routines into rejuvenating rituals that not only nourish your body but also calm your mind. Integrating herbalism into your daily life doesn't just enhance your physical well-being; it connects you with centuries of wisdom and the healing power of the earth. In this chapter, we explore how simple it can be to weave herbal practices into the rhythm of your day, from the moment you awaken to the quiet of the evening.

7.1 HERBAL ROUTINES FOR MORNING AND EVENING

Morning Herbal Kickstart

As dawn breaks, the world stirs to life with a promise of new beginnings, and what better way to greet the day than with herbs that awaken and invigorate your senses? Consider starting your morning with lemon balm and green tea, both renowned for their invigorating properties that boost mental clarity and energy. Lemon balm, with its soothing yet refreshing scent, can help to lift your spirits and calm morning anxiety, setting a positive tone for the day. Its benefits extend to enhancing cognitive function, making it a perfect herb to kickstart a busy day.

Green tea, on the other hand, is a well-loved energizer rich in antioxidants and nutrients that not only awaken the body but also offer long-term health benefits, including improved brain function and fat loss. To incorporate these herbs into your morning routine, try brewing a pot of green tea with a few leaves of lemon balm. This simple ritual not only hydrates but also infuses your body with antioxidants and calming properties, preparing you to face the day with vitality and clarity.

Relaxing Evening Herbs

As evening descends and the pace of the day slows, your nighttime routine should support a peaceful transition to rest. Herbs like chamomile and lavender are perfect for evening rituals due to their renowned calming and sleep-inducing properties. Chamomile, often referred to as the 'night-time' herb, is a gentle sedative that alleviates insomnia and induces a deep, restorative sleep. Its mildly sweet flavor and soothing aroma make it an ideal choice for a bedtime tea.

Lavender, known for its distinctive and soothing fragrance, is another excellent herb for your night-time routine. It reduces anxiety, soothes nervous tension, and improves sleep quality. You can use lavender in various forms, such as adding a few drops of essential oil to your bathwater or placing a lavender-filled pillow by your bed. These practices not only encourage relaxation but also immerse your senses in a healing, aromatic environment that promotes restful sleep.

Creating Rituals

Establishing personal morning and evening herbal rituals can significantly enhance your quality of life. These rituals are deeply personal and can be tailored to fit your individual health goals and lifestyle. For instance, if you are seeking mental clarity, your morning ritual might include journaling while sipping your lemon balm and green tea brew. If relaxation is your goal, your evening ritual might involve a meditative practice accompanied by your chamomile tea.

Consistency and Adaptation

The key to reaping the full benefits of herbal routines lies in consistency. Regular practice helps your body and mind integrate the benefits of the herbs, making them more effective over time. However, life is ever-changing, and your herbal practices should be flexible enough to adapt to different seasons and life circumstances. For example, during winter, you might add ginger to your morning tea for its warming properties, or if you're experiencing heightened stress, you might increase your use of calming herbs like lavender.

Embracing herbal routines is not about rigid practices but about infusing your days with moments of connection to nature's rhythms and remedies. Whether it's the energizing aroma of lemon balm in the morning or the soothing scent of chamomile at night, these simple rituals enrich your life, offering a daily touchstone that is both grounding and uplifting. This gentle integration of herbalism into your daily life not only enhances your well-being but also deepens your connection to the natural world, reminding you of the simple joys and profound healing that nature offers.

7.2 INTEGRATING HERBS WITH DIET FOR OPTIMAL HEALTH

Infusing your daily meals with herbs is not only a delightful culinary adventure but also a profound way to enhance your health. Imagine the aroma of fresh basil on a tomato salad or the invigorating zest of mint in your morning smoothie. These are simple pleasures that also pack a powerful health punch. Let's delve into the art of cooking with herbs, ensuring that you preserve their nutritional content and flavor, transforming everyday meals into a foundation for better health.

Herbal Cooking Techniques

Cooking with herbs can elevate the simplest dish to something extraordinary, but knowing how to use them effectively is key to maximizing their health benefits. When incorporating fresh herbs like parsley or cilantro, it's best to add them towards the end of the cooking process. This method preserves the integrity of their delicate oils, which are responsible for their aroma and therapeutic properties. For dried herbs, which are often more concentrated and potent than their fresh counterparts, it's beneficial to add them earlier in the cooking process. This allows their flavors to meld with the other ingredients and infuses the dish with their essence. Steaming herbs with vegetables or incorporating them into sauces are excellent ways to enhance flavor while retaining nutrients.

To preserve the nutritional content of herbs, avoid prolonged cooking at high temperatures. Instead, use techniques like quick sautéing or adding herbs to dishes that require minimal cooking, such as salads or dips. Another effective method is to use herbs in marinades. By mixing herbs with oil, vinegar, or citrus juice, you can create a marinade that not only flavors the food but also helps to reduce the formation of harmful compounds during cooking, particularly in grilled meat.

Herbs as Dietary Supplements

While herbs are wonderful for adding flavor to food, they also serve as potent dietary supplements that can address specific health issues and boost overall wellness. For example, turmeric, known for its anti-inflammatory properties, can be incorporated into your diet through capsules or powders. However, integrating turmeric directly into your meals, such as adding it to curries, soups, or golden milk, allows for better absorption, especially when paired with black pepper, which contains piperine—an alkaloid that enhances curcumin absorption.

Similarly, cinnamon, which can help regulate blood sugar levels, can be sprinkled on oatmeal or added to coffee. For those looking to improve digestive health, incorporating ginger into your diet can be particularly beneficial. Ginger can be taken as a supplement, or freshly grated into stir-fries, dressings, and teas. These practices ensure that you're not only enjoying the flavors of these herbs but also reaping their medicinal benefits.

Recipe Ideas

Bringing herbs into your daily meals can be both creative and health-promotive. Consider starting your day with a smoothie that blends fruits with herbs such as mint or basil, which not only add a fresh twist but also aid in digestion and enhance nutrient absorption. For lunch, a quinoa salad with chopped parsley, chives, and thyme offers a nutrient-packed meal, with herbs that support immune function and provide vital antioxidants.

For dinner, integrating herbs can be as simple as preparing a rosemary garlic chicken that fills your home with a mouth-watering aroma, or a basil pesto pasta that brings the fresh flavors of your garden to the table. Even desserts can benefit from the addition of herbs. Lavender-infused honey drizzled over fresh berries or a mint chocolate smoothie can be delightful ways to end your day on a sweet note.

Food and Herb Pairings

Understanding how to pair foods with herbs not only enhances flavor but also boosts your health by facilitating nutrient absorption. For instance, the classic pairing of tomatoes with basil is not only delicious but also nutritionally beneficial. Tomatoes are rich in lycopene, an antioxidant that is better absorbed when consumed with fat-soluble vitamins, which basil provides. Similarly, pairing iron-rich spinach with citrusy herbs like parsley can enhance iron absorption thanks to the vitamin C found in parsley.

Moreover, combining turmeric with black pepper not only improves curcumin absorption but also adds a depth of flavor to dishes. These thoughtful combinations ensure that your meals are not just nourishing to the palate but also to the body, optimizing the nutritional benefits of each meal and making every bite count towards your health.

Incorporating herbs into your diet is about more than just adding flavor—it's about enriching your life with nature's proven remedies, enhancing your health with every meal. As you continue to explore the vibrant world of herbs, let each dish be a step toward a healthier, more vibrant you, celebrating the natural healing power that comes with every spoonful.

7.3 CREATING A PERSONALIZED HERBAL WELLNESS PLAN

Embarking on a path toward using herbal remedies to enhance your health is a deeply personal process, one that involves understanding your specific needs and objectives. The first step in creating a personalized herbal wellness plan is to conduct a thorough assessment of your health needs and goals. This involves taking stock of your current health conditions, lifestyle factors, and what you hope to achieve through herbal remedies. Are you looking to alleviate stress? Perhaps you need support for digestive health or are seeking natural ways to boost your immune system. Understanding your specific needs helps in selecting the most appropriate herbs and determining the focus of your wellness plan.

Start by keeping a health diary for a couple of weeks. Note down issues like energy levels, digestive health, stress, sleep patterns, and any other health concerns. This record provides a baseline of your health and helps identify patterns or recurring issues that herbal remedies can address. Consulting with a healthcare provider or a certified herbalist can also provide insights into which areas of your health could benefit most from herbal supplementation. This professional guidance is invaluable, particularly if you have existing health conditions or are taking medications, as some herbs can interact with medicines.

Once you have a clear understanding of your health needs, the next step is choosing the right herbs. This selection process is crucial and should be approached with care. Each herb has its own profile of benefits, modes of action, and, sometimes, side effects. The choice of herbs should align with your health profile and your body's specific needs. For instance, if you are dealing with stress and anxiety, herbs like ashwagandha or lavender might be beneficial. For digestive issues, peppermint and ginger could be more appropriate. When selecting herbs, consider factors such as your body's reactions to certain plants, any allergies you might have, and how the herb is typically administered.

The efficacy of an herb can also be influenced by its form—whether as a tea, tincture, capsule, or oil. Some forms might be more effective or faster acting than others depending on the condition being treated. For example, teas can be soothing and provide immediate relief for issues like sore throats or menstrual cramps, while tinctures might be more effective for long-term support of conditions such as chronic anxiety.

Setting realistic goals is another fundamental aspect of your herbal wellness plan. Goals should be specific, measurable, achievable, relevant, and time-bound (SMART). For example, rather than a vague goal like "improve sleep," a SMART goal would be "use valerian root nightly for a month to assess improvements in sleep duration and quality." Setting such precise goals not only helps in tracking your progress but also in making adjustments as needed.

Monitoring your progress is crucial as it helps determine the effectiveness of the herbal regimen. Keep a journal of your symptoms and any changes you notice. Are the herbs making a difference? Do you feel better, worse, or the same? This documentation can help you or your herbalist adjust dosages, try different herbs, or change the method of delivery. Remember, the body's response to herbs can be subtle, and benefits might take time to manifest. Patience and consistency are key in any herbal therapy.

Flexibility in adjusting your plan is essential as well. Your body's needs may change due to various factors like age, stress, or changes in your environment or health status. Regularly review and adjust your herbal wellness plan in consultation with your herbalist or healthcare provider. This iterative process ensures that the plan remains aligned with your health needs and goals, allowing for a personalized approach that evolves with you.

Creating a personalized herbal wellness plan is a proactive step towards taking control of your health. It empowers you to make informed decisions about the herbs you use and how you use them, tailored specifically to your health needs and goals. This tailored approach not only enhances the effectiveness of the treatments but also aligns with a holistic view of health care, where the focus is on long-term wellness and prevention. As you continue to explore and adjust your herbal wellness plan, you'll gain deeper insights into the healing power of plants and their role in supporting your health journey.

7.4 ENGAGING COMMUNITY THROUGH HERBALISM

Building a vibrant community around herbalism offers a multitude of benefits, from sharing knowledge and experiences to supporting each other's health and wellness journeys. One of the most effective ways to foster such a community is by establishing or joining herbal study groups. These groups provide a structured yet flexible environment where individuals can come together to learn about different herbs, their uses, and how to incorporate them into daily life. Imagine regular meetings where you and your neighbors share herbal recipes, discuss the latest herbal health books, or even swap home-grown herbs. These interactions not only deepen your understanding of herbalism but also create a support network that encourages continual learning and practice.

Another impactful approach is to participate in or initiate community gardening projects focused on medicinal plants. This can be particularly rewarding as it involves members of the community in growing, maintaining, and harvesting herbs, which can then be used to create natural remedies shared among the group. Such gardens can become educational hubs, where workshops on sustainable gardening practices and the medicinal uses of plants are held. For instance, setting up a community herb garden in a local park or an unused lot can transform an underutilized space into a thriving source of health and education. It's also a way to reconnect with nature and the ancient traditions of herbal medicine, providing a hands-on experience that enhances physical and mental well-being.

Community service projects offer another avenue to promote herbalism while giving back to the wider community. Organizing public educational talks or workshops on the basics of herbal medicine can demystify herbal practices and introduce more people to their benefits. These events can cover topics such as how to safely use herbal remedies, understanding herb-drug interactions, and ways to integrate herbs into daily health routines. Alternatively, starting a community initiative that designs and maintains herb gardens in local schools, hospitals, or senior centers not only spreads herbal knowledge but also brings the therapeutic benefits of gardening to diverse groups. These projects not only raise awareness about herbalism but also encourage communal responsibility and active participation in health and wellness.

Integrating herbal practices within the family and social circles is equally crucial. It starts with simple steps, such as including family members in the process of planting and caring for herbs in the garden, or using herbal remedies at home for common ailments like colds or minor cuts. Over time, as your family sees the benefits of these natural remedies, their interest and trust in herbalism can grow. Social gatherings are also perfect opportunities to introduce friends to herbalism. Serving herbal teas and snacks or giving small, home-made herbal products as gifts can spark conversations about natural health and inspire others to explore herbal remedies. By making herbalism a part of your family and social life, you naturally promote wider acceptance and understanding, and these practices can ripple out through your community, inspiring more people to turn to herbalism for health and wellness.

Reflecting on the cultural and social impact of embracing herbalism reveals its profound potential to transform health care practices and wellness philosophies. As more individuals and communities recognize and embrace the benefits of natural remedies, a shift occurs in how society views health and wellness. Herbalism encourages a proactive approach to health, emphasizing prevention, natural balance, and holistic care, which contrasts sharply with the often reactive and fragmented approach seen in conventional medicine. This shift can lead to broader societal changes, where wellness is not just about treating symptoms but about fostering long-term health through natural, sustainable practices. The growing interest in herbalism also promotes a greater connection to the environment and a deeper respect for the plant world, principles that are increasingly important in our global efforts to ensure environmental sustainability and health equity. As you integrate herbalism into your community and social spheres, you contribute to these cultural shifts, paving the way for a healthier, more sustainable future where natural and holistic health practices are valued and embraced.

7.5 THE FUTURE OF PERSONAL HEALTH: EMBRACING HERBAL PRACTICES

As we navigate through the ever-evolving landscape of health and wellness, the integration of herbal practices into our daily lives represents not only a return to ancestral knowledge but also a stride toward future innovations in healthcare. The current trend sees a remarkable fusion of technology with traditional herbal wisdom, exemplified by the development of sophisticated apps designed to identify herbs, track their effects, and even guide users in creating personalized herbal remedies. These digital tools make herbalism more accessible, allowing individuals to gain knowledge and confidence in using herbs to support their health. Imagine the convenience of using your smartphone to scan a plant in your backyard and instantly receiving information about its medicinal properties and uses. Such technology not only empowers users but also promotes a deeper connection with the natural world around them.

Looking ahead, the role of herbal medicine in mainstream healthcare is poised for significant expansion. As more individuals seek natural and preventive approaches to health, we can anticipate a greater integration of herbal therapies alongside conventional medical treatments. This synergy promises a more holistic approach to healthcare, where the natural efficacy of herbal remedies complements medical advancements, offering a comprehensive treatment paradigm that caters to the whole person. This shift is likely to encourage more healthcare providers to gain expertise in herbal medicine, further legitimizing and expanding its role in public health.

Advocacy plays a crucial role in this transformative process. As herbal medicine gains popularity, it becomes imperative to advocate for regulatory frameworks that ensure the safety, efficacy, and quality of herbal products. Supporting policies that promote research in herbal medicine and protect natural resources ensures sustainable practices within the industry and helps maintain the integrity of herbal products. Moreover, by advocating for the inclusion of herbal medicine in healthcare policies and insurance coverage, we can facilitate broader access to these therapies, making them a viable option for more people.

Your personal commitment to herbalism is perhaps the most profound contribution to its future. By choosing to embrace herbal practices, you become an advocate for a more sustainable, healthful, and balanced approach to wellness. Engaging with herbalism not only enhances your personal health but also influences those around you, inspiring a community-wide shift towards more natural and mindful approaches to health. This commitment encourages continuous learning and adaptation, ensuring that herbal practices evolve with new scientific discoveries and societal needs.

As you integrate these practices into your life, remember that each choice to use a herbal remedy, to learn about a plant, or to share your knowledge contributes to a larger movement towards global sustainability. Herbalism offers more than just health benefits; it promotes a way of living that is in harmony with nature, fostering environmental stewardship and a healthier planet for future generations.

In this chapter, we have explored how embracing herbal practices can enrich your health and play a significant role in shaping the future of healthcare. As we move forward, let us carry with us the knowledge and insights gained, continuing to explore and advocate for the integration of herbal wisdom in our lives and communities. The journey towards a more holistic and integrated approach to health is not just a personal quest but a collective endeavor that promises a healthier, more sustainable future for all.

CONCLUSION

As we draw the curtains on this enriching journey through the realm of herbal remedies, it's essential to reflect on the ground we have covered together. From the very first pages, where we decoded herbal terminology and explored the historical tapestry of herbal medicine, to diving into advanced herbal applications and embracing sustainable practices, this book has been a comprehensive guide aimed at empowering you with the knowledge to integrate herbalism into your day-to-day life for wellness, beauty, and stress relief.

Throughout these chapters, we have emphasized a holistic approach to health that goes beyond the physical. Herbal remedies are unique in that they offer benefits that touch upon mental and emotional wellness, allowing for a balanced life that nurtures the mind, body, and spirit. This holistic perspective is not just a method but a lifestyle, encouraging a deeper connection with the healing powers of nature.

As we conclude, I hope this book serves not only as a guide but as an inspiration for you to embrace the transformative power of herbal remedies. These practices have the potential to change not just individual lives but to influence broader societal health and sustainability.

Thank you for joining me on this journey. May you find joy and health in the embrace of herbalism, and may you spread this knowledge to enrich the lives of others around you. Here's to a healthier, more sustainable future, one leaf at a time.

OTHER COMMON AILMENT RECIPES

Herbal Remedy Recipe for Ayurvedic Triphala

WHAT YOU NEED:

1. **Amalaki (Amla) Powder**: 1 part
2. **Haritaki Powder**: 1 part
3. **Bibhitaki Powder**: 1 part
4. **Water**: 1 cup (optional, for making a tea)
5. **Honey** (optional): For taste

STEPS TO PREPARE:

1. Prepare the Powders:

- Mix equal parts of Amalaki, Haritaki, and Bibhitaki powders. For example, use 1 teaspoon of each powder.

2. For Internal Use:

- **As a Powder**: Take 1 teaspoon of the Triphala powder blend with warm water before bed or first thing in the morning.
- **As a Tea**: Boil 1 cup of water. Add 1 teaspoon of the Triphala powder blend and let it steep for 5-10 minutes. Strain the mixture and add honey if desired.

3. For External Use:

- **As a Paste**: Mix the Triphala powder with a little water to make a paste. Apply it to the skin for its anti-inflammatory and healing properties.

BENEFITS OF TRIPHALA:

1. Digestive Health:

- **Aids Digestion**: Triphala helps improve digestion and alleviates constipation. It acts as a mild laxative, promoting regular bowel movements.
- **Detoxifies the Body**: It helps detoxify the gastrointestinal tract, promoting overall digestive health.

2. Antioxidant Properties:

- **Rich in Antioxidants**: Triphala is high in antioxidants, which help protect cells from oxidative stress and free radical damage.

3. Immune System Support:

- **Boosts Immunity**: The combination of Amalaki, Haritaki, and Bibhitaki helps strengthen the immune system and increase resistance to infections.

4. Anti-inflammatory:

- **Reduces Inflammation**: Triphala has anti-inflammatory properties that can help reduce inflammation in the body, benefiting conditions like arthritis.

5. Skin Health:

- **Promotes Healthy Skin**: When used externally, Triphala can help with skin conditions such as acne, eczema, and psoriasis due to its antimicrobial and anti-inflammatory properties.

6. Weight Management:

- **Supports Weight Loss**: Triphala may help support weight loss by improving digestion, enhancing metabolism, and reducing fat accumulation.

Herbal Remedy Recipe for Inflammatory Conditions with Circulation Support and Detoxification

INGREDIENTS:

1. **Turmeric Powder**: 1 teaspoon
2. **Fresh Ginger Root**: 1-inch piece (or 1 teaspoon of dried ginger powder)
3. **Dried Ginkgo Biloba Leaves**: 1 teaspoon
4. **Dried Milk Thistle Seeds**: 1 teaspoon
5. **Water**: 4 cups
6. **Honey or Lemon** (optional): For taste

STEPS TO PREPARE:

1. Boil the Water:

- Pour 4 cups of water into a saucepan and bring it to a boil.

2. Prepare the Ingredients:

- Peel and slice the fresh ginger root. If using dried ginger powder, measure out 1 teaspoon.

3. Steep the Ingredients:

- Add the turmeric powder, ginger (fresh or dried), dried ginkgo biloba leaves, and dried milk thistle seeds to the boiling water.
- Reduce the heat and let the mixture simmer for about 10-15 minutes.

4. Strain the Tea:

- After simmering, remove the saucepan from heat and let it cool slightly.
- Strain the tea through a fine strainer or cheesecloth to remove the solids.

5. Add Honey or Lemon (Optional):

- If desired, add honey for sweetness or a slice of lemon for additional flavor and health benefits.

6. Serve:

- Pour the strained tea into a cup and enjoy.

DOSAGE:

- **For Regular Use**: Drink 1-2 cups daily to enjoy the full benefits of this herbal remedy.

BENEFITS OF THE INGREDIENTS:

1. Turmeric:

- **Anti-inflammatory Properties**: Curcumin, the active compound in turmeric, has powerful anti-inflammatory effects that can help reduce inflammation and pain in conditions such as arthritis.
- **Antioxidant**: Turmeric is rich in antioxidants, which help protect cells from oxidative damage and support overall health.

2. Ginger:

- **Improves Circulation**: Ginger helps improve blood circulation, which can be beneficial for cardiovascular health and reducing symptoms of poor circulation.
- **Anti-inflammatory**: Ginger contains gingerols, which have strong anti-inflammatory and pain-relieving properties.
- **Digestive Health**: Ginger aids digestion and can help alleviate symptoms of nausea and indigestion.

3. Ginkgo Biloba:

- **Enhances Circulation**: Ginkgo biloba improves blood flow, particularly to the brain and extremities, supporting cognitive function and reducing symptoms of poor circulation.
- **Antioxidant Properties**: It contains flavonoids and terpenoids, which are antioxidants that help protect cells from damage.

4. Milk Thistle:

- **Liver Detoxification**: Milk thistle is known for its liver-protective properties. It helps detoxify the liver and supports its function.
- **Anti-inflammatory**: Silymarin, the active compound in milk thistle, has anti-inflammatory effects that can help reduce liver inflammation and support overall liver health.

Herbal Remedy Recipe for Diabetes Management

INGREDIENTS:

1. **Fenugreek Seeds**: 1 teaspoon
2. **Cinnamon Powder**: 1/2 teaspoon
3. **Ginger Root**: 1-inch piece (or 1/2 teaspoon dried ginger powder)
4. **Turmeric Powder**: 1/2 teaspoon
5. **Water**: 2 cups
6. **Honey** (optional): For taste

STEPS TO PREPARE:

1. Soak the Fenugreek Seeds:

- Soak 1 teaspoon of fenugreek seeds in water overnight. This helps to enhance their effectiveness and ease of digestion.

2. Boil the Water:

- Pour 2 cups of water into a saucepan and bring it to a boil.

3. Prepare the Ingredients:

- Peel and slice the ginger root if using fresh ginger.

4. Combine and Simmer:

- Add the soaked fenugreek seeds (along with the soaking water), cinnamon powder, ginger (fresh or dried), and turmeric powder to the boiling water.
- Reduce the heat and let the mixture simmer for about 10-15 minutes.

5. Strain the Tea:

- After simmering, remove the saucepan from heat and let it cool slightly.
- Strain the tea through a fine strainer to remove the solids.

6. Add Honey (Optional):

- If desired, add honey for sweetness. Stir well to combine.

7. Serve:

- Pour the strained tea into a cup and enjoy.

DOSAGE:

- **For Regular Use**: Drink 1 cup of this herbal tea daily, preferably in the morning or before meals, to help manage blood sugar levels.

BENEFITS OF THE INGREDIENTS:

1. Fenugreek Seeds:

- **Lowers Blood Sugar Levels**: Fenugreek seeds contain soluble fiber, which helps lower blood sugar by slowing down digestion and absorption of carbohydrates.

- **Improves Insulin Sensitivity**: Fenugreek may improve insulin sensitivity and reduce insulin resistance.

2. Cinnamon:

- **Reduces Blood Sugar**: Cinnamon can lower blood sugar levels by increasing insulin sensitivity and slowing the breakdown of carbohydrates in the digestive tract.
- **Antioxidant Properties**: It has powerful antioxidants that help reduce oxidative stress and inflammation.

3. Ginger:

- **Improves Glycemic Control**: Ginger has been shown to improve fasting blood sugar levels and HbA1c (a measure of long-term blood sugar levels).
- **Anti-inflammatory**: Ginger's anti-inflammatory properties can help reduce inflammation, which is beneficial for managing diabetes.

4. Turmeric:

- **Reduces Inflammation**: Curcumin, the active compound in turmeric, has potent anti-inflammatory effects that can help manage diabetes-related inflammation.
- **Improves Insulin Sensitivity**: Turmeric can improve insulin sensitivity and lower blood sugar levels.

Herbal Remedy Recipe for Chronic Fatigue Syndrome with Ashwagandha and Rhodiola

INGREDIENTS:

1. **Ashwagandha Root Powder**: 1 teaspoon
2. **Dried Rhodiola Root**: 1 teaspoon

3. **Water**: 2 cups
4. **Honey or Lemon** (optional): For taste

STEPS TO PREPARE:

1. Boil the Water:

- Pour 2 cups of water into a saucepan and bring it to a boil.

2. Prepare the Ingredients:

- Measure out 1 teaspoon of ashwagandha root powder and 1 teaspoon of dried rhodiola root.

3. Combine and Simmer:

- Add the ashwagandha root powder and dried rhodiola root to the boiling water.
- Reduce the heat and let the mixture simmer for about 10-15 minutes.

4. Strain the Tea:

- After simmering, remove the saucepan from heat and let it cool slightly.
- Strain the tea through a fine strainer to remove the solids.

5. Add Honey or Lemon (Optional):

- If desired, add honey for sweetness or a slice of lemon for additional flavor and health benefits.

6. Serve:

- Pour the strained tea into a cup and enjoy.

DOSAGE:

- **For Regular Use**: Drink 1 cup of this herbal tea daily, preferably in the morning or early afternoon, to help manage symptoms of chronic fatigue syndrome.

BENEFITS OF THE INGREDIENTS:

1. Ashwagandha:

- **Adaptogenic Properties**: Ashwagandha is an adaptogen, meaning it helps the body adapt to stress and promotes overall balance. It can help reduce cortisol levels and alleviate symptoms of stress and fatigue.
- **Improves Energy Levels**: Ashwagandha can help improve energy levels and reduce fatigue by supporting adrenal function and enhancing stamina.
- **Enhances Cognitive Function**: It can improve cognitive function and memory, which can be beneficial for those experiencing brain fog associated with chronic fatigue syndrome.

2. Rhodiola:

- **Adaptogenic Properties**: Rhodiola is also an adaptogen that helps the body resist physical, chemical, and environmental stress. It can help reduce fatigue and improve mental and physical performance.
- **Boosts Energy and Stamina**: Rhodiola enhances energy levels and physical stamina, making it helpful for combating the fatigue and weakness associated with chronic fatigue syndrome.
- **Improves Mood**: Rhodiola has mood-enhancing properties and can help alleviate symptoms of depression and anxiety.

Herbal Remedies for Heart Disease:

Heart disease is a serious condition that requires medical supervision and treatment. However, certain herbal remedies can support cardiovascular health alongside conventional treatments. Here are some herbal remedies that may help with heart disease:

1. Hawthorn (Crataegus spp.)

BENEFITS:

- **Improves Heart Function**: Hawthorn can enhance the function of the heart and cardiovascular system by increasing blood flow to the heart muscle and improving cardiac output.
- **Antioxidant Properties**: It is rich in flavonoids, which have antioxidant properties that help protect the heart from damage.
- **Reduces Blood Pressure**: Hawthorn can help lower blood pressure by dilating blood vessels.

HOW TO USE:

- **Tea**: Steep 1-2 teaspoons of dried hawthorn berries or leaves in hot water for 10-15 minutes. Drink 1-2 cups daily.
- **Extract**: Follow the dosage instructions on the product label, typically 300-500 mg taken two to three times daily.

2. Garlic (Allium sativum)

BENEFITS:

- **Lowers Blood Pressure**: Garlic is known to help lower blood pressure.
- **Reduces Cholesterol Levels**: It can help reduce total and LDL (bad) cholesterol levels.

- **Antiplatelet Effects**: Garlic has antiplatelet properties, which can help prevent blood clots.

How to Use:

- **Raw**: Eat 1-2 cloves of raw garlic daily.
- **Supplement**: Garlic supplements are available in capsules or tablets. Follow the dosage instructions on the product label, typically 600-1200 mg daily.

3. Ginger (Zingiber officinale)

Benefits:

- **Improves Circulation**: Ginger can improve blood circulation, which is beneficial for cardiovascular health.
- **Anti-inflammatory**: It has anti-inflammatory properties that help reduce inflammation in the blood vessels.
- **Lowers Cholesterol**: Ginger can help lower cholesterol levels and prevent blood clots.

How to Use:

- **Tea**: Steep 1 teaspoon of fresh grated ginger or 1/2 teaspoon of dried ginger powder in hot water for 10-15 minutes. Drink 1-2 cups daily.
- **Supplement**: Follow the dosage instructions on the product label, typically 250-500 mg taken two to three times daily.

4. Turmeric (Curcuma longa)

Benefits:

- **Anti-inflammatory**: Curcumin, the active compound in turmeric, has potent anti-inflammatory effects that can help reduce inflammation in the cardiovascular system.

- **Antioxidant Properties**: Turmeric is rich in antioxidants that help protect the heart from oxidative stress.
- **Improves Blood Vessel Function**: Turmeric can improve the function of the endothelium, the lining of the blood vessels.

How to Use:

- **Tea**: Steep 1 teaspoon of turmeric powder in hot water for 10-15 minutes. Add honey and lemon for taste. Drink 1-2 cups daily.
- **Supplement**: Follow the dosage instructions on the product label, typically 500-1000 mg taken twice daily.

5. Green Tea (Camellia sinensis)

Benefits:

- **Antioxidant Properties**: Green tea is rich in catechins, which have strong antioxidant properties.
- **Reduces Cholesterol Levels**: It can help lower total and LDL cholesterol levels.
- **Improves Blood Vessel Function**: Green tea can improve the function of the endothelium.

How to Use:

- **Tea**: Steep 1 teaspoon of green tea leaves in hot water for 3-5 minutes. Drink 1-3 cups daily.
- **Extract**: Follow the dosage instructions on the product label, typically 300-400 mg of green tea extract daily.

Herbal Remedies for Cancer Management and Prevention:

Cancer is a serious and complex disease that requires professional medical treatment. While herbal remedies cannot cure cancer, they may help support overall health and alleviate some symptoms associated with cancer and its treatments. It is crucial to consult with a healthcare provider before using any herbal remedies, especially when dealing with cancer. Here are some herbs that are commonly discussed for their potential supportive roles in cancer care:

1. Turmeric (Curcuma longa)

BENEFITS:

- **Anti-inflammatory**: Curcumin, the active compound in turmeric, has strong anti-inflammatory properties that may help reduce inflammation associated with cancer.
- **Antioxidant**: Turmeric has antioxidant properties that can help protect cells from damage by free radicals.
- **Anti-cancer Potential**: Some studies suggest that curcumin may inhibit the growth of certain cancer cells and prevent metastasis.

HOW TO USE:

- **Supplement**: Follow the dosage instructions on the product label, typically 500-1000 mg taken twice daily.
- **Tea**: Steep 1 teaspoon of turmeric powder in hot water for 10-15 minutes. Add honey and lemon for taste. Drink 1-2 cups daily.

2. Green Tea (Camellia sinensis)

BENEFITS:

- **Antioxidant**: Green tea is rich in catechins, which have strong antioxidant properties that can protect cells from damage.
- **Anti-cancer Properties**: Some studies suggest that green tea catechins may inhibit the growth of cancer cells and reduce the risk of certain cancers.

HOW TO USE:

- **Tea**: Steep 1 teaspoon of green tea leaves in hot water for 3-5 minutes. Drink 1-3 cups daily.
- **Extract**: Follow the dosage instructions on the product label, typically 300-400 mg of green tea extract daily.

3. Ginger (Zingiber officinale)

BENEFITS:

- **Anti-inflammatory**: Ginger contains gingerols that have anti-inflammatory properties.
- **Anti-nausea**: Ginger is well-known for its ability to reduce nausea, which can be helpful for cancer patients undergoing chemotherapy.

HOW TO USE:

- **Tea**: Steep 1 teaspoon of fresh grated ginger or 1/2 teaspoon of dried ginger powder in hot water for 10-15 minutes. Drink 1-2 cups daily.
- **Supplement**: Follow the dosage instructions on the product label, typically 250-500 mg taken two to three times daily.

4. Milk Thistle (Silybum marianum)

BENEFITS:

- **Liver Support**: Milk thistle is known for its liver-protective properties, which can help detoxify the liver and support its function during cancer treatment.
- **Antioxidant**: Silymarin, the active compound in milk thistle, has antioxidant properties that help protect cells from damage.

HOW TO USE:

- **Supplement**: Follow the dosage instructions on the product label, typically 150-300 mg taken two to three times daily.
- **Tea**: Steep 1 teaspoon of crushed milk thistle seeds in hot water for 10-15 minutes. Drink 1-2 cups daily.

5. Astragalus (Astragalus membranaceus)

BENEFITS:

- **Immune Support**: Astragalus is an adaptogen that can help boost the immune system and enhance the body's resistance to infections.
- **Anti-inflammatory**: It has anti-inflammatory properties that can help reduce inflammation associated with cancer.

HOW TO USE:

- **Supplement**: Follow the dosage instructions on the product label, typically 500-1000 mg taken two to three times daily.
- **Tea**: Steep 1 teaspoon of dried astragalus root in hot water for 10-15 minutes. Drink 1-2 cups daily.

Herbal Remedies for COPD:

Chronic pulmonary diseases, such as chronic obstructive pulmonary disease (COPD), asthma, and bronchitis, often require medical treatment and lifestyle changes. Herbal remedies can complement conventional treatments by helping to manage symptoms and improve respiratory health. It is crucial to consult with a healthcare provider before using any herbal remedies, especially when dealing with chronic pulmonary diseases. Here are some herbal remedies that may help support respiratory health:

1. Mullein (Verbascum thapsus)

BENEFITS:

- **Respiratory Support**: Mullein is known for its ability to soothe the respiratory tract and reduce inflammation.
- **Expectorant**: It helps clear mucus from the lungs, making it easier to breathe.

HOW TO USE:

- **Tea**: Steep 1-2 teaspoons of dried mullein leaves in hot water for 10-15 minutes. Drink 1-2 cups daily.

2. Licorice Root (Glycyrrhiza glabra)

BENEFITS:

- **Anti-inflammatory**: Licorice root has anti-inflammatory properties that can help reduce inflammation in the respiratory tract.
- **Soothes Mucous Membranes**: It helps soothe and protect the mucous membranes of the throat and lungs.

How to Use:

- **Tea**: Steep 1 teaspoon of dried licorice root in hot water for 10-15 minutes. Drink 1-2 cups daily.

3. Ginger (Zingiber officinale)

Benefits:

- **Anti-inflammatory**: Ginger has strong anti-inflammatory properties that can help reduce inflammation in the respiratory system.
- **Improves Circulation**: It helps improve blood circulation, which can enhance respiratory function.

How to Use:

- **Tea**: Steep 1 teaspoon of fresh grated ginger or 1/2 teaspoon of dried ginger powder in hot water for 10-15 minutes. Drink 1-2 cups daily.

4. Thyme (Thymus vulgaris)

Benefits:

- **Antimicrobial**: Thyme has antimicrobial properties that can help fight respiratory infections.
- **Expectorant**: It helps loosen and expel mucus from the lungs.

How to Use:

- **Tea**: Steep 1 teaspoon of dried thyme leaves in hot water for 10-15 minutes. Drink 1-2 cups daily.

5. Eucalyptus (Eucalyptus globulus)

BENEFITS:

- **Decongestant**: Eucalyptus helps clear nasal congestion and improve airflow.
- **Anti-inflammatory and Antimicrobial**: It has both anti-inflammatory and antimicrobial properties that can support respiratory health.

HOW TO USE:

- **Steam Inhalation**: Add a few drops of eucalyptus essential oil to a bowl of hot water. Cover your head with a towel and inhale the steam for 5-10 minutes.
- **Tea**: Steep 1 teaspoon of dried eucalyptus leaves in hot water for 10-15 minutes. Drink 1-2 cups daily.

Herbal Remedies for Alzheimer's Disease:

Alzheimer's disease is a complex neurodegenerative disorder that requires professional medical treatment. While herbal remedies cannot cure Alzheimer's, they may help support cognitive function and alleviate some symptoms. It's important to consult with a healthcare provider before using any herbal remedies, especially when dealing with Alzheimer's disease. Here are some herbal remedies that may help support cognitive function in Alzheimer's patients:

1. Ginkgo Biloba (Ginkgo biloba)

BENEFITS:

- **Improves Cognitive Function**: Ginkgo biloba is known for its ability to enhance memory and cognitive function by improving blood flow to the brain.

- **Antioxidant Properties**: It contains powerful antioxidants that protect brain cells from oxidative damage.

How to Use:

- **Supplement**: Follow the dosage instructions on the product label, typically 120-240 mg per day, divided into two to three doses.
- **Tea**: Steep 1 teaspoon of dried ginkgo biloba leaves in hot water for 5-10 minutes. Drink 1-2 cups daily.

2. Turmeric (Curcuma longa)

Benefits:

- **Anti-inflammatory**: Curcumin, the active compound in turmeric, has potent anti-inflammatory effects that can help reduce neuroinflammation associated with Alzheimer's disease.
- **Antioxidant**: Turmeric is rich in antioxidants that help protect brain cells from damage caused by free radicals.

How to Use:

- **Supplement**: Follow the dosage instructions on the product label, typically 500-1000 mg taken twice daily.
- **Tea**: Steep 1 teaspoon of turmeric powder in hot water for 10-15 minutes. Add honey and lemon for taste. Drink 1-2 cups daily.

3. Ashwagandha (Withania somnifera)

BENEFITS:

- **Reduces Stress and Anxiety**: Ashwagandha is an adaptogen that helps reduce stress and anxiety, which can be beneficial for overall brain health.
- **Neuroprotective**: It may help protect brain cells from damage and support overall cognitive function.

HOW TO USE:

- **Supplement**: Follow the dosage instructions on the product label, typically 300-500 mg taken twice daily.
- **Tea**: Steep 1 teaspoon of ashwagandha root powder in hot water for 10-15 minutes. Drink 1-2 cups daily.

4. Bacopa Monnieri (Brahmi)

BENEFITS:

- **Enhances Memory and Learning**: Bacopa is known for its ability to improve memory and cognitive function.
- **Reduces Anxiety**: It has anxiolytic properties that help reduce anxiety and stress.

HOW TO USE:

- **Supplement**: Follow the dosage instructions on the product label, typically 300-450 mg per day, divided into two doses.
- **Tea**: Steep 1 teaspoon of dried bacopa leaves in hot water for 10-15 minutes. Drink 1-2 cups daily.

5. Sage (Salvia officinalis)

BENEFITS:

- **Improves Cognitive Function**: Sage has been shown to enhance memory and cognitive function, making it beneficial for Alzheimer's patients.
- **Antioxidant Properties**: Sage is rich in antioxidants that protect brain cells from oxidative damage.

HOW TO USE:

- **Supplement**: Follow the dosage instructions on the product label, typically 300-600 mg per day.
- **Tea**: Steep 1 teaspoon of dried sage leaves in hot water for 5-10 minutes. Drink 1-2 cups daily.

Herbal Remedies for Diabetes:

Managing diabetes through herbal remedies can complement conventional treatments and help regulate blood sugar levels. Here are some herbal remedies that may support diabetes management:

1. Fenugreek (Trigonella foenum-graecum)

BENEFITS:

- **Lowers Blood Sugar Levels**: Fenugreek seeds contain soluble fiber, which helps control blood sugar by slowing digestion and absorption of carbohydrates.
- **Improves Insulin Sensitivity**: Fenugreek may improve insulin sensitivity and reduce insulin resistance.

How to Use:

- **Soak Seeds**: Soak 1-2 teaspoons of fenugreek seeds in water overnight and consume them in the morning on an empty stomach.
- **Powder**: Fenugreek seed powder can be taken in doses of 5-10 grams per day, mixed with water or food.

2. Cinnamon (Cinnamomum verum)

Benefits:

- **Reduces Blood Sugar**: Cinnamon can help lower fasting blood sugar levels by increasing insulin sensitivity and slowing the breakdown of carbohydrates.
- **Antioxidant Properties**: Cinnamon is rich in antioxidants, which help reduce oxidative stress and inflammation associated with diabetes.

How to Use:

- **Powder**: Add 1/2 to 1 teaspoon of cinnamon powder to your daily diet, such as in tea, oatmeal, or smoothies.
- **Supplement**: Cinnamon supplements are available in capsules or tablets. Follow the dosage instructions on the product label, typically 500-1000 mg per day.

3. Bitter Melon (Momordica charantia)

Benefits:

- **Lowers Blood Sugar**: Bitter melon contains compounds that act like insulin, helping to reduce blood sugar levels.
- **Improves Glucose Tolerance**: It can improve glucose tolerance and reduce fasting blood sugar levels.

How to Use:

- **Juice**: Drink fresh bitter melon juice (about 30 ml) on an empty stomach in the morning.
- **Cooked**: Bitter melon can be included in your diet as a vegetable, either cooked or stir-fried.

4. Ginger (Zingiber officinale)

Benefits:

- **Improves Glycemic Control**: Ginger has been shown to improve fasting blood sugar levels and HbA1c (a measure of long-term blood sugar levels).
- **Anti-inflammatory**: Ginger's anti-inflammatory properties can help reduce inflammation, which is beneficial for managing diabetes.

How to Use:

- **Tea**: Steep 1 teaspoon of fresh grated ginger or 1/2 teaspoon of dried ginger powder in hot water for 10-15 minutes. Drink 1-2 cups daily.
- **Supplement**: Follow the dosage instructions on the product label, typically 250-500 mg taken two to three times daily.

5. Aloe Vera (Aloe barbadensis)

Benefits:

- **Lowers Blood Sugar Levels**: Aloe vera juice can help lower fasting blood sugar levels.
- **Improves Lipid Profile**: It can improve lipid profiles by reducing cholesterol and triglycerides.

How to Use:

- **Juice**: Drink 1/4 cup of aloe vera juice daily. Ensure you are using a product meant for internal use and follow the dosage instructions on the product label.

6. Berberine

Benefits:

- **Lowers Blood Sugar**: Berberine, a compound found in several plants, helps lower blood sugar levels and improve insulin sensitivity.
- **Improves Glycemic Control**: It has been shown to reduce HbA1c levels and improve overall glycemic control.

How to Use:

- **Supplement**: Follow the dosage instructions on the product label, typically 500 mg taken two to three times daily before meals.

Herbal Remedies for Managing Kidney Disease:

Managing kidney disease requires professional medical treatment and lifestyle changes, but certain herbal remedies may help support kidney health and alleviate symptoms. It's important to consult with a healthcare provider before using any herbal remedies, especially when dealing with kidney disease. Here are some herbs that may support kidney health:

1. Dandelion Root (Taraxacum officinale)

BENEFITS:

- **Diuretic**: Dandelion root acts as a natural diuretic, helping to increase urine production and flush out toxins from the kidneys.
- **Detoxification**: It supports overall detoxification processes in the body, which can benefit kidney health.

HOW TO USE:

- **Tea**: Steep 1-2 teaspoons of dried dandelion root in hot water for 10-15 minutes. Drink 1-2 cups daily.
- **Supplement**: Follow the dosage instructions on the product label, typically 500-2000 mg per day.

2. Nettle Leaf (Urtica dioica)

BENEFITS:

- **Anti-inflammatory**: Nettle leaf has anti-inflammatory properties that can help reduce inflammation in the kidneys.
- **Diuretic**: It also acts as a mild diuretic, promoting urine production and helping to clear waste products from the kidneys.

HOW TO USE:

- **Tea**: Steep 1-2 teaspoons of dried nettle leaf in hot water for 10-15 minutes. Drink 1-2 cups daily.
- **Supplement**: Follow the dosage instructions on the product label, typically 300-500 mg taken twice daily.

3. Cranberry (Vaccinium macrocarpon)

BENEFITS:

- **Prevents UTIs**: Cranberry is well-known for its ability to prevent urinary tract infections (UTIs), which can help prevent further kidney complications.
- **Antioxidant Properties**: It is rich in antioxidants, which help protect kidney cells from damage.

HOW TO USE:

- **Juice**: Drink 100% pure cranberry juice (without added sugars) daily, about 8-16 ounces.
- **Supplement**: Follow the dosage instructions on the product label, typically 300-400 mg taken twice daily.

4. Parsley (Petroselinum crispum)

BENEFITS:

- **Diuretic**: Parsley has diuretic properties that help increase urine output and flush out toxins from the kidneys.
- **Anti-inflammatory**: It helps reduce inflammation and can support overall kidney health.

HOW TO USE:

- **Tea**: Steep 1-2 teaspoons of fresh or dried parsley in hot water for 10-15 minutes. Drink 1-2 cups daily.
- **Juice**: Blend fresh parsley with water and drink 1/4 cup of the juice daily.

5. Ginger (Zingiber officinale)

BENEFITS:

- **Anti-inflammatory**: Ginger has anti-inflammatory properties that can help reduce inflammation in the kidneys.
- **Antioxidant**: It helps protect kidney cells from oxidative damage.

HOW TO USE:

- **Tea**: Steep 1 teaspoon of fresh grated ginger or 1/2 teaspoon of dried ginger powder in hot water for 10-15 minutes. Drink 1-2 cups daily.
- **Supplement**: Follow the dosage instructions on the product label, typically 250-500 mg taken two to three times daily.

Herbal Remedies for Managing High Cholesterol:

Managing high cholesterol often involves dietary and lifestyle changes, but certain herbal remedies may help support cholesterol reduction. It is crucial to consult with a healthcare provider before using any herbal remedies, especially if you have underlying health conditions or are taking other medications. Here are some herbs that may help manage high cholesterol:

1. Garlic (Allium sativum)

BENEFITS:

- **Reduces Total and LDL Cholesterol**: Garlic has been shown to lower total cholesterol and LDL (bad) cholesterol levels.
- **Antioxidant Properties**: It contains antioxidants that protect against oxidative damage, which can contribute to cardiovascular health.

How to Use:

- **Raw**: Eat 1-2 cloves of raw garlic daily.
- **Supplement**: Garlic supplements are available in capsules or tablets. Follow the dosage instructions on the product label, typically 600-1200 mg daily.

2. Turmeric (Curcuma longa)

Benefits:

- **Lowers LDL Cholesterol**: Curcumin, the active compound in turmeric, can help reduce LDL cholesterol levels.
- **Anti-inflammatory and Antioxidant**: Turmeric's anti-inflammatory and antioxidant properties support overall cardiovascular health.

How to Use:

- **Supplement**: Follow the dosage instructions on the product label, typically 500-1000 mg taken twice daily.
- **Tea**: Steep 1 teaspoon of turmeric powder in hot water for 10-15 minutes. Add honey and lemon for taste. Drink 1-2 cups daily.

3. Psyllium (Plantago ovata)

Benefits:

- **Lowers LDL Cholesterol**: Psyllium husk is rich in soluble fiber, which can help lower LDL cholesterol levels by binding to cholesterol in the intestines and promoting its excretion.
- **Improves Digestion**: It also supports healthy digestion and regular bowel movements.

HOW TO USE:

- **Powder**: Mix 1 tablespoon of psyllium husk powder in a glass of water or juice and drink immediately. Take once or twice daily.
- **Supplement**: Follow the dosage instructions on the product label.

4. Green Tea (Camellia sinensis)

BENEFITS:

- **Lowers Total and LDL Cholesterol**: Green tea contains catechins, which have been shown to reduce total and LDL cholesterol levels.
- **Antioxidant Properties**: Green tea is rich in antioxidants that help protect against oxidative stress and inflammation.

HOW TO USE:

- **Tea**: Steep 1 teaspoon of green tea leaves in hot water for 3-5 minutes. Drink 1-3 cups daily.
- **Extract**: Follow the dosage instructions on the product label, typically 300-400 mg of green tea extract daily.

5. Red Yeast Rice (Monascus purpureus)

BENEFITS:

- **Lowers LDL Cholesterol**: Red yeast rice contains monacolin K, which is similar to the active ingredient in some statin drugs used to lower cholesterol.
- **Supports Cardiovascular Health**: It has been shown to reduce total and LDL cholesterol levels.

How to Use:

- **Supplement**: Follow the dosage instructions on the product label, typically 1200-2400 mg taken in divided doses with meals.

Herbal Remedies for High Blood Pressure:

Managing hypertension (high blood pressure) often involves lifestyle changes and medication, but certain herbal remedies may help support blood pressure regulation. It is crucial to consult with a healthcare provider before using any herbal remedies, especially if you have underlying health conditions or are taking other medications. Here are some herbs that may help manage hypertension:

1. Garlic (Allium sativum)

BENEFITS:

- **Lowers Blood Pressure**: Garlic has been shown to reduce both systolic and diastolic blood pressure.
- **Improves Circulation**: It helps improve blood flow and reduce the risk of cardiovascular diseases.

How to Use:

- **Raw**: Eat 1-2 cloves of raw garlic daily.
- **Supplement**: Garlic supplements are available in capsules or tablets. Follow the dosage instructions on the product label, typically 600-1200 mg daily.

2. Hibiscus (Hibiscus sabdariffa)

BENEFITS:

- **Lowers Blood Pressure**: Hibiscus tea has been shown to lower systolic and diastolic blood pressure.
- **Diuretic Properties**: It acts as a natural diuretic, helping to reduce blood volume and pressure.

HOW TO USE:

- **Tea**: Steep 1-2 teaspoons of dried hibiscus flowers in hot water for 10-15 minutes. Drink 1-2 cups daily.

3. Hawthorn (Crataegus spp.)

BENEFITS:

- **Cardiovascular Support**: Hawthorn can improve heart function and blood flow, reducing blood pressure.
- **Antioxidant Properties**: It contains flavonoids, which have antioxidant properties that help protect the heart.

HOW TO USE:

- **Tea**: Steep 1-2 teaspoons of dried hawthorn berries or leaves in hot water for 10-15 minutes. Drink 1-2 cups daily.
- **Supplement**: Follow the dosage instructions on the product label, typically 300-500 mg taken two to three times daily.

4. Ginger (Zingiber officinale)

BENEFITS:

- **Lowers Blood Pressure**: Ginger can help reduce blood pressure by improving circulation and relaxing the blood vessels.
- **Anti-inflammatory**: It has anti-inflammatory properties that support overall cardiovascular health.

HOW TO USE:

- **Tea**: Steep 1 teaspoon of fresh grated ginger or 1/2 teaspoon of dried ginger powder in hot water for 10-15 minutes. Drink 1-2 cups daily.
- **Supplement**: Follow the dosage instructions on the product label, typically 250-500 mg taken two to three times daily.

5. Celery Seed (Apium graveolens)

BENEFITS:

- **Diuretic Properties**: Celery seed acts as a natural diuretic, helping to reduce blood volume and pressure.
- **Lowers Blood Pressure**: It has been shown to help lower blood pressure and improve overall cardiovascular health.

HOW TO USE:

- **Tea**: Steep 1 teaspoon of crushed celery seeds in hot water for 10-15 minutes. Drink 1-2 cups daily.
- **Supplement**: Follow the dosage instructions on the product label, typically 600-1000 mg taken two to three times daily.

Herbal Remedies for Crohn's Disease:

Crohn's disease is a chronic inflammatory bowel disease that requires medical management. While herbal remedies cannot cure Crohn's disease, they can help manage symptoms and support overall gut health. Always consult with a healthcare provider before starting any new herbal remedy. Here are some herbal remedies that may help support individuals with Crohn's disease:

1. Turmeric (Curcuma longa)

BENEFITS:

- **Anti-inflammatory**: Curcumin, the active compound in turmeric, has strong anti-inflammatory properties that can help reduce inflammation in the digestive tract.
- **Antioxidant**: Turmeric is rich in antioxidants that help protect cells from damage caused by oxidative stress.

HOW TO USE:

- **Supplement**: Follow the dosage instructions on the product label, typically 500-1000 mg taken twice daily.
- **Tea**: Steep 1 teaspoon of turmeric powder in hot water for 10-15 minutes. Add honey and lemon for taste. Drink 1-2 cups daily.

2. Ginger (Zingiber officinale)

BENEFITS:

- **Anti-inflammatory**: Ginger has anti-inflammatory properties that can help reduce inflammation in the digestive tract.
- **Aids Digestion**: It can help alleviate symptoms of nausea and indigestion, which are common in Crohn's disease.

How to Use:

- **Tea**: Steep 1 teaspoon of fresh grated ginger or 1/2 teaspoon of dried ginger powder in hot water for 10-15 minutes. Drink 1-2 cups daily.
- **Supplement**: Follow the dosage instructions on the product label, typically 250-500 mg taken two to three times daily.

3. Aloe Vera (Aloe barbadensis)

Benefits:

- **Soothes Inflammation**: Aloe vera has soothing properties that can help reduce inflammation in the digestive tract.
- **Supports Gut Health**: It helps promote healing of the intestinal lining and supports overall digestive health.

How to Use:

- **Juice**: Drink 1/4 cup of aloe vera juice daily. Ensure you are using a product meant for internal use and follow the dosage instructions on the product label.

4. Slippery Elm (Ulmus rubra)

Benefits:

- **Soothes Mucous Membranes**: Slippery elm helps soothe and protect the mucous membranes of the digestive tract.
- **Reduces Inflammation**: It can help reduce inflammation and alleviate symptoms of diarrhea and abdominal pain.

How to Use:

- **Tea**: Steep 1-2 teaspoons of slippery elm powder in hot water for 10-15 minutes. Drink 1-2 cups daily.

- **Supplement**: Follow the dosage instructions on the product label, typically 400-500 mg taken two to three times daily.

5. Marshmallow Root (Althaea officinalis)

BENEFITS:

- **Soothes Irritation**: Marshmallow root helps soothe irritation and inflammation in the digestive tract.
- **Protects Mucous Membranes**: It forms a protective layer over the mucous membranes, helping to reduce symptoms of Crohn's disease.

HOW TO USE:

- **Tea**: Steep 1-2 teaspoons of dried marshmallow root in cold water for 4-8 hours. Strain and drink 1-2 cups daily.
- **Supplement**: Follow the dosage instructions on the product label.

Herbal Remedies for Gout:

Gout is a form of arthritis characterized by severe pain, redness, and tenderness in joints. Herbal remedies can help manage symptoms and reduce the frequency of gout attacks. It's important to consult with a healthcare provider before starting any new herbal remedies. Here are some herbal remedies and recipes that may help with gout:

1. Cherry Juice

BENEFITS:

- **Reduces Uric Acid Levels**: Cherries are known to lower uric acid levels in the blood, which can help prevent gout attacks.
- **Anti-inflammatory**: They have anti-inflammatory properties that can reduce swelling and pain.

How to Use:

- **Juice**: Drink 8-16 ounces of pure cherry juice daily.
- **Fresh or Dried Cherries**: Eat a handful of fresh or dried cherries daily.

2. Turmeric (Curcuma longa)

Benefits:

- **Anti-inflammatory**: Curcumin, the active compound in turmeric, has potent anti-inflammatory effects that can help reduce pain and inflammation associated with gout.

How to Use:

- **Supplement**: Follow the dosage instructions on the product label, typically 500-1000 mg taken twice daily.
- **Tea**: Steep 1 teaspoon of turmeric powder in hot water for 10-15 minutes. Add honey and lemon for taste. Drink 1-2 cups daily.

3. Ginger (Zingiber officinale)

Benefits:

- **Anti-inflammatory**: Ginger has anti-inflammatory properties that can help reduce swelling and pain.
- **Improves Circulation**: It helps improve blood circulation, which can benefit joint health.

How to Use:

- **Tea**: Steep 1 teaspoon of fresh grated ginger or 1/2 teaspoon of dried ginger powder in hot water for 10-15 minutes. Drink 1-2 cups daily.

- **Compress**: Apply a warm ginger compress to the affected area for 15-30 minutes daily.

4. Nettle (Urtica dioica)

BENEFITS:

- **Anti-inflammatory**: Nettle has anti-inflammatory properties that can help reduce swelling and pain.
- **Diuretic**: It helps promote urine production, which can aid in the elimination of uric acid from the body.

HOW TO USE:

- **Tea**: Steep 1-2 teaspoons of dried nettle leaves in hot water for 10-15 minutes. Drink 1-2 cups daily.
- **Supplement**: Follow the dosage instructions on the product label, typically 300-500 mg taken twice daily.

5. Celery Seed (Apium graveolens)

BENEFITS:

- **Reduces Uric Acid Levels**: Celery seeds can help lower uric acid levels in the blood.
- **Anti-inflammatory**: They have anti-inflammatory properties that can help reduce pain and inflammation.

HOW TO USE:

- **Tea**: Steep 1 teaspoon of crushed celery seeds in hot water for 10-15 minutes. Drink 1-2 cups daily.
- **Supplement**: Follow the dosage instructions on the product label, typically 600-1000 mg taken twice daily.

Herbal Tea Recipe for Gout Relief

INGREDIENTS:

- 1 teaspoon dried nettle leaves
- 1 teaspoon dried ginger root or 1/2 teaspoon ginger powder
- 1 teaspoon dried turmeric powder
- 1 teaspoon crushed celery seeds
- 4 cups water
- Honey and lemon (optional)

STEPS TO PREPARE:

1. **Boil the Water**: Pour 4 cups of water into a saucepan and bring it to a boil.
2. **Add Herbs**: Add the dried nettle leaves, dried ginger root, turmeric powder, and crushed celery seeds to the boiling water.
3. **Simmer**: Reduce the heat and let the mixture simmer for about 10-15 minutes.
4. **Strain**: Remove the saucepan from heat and let it cool slightly. Strain the tea through a fine strainer to remove the solids.
5. **Add Honey and Lemon**: Add honey and lemon to taste, if desired.
6. **Serve:** Pour the strained tea into a cup and enjoy.

Herbal Remedies for Shingles:

Shingles, also known as herpes zoster, is a viral infection that causes a painful rash. Herbal remedies can help alleviate symptoms and support the healing process. Always consult with a healthcare provider before starting any new herbal remedy, especially if you have underlying health conditions or are taking other medications. Here are some herbal remedies and recipes that may help with shingles:

1. Lemon Balm (Melissa officinalis)

BENEFITS:

- **Antiviral Properties**: Lemon balm has antiviral properties that can help fight the herpes zoster virus.
- **Soothes Skin**: It can help soothe and heal the skin affected by shingles.

HOW TO USE:

- **Topical Application**: Apply lemon balm cream or ointment to the affected area several times a day.
- **Tea**: Steep 1-2 teaspoons of dried lemon balm leaves in hot water for 10-15 minutes. Drink 1-2 cups daily.

2. Aloe Vera (Aloe barbadensis)

BENEFITS:

- **Soothes Skin**: Aloe vera has soothing properties that can help relieve pain and inflammation associated with shingles.
- **Promotes Healing**: It supports skin healing and reduces itching.

HOW TO USE:

- **Topical Application**: Apply pure aloe vera gel directly to the affected area several times a day.

3. Licorice Root (Glycyrrhiza glabra)

BENEFITS:

- **Antiviral Properties**: Licorice root has antiviral properties that can help inhibit the replication of the herpes zoster virus.

- **Reduces Inflammation**: It has anti-inflammatory properties that can help reduce pain and inflammation.

HOW TO USE:

- **Topical Application**: Apply licorice root cream or ointment to the affected area several times a day.
- **Tea**: Steep 1 teaspoon of dried licorice root in hot water for 10-15 minutes. Drink 1-2 cups daily.

4. Oatmeal (Avena sativa)

BENEFITS:

- **Soothes Skin**: Oatmeal has soothing properties that can help relieve itching and irritation.
- **Reduces Inflammation**: It can help reduce inflammation and promote healing of the skin.

HOW TO USE:

- **Oatmeal Bath**: Add 1-2 cups of colloidal oatmeal to a warm bath and soak for 15-20 minutes. Repeat daily as needed.

5. Peppermint (Mentha piperita)

BENEFITS:

- **Pain Relief**: Peppermint has analgesic properties that can help relieve pain associated with shingles.
- **Cooling Effect**: It provides a cooling sensation that can help soothe itching and irritation.

How to Use:

- **Topical Application**: Dilute peppermint essential oil with a carrier oil (such as coconut oil) and apply to the affected area. Do a patch test first to ensure there is no allergic reaction.

Herbal Tea Recipe for Shingles Relief

Ingredients:

- 1 teaspoon dried lemon balm leaves
- 1 teaspoon dried licorice root
- 1 teaspoon dried peppermint leaves
- 4 cups water
- Honey (optional)

Steps to Prepare:

1. **Boil the Water**: Pour 4 cups of water into a saucepan and bring it to a boil.
2. **Add Herbs**: Add the dried lemon balm leaves, licorice root, and peppermint leaves to the boiling water.
3. **Simmer**: Reduce the heat and let the mixture simmer for about 10-15 minutes.
4. **Strain**: Remove the saucepan from heat and let it cool slightly. Strain the tea through a fine strainer to remove the solids.
5. **Add Honey**: Add honey to taste, if desired.
6. **Serve**: Pour the strained tea into a cup and enjoy.

Herbal Remedies for Strep Throat:

Strep throat is a bacterial infection that requires medical attention and antibiotics prescribed by a healthcare provider. However, certain herbal remedies can help soothe symptoms and support the healing process alongside conventional treatment.

Always consult with a healthcare provider before starting any new herbal remedy, especially when dealing with infections. Here are some herbal remedies that may help with the symptoms of strep throat:

1. Echinacea (Echinacea purpurea)

BENEFITS:

- **Boosts Immune System**: Echinacea can help enhance the immune system, aiding the body in fighting off infections.
- **Anti-inflammatory**: It has anti-inflammatory properties that can help reduce throat swelling and pain.

HOW TO USE:

- **Tea**: Steep 1 teaspoon of dried echinacea root or leaves in hot water for 10-15 minutes. Drink 1-2 cups daily.
- **Supplement**: Follow the dosage instructions on the product label, typically 300-500 mg taken two to three times daily.

2. Licorice Root (Glycyrrhiza glabra)

BENEFITS:

- **Soothes Throat**: Licorice root can help soothe a sore throat and reduce pain.
- **Antiviral and Anti-inflammatory**: It has antiviral and anti-inflammatory properties that can help reduce throat inflammation and fight infection.

HOW TO USE:

- **Tea**: Steep 1 teaspoon of dried licorice root in hot water for 10-15 minutes. Drink 1-2 cups daily.
- **Gargle**: Make a gargle solution by steeping licorice root in hot

water, then letting it cool. Gargle with the solution several times a day.

3. Slippery Elm (Ulmus rubra)

BENEFITS:

- **Soothes Irritation**: Slippery elm contains mucilage, which coats and soothes the throat, reducing irritation and pain.
- **Anti-inflammatory**: It helps reduce inflammation in the throat.

HOW TO USE:

- **Tea**: Steep 1-2 teaspoons of slippery elm powder in hot water for 10-15 minutes. Drink 1-2 cups daily.
- **Lozenges**: Slippery elm lozenges are available and can be taken as directed.

4. Marshmallow Root (Althaea officinalis)

BENEFITS:

- **Soothes Throat**: Marshmallow root contains mucilage that can soothe and coat the throat, reducing pain and irritation.
- **Anti-inflammatory**: It helps reduce inflammation in the throat.

HOW TO USE:

- **Tea**: Steep 1-2 teaspoons of dried marshmallow root in hot water for 10-15 minutes. Drink 1-2 cups daily.
- **Gargle**: Make a gargle solution by steeping marshmallow root in hot water, then letting it cool. Gargle with the solution several times a day.

5. Sage (Salvia officinalis)

BENEFITS:

- **Antimicrobial**: Sage has antimicrobial properties that can help fight the bacteria causing strep throat.
- **Anti-inflammatory**: It helps reduce inflammation and soothe the throat.

HOW TO USE:

- **Tea**: Steep 1 teaspoon of dried sage leaves in hot water for 10-15 minutes. Drink 1-2 cups daily.
- **Gargle**: Make a gargle solution by steeping sage leaves in hot water, then letting it cool. Gargle with the solution several times a day.

REFERENCES

Historical review of medicinal plants' usage. (n.d.). PMC. Retrieved from https://www.ncbi.nlm.nih.gov/pmc/articles/PMC3358962/

Herb-drug interactions. (n.d.). NCCIH. Retrieved from https://www.nccih.nih.gov/health/providers/digest/herb-drug-interactions

How to read supplement labels like a pro. (n.d.). Healthline. Retrieved from https://www.healthline.com/nutrition/how-to-read-supplement-labels

History of herbalism. (n.d.). Wikipedia. Retrieved from https://en.wikipedia.org/wiki/History_of_herbalism

Natural remedies for everyday illnesses. (n.d.). Allina Health. Retrieved from https://www.allinahealth.org/healthysetgo/heal/natural-remedies-for-everyday-illnesses

What you need to know about herbal tinctures. (n.d.). Healthline. Retrieved from https://www.healthline.com/health/what-is-a-tincture

9 popular herbal medicines: Benefits and uses. (n.d.). Healthline. Retrieved from https://www.healthline.com/nutrition/herbal-medicine

Dietary supplements and herbal remedies for premenstrual syndrome. (n.d.). NCBI. Retrieved from https://www.ncbi.nlm.nih.gov/books/NBK72353/

Hormone-balancing effect of pre-gelatinized organic maca. (n.d.). PMC. Retrieved from https://www.ncbi.nlm.nih.gov/pmc/articles/PMC3614604/

Herbal medicines—are they effective and safe during pregnancy? (n.d.). PMC. Retrieved from https://www.ncbi.nlm.nih.gov/pmc/articles/PMC8802657/

Black cohosh - health professional fact sheet. (n.d.). NIH. Retrieved from https://ods.od.nih.gov/factsheets/BlackCohosh-HealthProfessional/

Adaptogens: Top 9 adaptogenic herbs for stress and more. (n.d.). Dr. Axe. Retrieved from https://draxe.com/nutrition/adaptogenic-herbs-adaptogens/

Nutritional and herbal supplements for anxiety. (n.d.). PMC. Retrieved from https://www.ncbi.nlm.nih.gov/pmc/articles/PMC2959081/

Therapeutic effects of phytochemicals and medicinal herbs. (n.d.). PMC. Retrieved from https://www.ncbi.nlm.nih.gov/pmc/articles/PMC5414506/

Popular herbal and natural remedies used in psychiatry. (n.d.). PMC. Retrieved from https://www.ncbi.nlm.nih.gov/pmc/articles/PMC6519573/

Safe and beneficial herbs for kids. (n.d.). Euphoric Herbals. Retrieved from https://www.euphoricherbals.com/blogs/blog/safe-and-beneficial-herbs-for-kids

Make an herbal first aid kit. (n.d.). Wholly Rooted. Retrieved from https://www.wholly-rooted.com/blog/herbal-first-aid-kit-dayweekend-prep

Common herbal dietary supplement–drug interactions. (n.d.). AAFP. Retrieved from https://www.aafp.org/pubs/afp/issues/2017/0715/p101.html

Herbal remedies for dogs. (n.d.). PetMD. Retrieved from https://www.petmd.com/dog/wellness/evr_dg_herbs

Herbal medicines: Where is the evidence? (n.d.). PMC. Retrieved from https://www.ncbi.nlm.nih.gov/pmc/articles/PMC1127780/

Techniques for extraction and isolation of natural products. (n.d.). PMC. Retrieved from https://www.ncbi.nlm.nih.gov/pmc/articles/PMC5905184/

Sustainable herbs program. (n.d.). Retrieved from https://sustainableherbsprogram.org/explore/what-is-sustainable-medicine/

Advancing herbal medicine: Enhancing product quality and safety. (n.d.). PMC. Retrieved from https://www.ncbi.nlm.nih.gov/pmc/articles/PMC10561302/

Sustainable harvesting of medicinal plants: Some thoughts for conservation. (n.d.). PMC. Retrieved from https://www.ncbi.nlm.nih.gov/pmc/articles/PMC3733198/

Ethical foraging: A strategy for sustainability. (n.d.). Scriver. Retrieved from https://scriver.org/ethical-foraging-a-strategy-for-sustainability/

How to start a community garden in your area. (n.d.). Bonnie Plants. Retrieved from https://bonnieplants.com/blogs/garden-ideas-inspiration/working-tips-for-organizing-a-community-effort

Plants and climate change. (n.d.). U.S. National Park Service. Retrieved from https://www.nps.gov/articles/000/plants-climateimpact.htm

10 simple herbal remedies from your garden. (n.d.). Healthline. Retrieved from https://www.healthline.com/health/herbal-remedies-from-your-garden

Clinical implications of herbal supplements in healthcare. (n.d.). PMC. Retrieved from https://www.ncbi.nlm.nih.gov/pmc/articles/PMC9375827/

Florida school of holistic living: Home. (n.d.). Retrieved from https://www.holisticlivingschool.org/

Incorporating herbs into your daily life. (n.d.). Wishgarden Herbs. Retrieved from https://www.wishgardenherbs.com/blogs/wishgarden/incorporating-herbs-into-your-daily-life

Made in the USA
Las Vegas, NV
06 February 2025